PLEASING
PEOPLE

PLEASING PEOPLE

How Not to Be an "Approval Junkie"

LOU PRIOLO

PUBLISHING
P.O. BOX 817 • PHILLIPSBURG • NEW JERSEY 08865-0817

For clarity, some of the quotations from Puritan authors contained in this volume have
been slightly modified (rephrased into modern English).

Unless otherwise indicated, Scripture quotations are from the NEW AMERICAN STAN-
DARD BIBLE®. © Copyright The Lockman Foundation 1960, 1962, 1963, 1968, 1971,
1972, 1973, 1975, 1977. Used by permission.

Verses marked (KJV) are taken from the King James Version of the Bible.

Scripture quotations marked (NKJV) are from The Holy Bible, New King James Version.
Copyright © 1979, 1980, 1982, Thomas Nelson, Inc.

Scripture quotations marked (NIV) are from the HOLY BIBLE, NEW INTERNATIONAL
VERSION®. NIV®. Copyright © 1973, 1978, 1984 by International Bible Society. Used
by permission of Zondervan Publishing House. All rights reserved.

Italics within Scripture quotations indicate emphasis added.

Printed in the United States of America

Library of Congress Control Number: 2006934628

ISBN-13: 978-1-59638-055-4

To Bob Carroll

If a friend loves at *all* times,
you are one of my *truest* friends.

CONTENTS

CONTENTS

PREFACE

As you may have noticed, this book is divided into two sections. The first deals with a problem with which most of us struggle; the second addresses how to solve our problem biblically. Right up front, I would like to give you a warning as you read Part One as well as make a request as you study and apply Part Two. Both have a common denominator: the grace of God as found in the gospel of Jesus Christ.

First, the warning: Part One of this book may well contain some of the most convicting material you have ever read. It is intended to be so. You see, most of us would never change the things in our lives that are out of sync with God's Word apart from being convicted of our sin. That is why as a father, an elder, a counselor, and an author, I strive to use great precision as I convict with the Scriptures those to whom I minister. Of course, conviction is only a small part of the process of change. Indeed, all Scripture is useful for doctrine, for conviction, for correction, and for disciplined training in righteousness (2 Tim. 3:16).

The thought of my trying to convict you of your sin may seem like a rather severe (if not unsympathetic) approach to encourage you to change, but it is actually a very loving approach. The truth is, what we will be discussing in this book is not a sickness (or a psychological disorder) for which there is no cure; it is not a genetic predisposition that you as a Christian will be forced to live with for the rest of your life. It is simply a sin![1] And Jesus Christ came to do away with our sin. That is

---

1. I trust that as you read this book, it will become apparent that I have not diminished the malevolence or misery of sin—or how egregious it is to our thrice-holy God.

where the gospel comes in. To help you see your problem as a sin is one of the most hopeful things I can do for you because there is a powerful cure for this type of problem—the gospel of Jesus Christ.

For those of us who have trusted in Christ, we understand that our justification is by faith in Christ apart from works we have done or righteousness we possess within ourselves. We understand that any righteousness that we may possess apart from Christ is as filthy rags. We understand that we were born into this world dead in our trespasses and sins and therefore needed to be quickened. We understand that despite the guilt of our sin, former bondage to it, and current struggle against it, we have been declared righteous by virtue of Christ's substitutionary death and therefore are (or should be) conscious at all times of His imputed righteousness and of our adoption as sons and daughters of Almighty God.

Despite our indwelling sin, we have been reckoned to be righteous. We have been legally declared "not guilty." The guilt that we experienced as a result of our sin is covered by the blood of Christ who ever lives to make intercession for us. Because of Him, we no longer relate to God as a judge, but as a father. This is a wonderful thing, a cause of great rejoicing, and a very present help in times of unholy self-condemnation and satanic accusation.

As sons and daughters, however, Christians still can and do experience guilt. And though justified, "they may, by their sins, fall under God's fatherly displeasure, and not have the light of His countenance restored unto them, until they humble themselves, confess their sins, beg pardon, and renew their faith and repentance."[2]

This leads us to the request: As we consider the specific biblical remedies of this problem given in Part Two, please don't lose sight of the fact that you will not be able to change apart from the Spirit of God applying the Word of God in sanctifying power to your mind and will. An unsaved individual may be able to *reform* his life to a certain degree and perhaps *conform* to his own self-imposed standards (or those of

---

2. *Westminster Confession of Faith* XI:5.

his therapist). But what he cannot do without the Holy Spirit is to *trans-form* himself into the image of Christ. What's more, the changes that he is able to make "in the flesh" do not please God. "Those who are in the flesh [unbelievers] cannot please God" (Rom. 8:8).

It is possible to open up this volume at any point and read for pages without any apparent reference to *justification by faith, the gospel of Christ,* or *the ministry of the Holy Spirit*, but these truths are to be understood throughout. Who would disagree that these fundamentals of the faith are woven through the entire Bible and underlie all of Scripture even when not apparent in each section? The Bible does not balance every doctrine with its counterpart on every page. In some places, the righteous requirement of the law is emphasized; in other places, the grace of God is clearly the predominant theme. In some places, faith apart from works is taught; elsewhere, faith is tied to one's works. When you put it all together, you understand that we are saved by faith alone, but not the kind of faith that is alone. What I want you to keep in mind as you read this book is that these precious truths undergird every page, whether or not I point them out to you. Sure, I try to remind you of them at various points on our journey, but it is your job to never lose sight of them as you move closer and closer to the goal.

ACKNOWLEDGMENTS

I would like to express my gratitude to several individuals who have helped me with this project.

To my wife, Kim, who has prayed diligently for this book.

To Fern Gregory (the best proofreader I have ever known), who has invested many hours in editing this manuscript.

To Chas and Patti Morse, who have also helped with the editing process.

To Marvin Padgett at P&R Publishing, with whom it has been a delight to work.

INTRODUCTION:
ME, AN APPROVAL JUNKIE?

I never thought of myself as a people-pleaser. I had confronted hundreds of counselees about the sin in their lives. I'd done the same for many of my friends (some of whom turned into enemies). I faced ridicule and censure from other "Christian counselors" and from some of my colleagues for the position I held on the sufficiency of Scripture. I even stood up to people in positions of authority who I believed were in error. Once, my opposing position contributed to costing me a job. Surely I didn't have a problem with the love of approval.

But I did! As I was confronted with the material you will encounter in this book (initially as a result of preparing a series of sermons on the subject), I had to confess that I was not as free from the love of approval as I'd thought. You see, the sin of pride, which is at the heart of being a people-pleaser, is an insidious thing. Like a cataract that slowly covers the eye of its victim, pride keeps us from seeing our sins, thus preventing us from properly dealing with them.

In my case, there had always been a few individuals (usually people in positions of authority over me) whom I inordinately wanted to please. Moreover, even with all my training as a biblical counselor, I occasionally found myself struggling to accommodate the nonbiblical views and goals of my counselees rather than boldly (albeit gently) confronting them. The more I looked into the Bible, the more I realized the degree to which the sin of pride and the idol of man's approval had taken root in my heart.

So before I go any further, I must tell you that I can't take credit for the contents of this book. They didn't originate with me. I am indebted to men who were promoted to glory long before I was born. Godly men such as Timothy Dwight, Hugh Blair, Jeremiah Burroughs, and especially Richard Baxter wrote much about this problem years before anyone ever thought to coin the term *codependency*. Since these saints lived before the advent of modern psychology, they diagnosed life's problems "not in words taught us by human wisdom but in words taught by the Spirit, expressing spiritual truths in spiritual words" (1 Cor. 2:13 NIV). Their writings were refreshingly free from the psychobabble associated with the majority of today's "Christian literature."[1]

I don't know exactly what motivated you to pick up this book, but I suspect that you or someone you love struggles with wanting to please people too much. It is my prayer that the Holy Spirit will use the truths contained in this volume to remove any spiritual cataracts from your eyes and enable you (and the people you love) to love the approval of God rather than the approval of man.

---

1. The only notable exception I've found is the Puritans' reference to the "four temperaments," which Dr. Hippocrates first postulated some 450 years before Christ. Perhaps we should take a lesson from these Puritans, who placed a little too much confidence in the medical models of their day.

Part One

OUR PROBLEM

No passion of the human mind is stronger than this. After it has been sufficiently indulged, it becomes so habitual that it occupies all the energy of the soul—or perhaps more accurately, it becomes all the energy of the soul, transforming all of the soul's faculties and all its efforts into servants of its own selfish purposes. In such cases, the soul is changed into a mere mass of ambition; and nothing in heaven, or in earth, is valued except to the extent that it can serve this master ambition . . . There is no excess, no length to which this passion will not go. There is no authority of God or man against which it will not rebel; no law which it will not violate; no obligation which it will not neglect; no pure motive which it will not overcome. There is no other form of wickedness that can become more intense, nor its plans more vast, nor its obstinacy more enduring, nor its destruction more extensive, or more dreadful than the love of distinction.

—Timothy Dwight, President of Yale College in the late 1700s to early 1800s, from his sermon "On the Love of Distinction" (paraphrased).

One

CHARACTERISTICS OF
A PEOPLE-PLEASER

The notion of "codependency" has been given lots of attention in recent years. Countless books, articles, seminar workshops, college courses, radio programs, and even sermons have arisen to help people get a handle on this new pop-psychology buzzword. But the term has become so prevalent that it is now difficult to find two people who define it in exactly the same way. As Christians, however, we must take care to define and diagnose man's problems "not in words taught us by human wisdom but in words taught by the Spirit, expressing spiritual truths in spiritual words" (1 Cor. 2:13 NIV).

So what does God's Word call this not-so-new phenomenon? Actually, several biblical words describe it. In the most general terms, the concept of codependency seems to best fall under the biblical category of "idolatry"—looking to someone (or something) else to do for me those things that only God can do. In terms of a type of person who is characterized by this particular kind of behavior, "people-pleaser" is the more specific diagnosis. The motive of such an individual is identified in John 12:43: he "loved the approval of men rather than [or at least *more than*] the approval of God."

All of this will be developed more fully in subsequent chapters, but before we go any further, let me try to help you evaluate how much of a people-pleaser you may be. The People-Pleasing Inventory is designed to help individuals get a general sense of their tendencies to fall into the sin of people-pleasing. Respond to each of the following twenty statements, using the rating scale below.

PEOPLE-PLEASING INVENTORY

RATING SCALE	POINTS
Never (or Hardly Ever)	5
Seldom	4
Sometimes	3
Frequently	2
Always (or Almost Always)	1

1. I listen with anxious attentiveness when others discuss that which pleases or displeases them. _____

2. I strive to be politically correct more than biblically correct. _____

3. I like to go "fishing" for compliments. _____

4. I gossip about others to people whom I believe will be pleased with me for giving them such luscious tidbits of information. _____

5. My desire for a good reputation is predominantly based on how such a reputation will benefit me rather than how that reputation will serve as a means to a greater end, such as the glory of God, the good of others, or some other unselfish objective. _____

6. I value the approval of certain individuals from whom I expect to receive certain honors more than the approval of those from whom I do not expect to receive such honors. _____

7. I worry about what people think of me. _____

8. I am willing to sin rather than face the rejection of certain individuals. _____

9. I struggle with being a respecter of persons and showing favoritism. _____

10. I believe that being rejected is one of the worst things that a person could possibly experience. _____

11. I avoid conflicts rather than trying to resolve them. _____

12. I take unnecessary precautions to protect my good name. _____

13. I become angry when I am contradicted by others, especially when being publicly contradicted. _____

14. When meeting new people, I spend more time thinking about how to impress them than how to minister to them. _____

15. My fear of being rejected paralyzes me to the extent that it keeps me from getting close to others. _____

16. I forget that being rejected by others is part of the "suffering for righteousness' sake" that is my reasonable service to God and part of my calling as a Christian. _____

17. I long to be noticed more than I long to be godly. _____

18. I give in to peer pressure rather than standing up for what I know is right. _____

19. I do not witness to others as I should because I fear being criticized or rejected. _____

20. I overreact to criticism by dwelling on it too long or unnecessarily allowing it to depress me. _____

TOTAL POINTS _____

YOUR APPROVAL RATING

Here is a simple, albeit nonscientific,[1] way to determine the level of your struggle with approval. If you've not yet done so, please take a

1. The People-Pleasing Inventory is not a scientifically normed instrument. Because the questions were developed from biblical constructs, persons taking the test are being compared more closely to the character of Jesus Christ than to the character of those in our secular society.

moment right now to tally your inventory score. If you scored between 96 and 100, you do not have a problem with people-pleasing. (You may have a problem with being insensitive, callous, or even hard hearted, but you're definitely not a people-pleaser.) If your total points fall between 90 and 95, you're probably free from the love of approval. If your total was between 80 and 89, you are probably a bit too concerned with the approval of others. If you scored between 70 and 79, you may, in fact, be a bona fide people-pleaser. If your score was 69 or below, you may very well be an approval addict. (You are probably somewhat enslaved to the approval of man.) The lower your score, the more helpful you should find the contents of this book.

How'd you do? Perhaps you scored better than you thought you would. Perhaps your score was worse than you had hoped. Because the problem of approval is rooted in pride, and pride is <u>endemic</u> to every human heart, each of us will, in varying degrees, struggle with the temptation to be people-pleasers. So don't be too discouraged with your score, and don't be too proud of yourself if you obtained a high score on this preliminary evaluation. The real test of your approval addiction will come as we take a closer look at characteristics of a people-pleaser below. But before we do that, I'd like to digress momentarily to make an important point about idolatry.

THE TWO SIDES OF IDOLATRY

As there are two sides to a coin, so there are usually two sides to idolatry. The <u>first side involves neglecting God</u>. The <u>other involves replacing Him</u> with a cheap substitute. The "heads" side of the coin says, "Inordinate Desire for Something." The "tails" side says, "Inordinate Fear of Losing Something." People who love money fear losing their wealth. Those who love to be in control fear being unable to control the circumstances and people that surround them. The person who loves pleasure is often afraid of missing out on opportunities to gratify his fleshly desires.

22

As with any other form of idolatry, the sin of people-pleasing also has two sides. For the people-pleaser, love of man's approval is accompanied by the flip side of the coin: fear of losing someone's approval (or respect, or favorable opinion), or fear of being rejected, or sometimes even fear of conflict. Keep this in mind as you evaluate your own struggle with people-pleasing.

DIAGNOSING THE SPIRITUAL DISORDER OF PEOPLE-PLEASERS

What does an approval addiction look like? This spiritual malady can manifest itself in many symptoms. The list that follows is far from exhaustive. Yet the presence of even one characteristic should be all that is necessary to convict a sincere Christian of the presence of a toxic level of pride in his heart.

1. He fears the displeasure of man more than the displeasure of God. Not only does the people-pleaser love the wrong thing (the approval of man rather than the approval of God), he *fears* the wrong thing as well—he fears the disapproval of man more than the disapproval of God.

Fear is a powerful emotion. It has power for good as well as for evil. The right kind of fear (the fear of God, for example, or the fear of sin and its consequences) keeps us from danger. The wrong kind of fear leads us into danger. "The fear of man brings a snare" (Prov. 29:25).

Let's take a look into a key passage of Scripture:

> Nevertheless many even of the rulers believed in Him, but because of the Pharisees they were not confessing Him, for fear that they would be put out of the synagogue; for they *loved* the approval of men *rather than* the approval of God. (John 12:42–43)

These rulers did not sin because they wanted to enjoy a bit of recognition. Rather, it was their loving man's approval rather than (or perhaps "more than," as the Greek might be rendered) God's approval that drew John's criticism. It's bad enough to inordinately long for the approval of others. It's much worse when such longings transcend one's longing for God. These rulers feared the wrong things. They were afraid of being excommunicated from the synagogue, which meant that they stood to lose quite a bit more than a good seat in church. As Timothy Dwight pointed out in his sermon titled "On the Love of Distinction," they feared man rather than God:

> The dread of this punishment prevented these rulers from acknowledging their belief in the Redeemer. Excommunication among the Jews was followed by the loss of all the ecclesiastical privileges which a Jew could claim as his birthright. At the same time, it assured to the unfortunate subject the hatred and contempt of his nation: and this seems to have been the evil principally dreaded by these rulers: so dreaded, that neither the wisdom and excellence of the Redeemer, nor the stupendous miracle, of which they had just been witnesses,[2] could induce them to encounter it: "For," says the evangelist, "they loved the praise of men more than the praise of God."3

The love of man's approval is inextricably bound to the fear of man's disapproval. When a people-pleaser interacts with others, his thoughts immediately and instinctively run in the direction of selfishness, anxiety, and fear.

▤ "I'm not prepared to meet this person."

▤ "What does he think of me?"

2. God the Father answering the prayer of God the Son in an audible voice: "'Father, glorify Your name.' Then a voice came out of heaven: 'I have both glorified it, and will glorify it again.' So the crowd of people who stood by and heard it were saying that it had thundered; others were saying, 'An angel has spoken to Him.' Jesus answered and said, 'This voice has not come for My sake, but for your sakes'" (John 12:28–30).

3. Timothy Dwight, *Sermons in Two Volumes* (New Haven, CT: Hezekiah How and Durrie and Peck, 1831), 1:497.

- ▤ "I'll probably make a fool of myself."
- ▤ "I can't reveal too much of myself or he will know what I'm really like and reject me."
- ▤ "I can't bear the thought of being hurt again."
- ▤ "I have to get away from this person as quickly as possible."
- ▤ "I have to be careful not to say anything that might get me into a conflict."

A people-pleaser is not a peacemaker, but rather a peace-lover. A peacemaker is willing to endure the discomfort of a conflict in the hope of bringing about a peaceful resolution. (Peace not only is the absence of conflict, but is often the result of it.) A peace-lover is so afraid of conflict that he will avoid it at almost all costs. He is so concerned about "keeping the peace" with his fellow man that he is often willing to forfeit the peace of God that comes from standing up and suffering for the truth. He is essentially a coward at heart.

2. He desires the praise of man above the praise of God. Unless he was backed into a corner with the evidence, the approval junkie might never admit that he loves anything more than the Lord. "Of course I love God more than anything else![4] Look at all the good things I do for Him! Look at all the time I've invested in serving him. My whole life is built around my faith. Surely I don't love the approval of man above the approval of God!"

I wonder whether that's what the scribes and Pharisees thought. They could certainly have made such claims. But although they were outwardly religious, they were among the clearest examples of people-pleasers in the Bible. They wanted approval so much that they spent a great deal of their time and effort doing those things that would bring them glory from men.

4. Peter, the disciple of Jesus, made a similar boast. But when the time came for him to prove his loyalty, he lied rather than face persecution. He had more of a problem with desiring approval than he realized.

But they do all their deeds *to be noticed by men*; for they broaden their phylacteries and lengthen the tassels of their garments. They *love the place of honor* at banquets and *the chief seats* in the synagogues, and *respectful greetings* in the market places, and *being called Rabbi by men*. (Matt. 23:5–7)

Even those things that are religious in nature (such as prayer, fasting, and giving) can be done with a hypocritical motive to gain man's approval.

Beware of practicing your righteousness before men to be noticed by them; otherwise you have no reward with your Father who is in heaven.

So when you give to the poor, do not sound a trumpet before you, as the hypocrites do in the synagogues and in the streets, so that they may be honored by men. Truly I say to you, they have their reward in full. But when you give to the poor, do not let your left hand know what your right hand is doing, so that your giving will be in secret; and your Father who sees what is done in secret will reward you.

When you pray, you are not to be like the hypocrites; for they love to stand and pray in the synagogues and on the street corners so that they may be seen by men. Truly I say to you, they have their reward in full. (Matt. 6:1–5)

The people-pleaser is a hypocrite. He is a Pharisee at heart. His service to man and to God is contaminated by impure desires. His religion is more external than it is internal. What he does is done outwardly, with his motive being a strong desire to draw attention to himself. His first thought is not "How will God be glorified by what I am about to do?" but rather "How will others perceive me when I do what I am about to do?" For him the question is not "What will God gain if I do this?" His question is, "What will I gain?" He is not concerned primarily with "How can I edify others with my words?" He is concerned instead with "Will the words I choose cast me in a favorable light?" Phrases such as "approved to God" (2 Tim. 2:15), "well-pleasing to God" (Phil. 4:18), "acceptable to God" (Rom. 12:1), and even "glorifying God" (Luke 17:15) rarely cross his mind because he's not accustomed to thinking in these terms. His selfish focus forces him to think almost exclusively of himself. He is concerned (if not consumed) with the establishment and maintenance of his own reputation. His heart so craves being held in high esteem by others (and to hear their praises) that little room is left to entertain thoughts of what he might do to acquire God's praise. In reality, pleasing God doesn't matter much to him because he is so intent on pleasing man. The truth is, he simply puts a much higher value on pleasing man than on pleasing God. He values the approval of man before and above the approval of God, for he loves "the approval of men rather than the approval of God" (John 12:43).

3. He studies what it takes to please man as much as (if not more than) what it takes to please God. The people-pleaser is so intent on gaining approval that he spends much of his time studying the interests, aversions, words, inflections, and body language of people. He is often inordinately sensitive to the countenances of those he is trying to please. When passing people on the street or in the hall, he studies their faces, looking for clues that might reveal their level of approval—usually reading more into facial expressions than one can possibly know without some sort of verbal verification.

Of course, studying people for the purpose of discovering their genuine needs so that you can minister to them is a manifestation of biblical love. But the motives of the people-pleaser are usually not so noble. When he does attempt to "meet the needs" of others, he often does so *not* because he is trying to love (to give without expecting anything in return), but in order to enhance his own reputation or find favor in the eyes of those he is "loving." In time, this self-oriented sensitivity to the needs of others often backfires on the people-pleaser as others see through his insincerity (hypocrisy) and are repulsed by it (cf. Prov. 23:6–8).

4. His speech is designed to entice and flatter others into thinking well of him. The speech of the people-pleaser betrays him. He may or may not do it consciously, but his words are designed to cover his flaws and foibles and to cajole others into seeing him in the best possible light. He is motivated by fear rather than by love. The Bible makes a very clear connection between flattery and people-pleasing.

> But just as we have been approved by God to be entrusted with the gospel, so we speak, not as *pleasing men* but God who examines our hearts. For we never came with *flattering speech*, as you know, nor with a *pretext* for greed—God is witness . . . (1Thess. 2:4–5)

A person who knows he is faithful and has therefore been approved by God can speak freely and boldly to others. He does not use flattering speech because he really doesn't care much about pleasing man. It is the person who seeks to please man who doesn't care much about pleasing God and so resorts to flattery or pretext. The Greek word for *pretext* means "pretense," especially in the disguising or cloaking of one's real motives. The people-pleaser is a hypocrite who, for fear of being found out or for the purpose of making others think better of him than he really is, disguises himself.

The makeup he uses to camouflage his true appearance consists largely of communication. Here are some characteristics of the communication style of an approval addict.

The people-pleaser . . .

- ▤ Rarely confronts sin in the life of another believer.
- ▤ Rarely challenges or even questions the opinions of others.
- ▤ Prematurely terminates conflicts (usually by yielding, withdrawing, or changing the subject).
- ▤ Rarely reveals to others the truth about who he really is inside (especially his struggles with sin).

- Steers conversations away from those topics that might cause others to realize what he is really like inside.
- Shades the truth (lies) in order "not to offend others."
- Finds clever ways to subtly introduce his accomplishments into conversations.
- Fishes for compliments.
- Listens attentively when others talk of things that displease him (so as not to say or do anything that might result in rejection).
- Frequently puts himself down in the hope that others will disagree with his purposely exaggerated negative self-assessment.
- Finds it difficult to say "no" to those who make requests of him, even when he knows that saying "yes" will not be the best choice.

5. He is a respecter of persons. Because the people-pleaser esteems the power and influence of men more than the authority and rule of Christ (cf. Prov. 29:26), he respects certain persons above others. His penchant to show favoritism is the result of seeking the glory of men above the glory of God.

> My brethren, do not hold your faith in our glorious Lord Jesus Christ with an attitude of *personal favoritism*. For if a man comes into your assembly with a gold ring and dressed in fine clothes, and there also comes in a poor man in dirty clothes, and you *pay special attention* to the one who is wearing the fine clothes, and say, "You sit here in a good place," and you say to the poor man, "You stand over there, or sit down by my footstool," have you not made *distinctions* among yourselves, and become judges with evil motives? (James 2:1–4)

It's not just the wealthy who are respected by people-pleasers—it is also those who are held in high esteem by others. People who have a reputation for almost any temporal achievement are prone to be treated with more respect than the average Joe or Jane by approval-seekers. Why? Because being approved by an "important person" is going to make them "feel important."[5] In the final analysis, this is more valuable to them than being approved by God.

A respecter of persons finds some temporal characteristic in his subject with which he is enthralled. He is enamored of it because he values it too much. Whether that trait is the by-product of sin or of righteousness is of little concern to him because he loves it more than he loves the Lord. Consequently, he courts the favor of those who possess it because they can give him that for which he is longing. He prefers to be with those who can give him what he wants. His kindness to them is based not on their need or God's glory, but rather on gaining advantage.

The people-pleaser also has a difficult time being objective in judgment because his desire for approval is often stronger than his desire for justice. He wrongly makes "distinctions" because he evaluates others on the basis of what is important to him (according to the things he values most) rather than on the basis of what's important to God (according to the things God values most).

> You shall do no injustice in judgment. You shall not be *partial* to the poor, nor *honor the person* of the mighty. In righteousness you shall judge your neighbor. (Lev. 19:15 NKJV)

It is not only the rich who can be wrongly preferred. Some show favoritism to the poor not because they truly care about poverty but because they want to gain approval from others for being charitable (cf. Matt. 6:1–4). The person who is preferred may not himself possess that characteristic coveted by the respecter of persons. He may simply be a convenient pawn who provides an opportunity to gain some selfish benefit from a third party.

---

5. Actually, approval-seekers judge or evaluate themselves as being important persons on the basis of being approved by other important people and consequently "feel" good about such a prestigious self-evaluation.

6. **He is oversensitive to correction, reproof, and other allusions of dissatisfaction or disapproval on the part of others.** The people-pleaser overreacts to any hint of disapproval. He feels a pinprick as keenly as a knife in the back. He is overly sensitive because he is too concerned about his own glory (and popularity). He sees any constructive criticism or suggestion for improvement as a threat to his reputation rather than as an opportunity to grow or as an indication of the reprover's love for him.

Being oversensitive is usually nothing less than pride. And as we have noted, pride is at the heart of people-pleasing. Richard Baxter, the prolific Puritan author, nicely connected the biblical dots for us on this point over three hundred years ago:

> Pride causes men to hate reproof. The proud are presumptuous in finding fault with others, but do not love the person who reproves them. Though it is a duty which God himself commands (Lev. 19:17) as an expression of love and is contrary to hatred, yet it will make a proud man to be your enemy. "A scorner loveth not one that reproveth him, neither will he go unto the wise" (Prov. 15:12). "He that reproveth a scorner, getteth himself shame; and he that rebuketh a wicked man, getteth himself a blot. Reprove not a scorner, lest he hate thee: rebuke a wise man, and he will love thee" (Prov. 9:7–8). It embitters their hearts, and they consider themselves to be injured, and they will bear a grudge against you for it as though you were their enemy.[6]

This oversensitivity may take the form of anger, bitterness, or hatred. It may show up in the form of withdrawing, sulking, or pouting. But remember, the approval-seeking person does not want to face rejection, so these vindictive forms of oversensitivity (at least the outward evidences of them) may be short-lived. They are counterproductive and contrary to his goal of being highly esteemed. It is possible, therefore, that in the long run, the people-pleaser will show his oversensitivity by

---

[6.] Richard Baxter, *Baxter's Practical Works*, vol. 1, *A Christian Directory* (Ligonier, PA: Soli Deo Gloria Publications, 1990) 204.

trying too hard to cover or correct (for wrong motives) that which has caused him to be corrected, reproved, or otherwise disapproved.

7. He outwardly renders eye service to man rather than inwardly rendering sincere (from the heart) ministry to the Lord. The word for *eye service* (*ophthalmodoulia*) appears twice in the Greek New Testament (Eph. 6:6; Col. 3:22). Both times it is in reference to slaves. The implicit idea of this compound term is a service that is provided only while under scrutiny, or only for the sake of appearance. Since it is contrasted in both passages with a heartfelt sincerity, it involves a kind of service that is both hypocritical and reluctant.

> Slaves, be obedient to those who are your masters according to the flesh, with fear and trembling, in the sincerity of your heart, as to Christ; not by way of eyeservice, as men-pleasers, but as slaves of Christ, doing the will of God from the heart. With good will render service, as to the Lord, and not to men. (Eph. 6:5–7)

> Bondservants, obey in all things your masters according to the flesh, not with eyeservice, as men-pleasers, but in sincerity of heart, fearing God. (Col. 3:22 NKJV)

Regardless of the service or ministry rendered, the people-pleaser struggles to do it with the right motive. Pleasing and glorifying God by serving others takes a backseat to serving others to promote and glorify self.

When the eye-serving employee speaks to his boss, he is more concerned with impressing him than he is with telling the truth. When the people-pleasing lawyer tries his case, he is more concerned with convincing his client that he is earning his fee than convincing the jury that justice must be done. When the approval-seeking housewife over-commits herself to activities outside the home to the neglect of her husband or children, she is more concerned about her reputation among her friends than she is about the Lord's reputation. When the approval-loving pastor is more consumed with how his congregants will see him than he is with how they will be edified through his message, he is more concerned with pleasing man than with pleasing God.

The person who gives eye service evaluates his success or failure not on the basis of whether God was pleased with his service, but rather on how well he performed. For example, although that lawyer may have thrown away the case through his grossly deleterious preparation, as long as the client is convinced that he "put up a good fight" in the courtroom, objected often enough to the opposition, was condescending and sarcastic enough on cross-examination, and effectively reduced a few witnesses to tears, he considers himself to have succeeded. And that pastor who was too consumed with his performance, even though he knows his message convicted and challenged God's people, will find himself battling depression over the fact that no one complimented him on his delivery and that he caught two people snoozing during his sermon.

8. He selfishly uses the wisdom, abilities, and gifts that have been given to him for God's glory and the benefit of others for his own glory and personal benefit. It's not just opportunities to minister that the people-pleaser squanders on his own selfish ends. He tries to use virtually every divine endowment given to him for the benefit of others and for the glory of God to make himself look good. Whatever he has been given, he views as a means of bringing honor to himself, rather than as an instrument to honor God.

> For who regards you as superior? What do you have that you did not receive? And if you did receive it, why do you boast as if you had not received it? (1 Cor. 4:7)

It's bad enough for a person to think he is responsible for the blessings and achievements in life. It is far worse to use those blessings to promote one's own glory and reputation rather than the glory and reputation of the One who is truly responsible for them. Yet this is what

33

the people-pleaser does continually. "Every good thing given and every perfect gift is from above, coming down from the Father . . ." (James 1:17). What are the good things given by God and abused by the approval junkie? The list is almost endless. Here are just a few.

- Personal Wealth
- Physical Beauty
- Spiritual Gifts
- Wisdom
- Honor of One's Vocation
- Artistic Ability
- Athletic Ability
- Verbal Ability
- Musical Ability
- Intellectual Ability
- Financial Status
- Family Heritage
- Position in the Community
- Position at Work
- Bible Knowledge
- Managerial Skill
- Good Reputation
- Spiritual Accomplishments
- Location of One's Home
- Appearance of One's Home
- Accomplishments of Children
- Worldly Possessions

To use any of these gifts to promote self is to use them for purposes other than those for which they were given. Not that it is wrong to take pleasure in these things—or even to enjoy a certain sense of satisfaction as they are used for God's purposes. But to expend them on one's lusts is to pervert the ends to which they were given and to rob the Giver of the glory that is due him.

9. He invests more of his personal resources in establishing his own honor than he does in establishing God's honor. The person who loves approval invests more of his time, effort, thought, or money in establishing and maintaining his own reputation (well above that which is necessary to establish and maintain "a good name") than he does in furthering the reputation of Christ. His daily preoccupation with his own honor drains his resources, preventing him from fully using them for eternal purposes. His treasure is laid up on earth ("where moth and rust [can] destroy, and where thieves break in and steal") rather than

in heaven ("where neither moth nor rust destroys, and where thieves do not break in or steal").[7] His treasure is invested where his heart is— in this life, not the next one, and in temporal glory, not in eternal glory. He seeks and will receive his reward on earth rather than in heaven.

Richard Baxter describes what lies behind the giving of such an individual:

> A proud man will give more to his own honor than to God. His estate is more under the control of his pride than of God. He gives more in the view or with the knowledge of others, than he could persuade himself to give in secret. He is more generous in gifts that tend to maintain the good name of his liberality, than he is to truly indigent persons. It is not the good that is done, but the honor which he expects to receive by doing it, which is his principal motive.[8]

This principle applies not just to the giving of material gifts but also to the giving of time, service, encouragement, and any other investment that the people-pleaser might seem to make in the lives of others.

10. He is discontented with the condition and proportion that God has appointed for him. By "condition" I mean one's state of being—from the state of a person's health to his IQ, his social standing, or anything else that might cause others to esteem him more highly. In other words, a man's condition is the situation or circumstances (and the honor associated with them) into which the Lord has chosen to place him. By "proportion" I mean the relative magnitude, quantity, or degree of those conditions (or circumstances) that God has chosen for him.

The people-pleaser is discontented with his status in life. He longs to have more authority, greater honor, more influence, and more wealth. Rather than being thankful for what has been given to him and

7. Matt. 6:19–20.
8. Baxter, *A Christian Directory*, 197.

for God's wise distribution of blessings to all men for his purposes, the approval-seeking idolater covets the honor-producing blessings that God has given to others, as though all of God's purposes revolved around bestowing honor on himself. Perhaps the saddest thing about such a person is that he will never be satisfied, no matter how much approval he is able to generate. What Solomon says to us about material wealth—"He who loves money will not be satisfied with money, nor he who loves abundance with its income" (Eccl. 5:10)—applies to any heart idol. Temporal things do not satisfy; they only tempt us to further discontentment.

This list of ten criteria is not exhaustive. There are perhaps dozens of other identifying features of one who is in bondage to approval. But I hope this little inventory will give you a better understanding of the extent to which you may be bound.

You may be wondering if it's really possible to be set free from such addictive behavior. It is! Come with me through the chapters that follow, and you will discover more about this ruthless master of pride and how to break its yoke by clothing yourself with the humility of Jesus Christ.

Two

IS IT EVER RIGHT TO PLEASE PEOPLE?

Some idolatrous desires are, of course, wrong in and of themselves (coveting another man's wife, for instance, or wanting to take your own revenge by lying about someone who hurt you, or wanting to cheat another out of something that is rightfully his). These desires are always wrong because there would never be an occasion in which such desires were *not* sinful.

But other desires are normal and natural and become sinful only by abuse. Good and lawful desires become corrupted when they are desired *inordinately*. When you want something good (such as desiring your spouse to love you, or your children to honor you, or your boss to treat you with respect) so much that you are willing to sin in order to fulfill your desire (or to sin as a result of your desire not being fulfilled), your desire becomes idolatrous. Such desires are sinful not because some new verse suddenly appeared in your Bible that says, "You shall not want your spouse to love you," or "You shall not desire your children to honor you," or "You shall not try to please your boss." They are wrong because you have longed for them *too intently*. What may have begun as a legitimate God-given desire has now metastasized and mutated into an inordinate one.

The Bible says, "Each one is tempted when he is drawn away by his own desires and enticed" (James 1:14 NKJV). The word for *desire* used in the Greek New Testament (*epithumia*) is a term that can be used of any strong desire (good or bad).

Is it a sin for the Christian to use money? Certainly not. It's a sin for him to *love* money (or to be a *lover* of money). Is it a sin to want to have some money? No, it's a sin to long for it to the point of idolatry—to look to it for provision more than one looks to God. And it's a sin to "*want* to get rich":

> But those who *want* to get rich fall into temptation and a snare and many foolish and harmful *desires* which plunge men into ruin and destruction. For the *love of money* is a root of all sorts of evil, and some by *longing* for it have wandered away from the faith and pierced themselves with many griefs. (1 Tim. 6:9–10; see also Luke 16:14; 2 Tim. 3:2)

Is it a sin to enjoy pleasure? No, it's a sin to *love* pleasure rather than (or more than) God (cf. Prov. 21:17; 2 Tim. 3:4). Is it a sin to want to manage those under your spiritual care? No. But it is a sin to be like Diotrephes, who so "*love*[*d*] to be first" (3 John 9; literally, "loved the presidency") that he abused his spiritual authority. Similarly, it is not necessarily wrong to desire approval. In fact, in some contexts the desire for approval is presumed, if not encouraged. But it is wrong to *love* "the approval of men rather than the approval of God" (John 12:43). It's also wrong to (like the scribes and Pharisees) "love the place of honor at banquets and the chief seats in the synagogues, and respectful greetings in the market places, and being called Rabbi by men" (Matt. 23:6–7).

To desire the approval of others is not necessarily wrong. If it were, to praise or commend one's child would be to necessarily tempt him to sin. Our desire for praise is part of our makeup, which allows us to more readily sense the shame and reproach associated with our sin. To experience no desire for praise is to experience no sense of shame.

WHEN IS IT RIGHT TO PLEASE PEOPLE?

Before we endeavor to further explore the sinfulness of people-pleasing, we must understand the extent to which it is lawful and right to please man.

1. It is right to please people to the extent that doing so is not the leading principle of conduct or primary motive of your actions, but subordinate to the love of God and the love of neighbor. The Bible assumes that man, to a certain extent, naturally desires approval from others. It nowhere cautions him against having a sober-minded desire for such approval.

> And He began speaking a parable to the invited guests when He noticed how they had been picking out the places of honor at the table, saying to them, "When you are invited by someone to a wedding feast, do not take the place of honor, for someone more distinguished than you may have been invited by him, and he who invited you both shall come and say to you, 'Give your place to this man,' and then in disgrace you proceed to occupy the last place. But when you are invited, go and recline at the last place, so that when the one who has invited you comes, he may say to you, 'Friend, move up higher'; then you will have honor in the sight of all who are at the table with you. For everyone who exalts himself will be humbled, and he who humbles himself will be exalted." (Luke 14:7–11)

Jesus does not condemn the man who, after humbling himself, receives honor in the sight of all who dine with him. Contrarily, he seems to use this innate desire for esteem as a motivation to be humble,[1] much like Solomon did by his truism, "Before honor comes humility" (Prov. 15:33; see also Prov. 18:12). We step over the line into sin when our hearts are governed by the desire to please people (rather than by the desire to love God and neighbor).

---

1. There is a purpose clause ("so that") in the original *hina*, suggesting that part of the rationale for taking a lower seat may be to receive "honor in the sight of all who are at the table with you."

2. It is right to please people to the extent that establishing a good name for the cause of Christ is your motive. "A good name is to be more desired than great wealth, favor is better than silver and gold" (Prov. 22:1).

As with so much in the Christian's life, that which distinguishes right from wrong is simply our motives. When we seek a good reputation in order to use it for our own selfish purposes, our prayer is wrong. "You ask and do not receive, because you ask with wrong motives, so that you may spend it on your pleasures" (James 4:3). When we want to establish and maintain a good name for the cause of Christ, our motivation is biblical and our efforts are likely to produce good fruit.

As Hugh Blair points out, our reputation can greatly help or hinder our service for God:

> The sphere of our influence is contracted or enlarged in proportion to the degree in which we enjoy the good opinion of the public. Men listen with an unwilling ear to one whom they do not honor; while a respected character adds weight to [a man's] example, and authority to [his] counsel. To desire the esteem of others for the sake of its *effects*, is not only allowable, but in many cases is our duty; and to be totally indifferent to praise or censure, is so far from being a virtue, that it is a real deficit in character.[2]

The Scriptures speak of the importance of possessing a good reputation. Some of these passages address the dangers associated with not having one. Solomon warns us that even a small amount of folly can ruin a good name:

> Dead flies putrefy the perfumer's ointment, and cause it to give off a foul odor; so does a little folly to one respected for wisdom and honor. (Eccl. 10:1 NKJV)

Moreover, those who aspire to church office must have a good reputation:

2. *Sermons by Hugh Blair, D.D.* (London: T. Cadell; C & J Rivington, 1827), 187.

> An overseer, then, must be above reproach . . . He must have a good reputation with those outside the church, so that he will not fall into reproach and the snare of the devil. (1 Tim. 3:2, 7)

Those who seek after the office are to first strive to meet the biblical qualifications. Paul's concern is that a man whose reputation is less than good may ultimately bring reproach (disgrace) on the local church and the cause of Christ and that such a man will somehow be ensnared by the devil. There are other places in the Bible where specific groups of people (e.g., widow, 1 Tim. 5:14, and servant, 1 Tim. 6:1) are encouraged to behave in certain ways to avoid reproach (cf. 2 Sam. 12:14; Rom. 2:24). It is clear that pleasing man for the purpose of not embarrassing God is not only lawful, but commendable.

3. It is right to please people to the extent that the Bible commands you to please, honor, and obey your parents, your rulers, and your superiors. Those whom God has placed in positions of authority are to be honored and, up to a point, obeyed. Implicit in these biblical directives is a divine sanction to please man. But again, such license is not without limit. It may not supersede one's responsibility to please God.

God is the one who ordains *all* human authority, both good and bad. As Paul reminds us, "There is no authority except from God, and those which exist are established by God" (Rom. 13:1). But he doesn't give anyone *absolute* authority. Nobody, regardless of his position, may lawfully ask another to sin. This is true of husbands, parents, employers, church officers, and government officials. At the point where an authority crosses the line and instructs his subordinate to sin, his instructions must be disobeyed. In such cases, efforts to please those in authority must be halted or at least redirected.[3]

3. There may be another way for the subordinate to please his authority. Perhaps some appeal could be made that would be just as pleasing to him as, if not more than, the original directive would have been. Daniel made such an appeal in Daniel 1:8–14.

Take a look at the following Scripture passages from the perspective of pleasing your superiors. In most cases it would be difficult to honor and obey them apart from making some effort to please them.

Pleasing Our Parents	Honor your father and your mother, that your days may be prolonged in the land which the Lord your God gives you. (Exod. 20:12)
	A wise son makes a father glad, but a foolish son is a grief to his mother. (Prov. 10:1)
	A wise son makes a father glad, but a foolish man despises his mother. (Prov. 15:20)
	The father of the righteous will greatly rejoice, and he who sires a wise son will be glad in him. Let your father and your mother be glad, and let her rejoice who gave birth to you. (Prov. 23:24–25)
	A man who loves wisdom makes his father glad, but he who keeps company with harlots wastes his wealth. (Prov. 29:3)
Pleasing Our Rulers	The fury of a king is like messengers of death, but a wise man will appease it. In the light of a king's face is life, and his favor is like a cloud with the spring rain. (Prov. 16:14–15)
	Submit yourselves for the Lord's sake to every human institution, whether to a king as the one in authority, or to governors as sent by him for the punishment of evildoers and the praise of those who do right. (1 Peter 2:13–14)
	Every person is to be in subjection to the governing authorities. For there is no authority except from God, and those which exist are established by God. Therefore whoever resists authority has opposed the ordinance of God; and they who have opposed will receive condemnation upon themselves. For rulers are not a cause of fear for good behavior, but for evil. Do you want to have no fear

of authority? Do what is good and you will have praise from the same; for it is a minister of God to you for good. But if you do what is evil, be afraid; for it does not bear the sword for nothing; for it is a minister of God, an avenger who brings wrath on the one who practices evil. Therefore it is necessary to be in subjection, not only because of wrath, but also for conscience' sake. For because of this you also pay taxes, for rulers are servants of God, devoting themselves to this very thing. Render to all what is due them: tax to whom tax is due; custom to whom custom; fear to whom fear; honor to whom honor. (Rom. 13:1–7)

They came and said to Him, "Teacher, we know that You are truthful and defer to no one; for You are not partial to any, but teach the way of God in truth. Is it lawful to pay a poll-tax to Caesar, or not? Shall we pay, or shall we not pay?" But He, knowing their hypocrisy, said to them, "Why are you testing Me? Bring Me a denarius to look at." They brought one. And He said to them, "Whose likeness and inscription is this?" And they said to Him, "Caesar's." And Jesus said to them, "Render to Caesar the things that are Caesar's, and to God the things that are God's." And they were amazed at Him. (Mark 12:14–17)

Pleasing Our Earthly Masters (Employers)

Slaves, in all things obey those who are your masters on earth, not with external service, as those who merely please men, but with sincerity of heart, fearing the Lord. (Col. 3:22)

Urge bondslaves to be subject to their own masters in everything, to be well-pleasing, not argumentative, not pilfering, but showing all good faith so that they will adorn the doctrine of God our Savior in every respect. (Titus 2:9–10)

4. It is right to please people to the extent that the Bible allows you to please your spouse. For those who are married, pleasing one's spouse comes second only to pleasing the Lord. Because this is a very important but often-misunderstood biblical principle (which when violated produces serious marital problems), let's take a moment to study it carefully.

> But I want you to be free from concern. One who is unmarried is concerned about the things of the Lord, how he may *please* the Lord; but one who is married is concerned about the things of the world, how he may *please* his wife, and his interests are divided. The woman who is unmarried, and the virgin, is concerned about the things of the Lord, that she may be holy both in body and spirit; but one who is married is concerned about the things of the world, how she may *please* her husband. (1 Cor. 7:32–34)

Marriage is unlike any other human relationship. When a man and woman marry, they become one flesh: "For this reason a man shall leave his father and his mother, and be joined to his wife; and they shall become one flesh" (Gen. 2:24). The Hebrew word for *one* in this passage (*echad*) is the same word used to describe the Trinity in the first line of the Shema:[4] "Hear, O Israel! The LORD is our God, the LORD is one!" (Deut. 6:4). It is sometimes used to describe the coming together of individual entities to make one unified entity (Gen. 34:16; Exod. 26:6, 11; 36:13; Ezek. 37:17).

No other human relationship is as intimate as the marriage bond. When a couple get married, they leave both father and mother. The Hebrew term for *leave* (*azab*) is translated elsewhere as "abandon" or "forsake." More is implied in this leaving one's parents besides mere geographic location.[5] For example, the couple leaves behind *parental provision*. Up to this point, they have been largely dependent upon their parents to provide for their needs. After marriage, they break all such

4. *Shema* is Hebrew for *hear*. This passage is considered by some to be the Jewish "confession of faith."
5. In biblical times, newlyweds often did not move very far away from their parents, sometimes living in the same household.

dependence and depend on each other (and of course on the Lord). The newlywed couple also leaves behind *emotional dependence*. Whereas their "emotional umbilical cords" have previously been attached to their parents, they must now be attached to the new spouse.[6] Another important part of leaving and cleaving has to do with abandoning parental beliefs, lifestyles, values, and traditions that are not clearly delineated in the Scriptures. Unless both husband and wife agree, such extrabiblical standards should not be automatically carried over from one family to another.

This same principle holds true about whom you please. One who is married is concerned not about how he may please his parents, but rather about how he may please his wife.

In a previous book, I have explained the meaning of the word for *to please* in 1 Corinthians 7:32–34:

> The Greek verb used in verse 33, which is translated *to please*, is a word that has several nuances of meaning. Its root means "to fit in with." It can also mean "to conform," "to adapt," "to satisfy," "to soften one's heart to," "to meet with one's approval" or "to accommodate." The word implies a preexisting relationship between the one doing the pleasing and the one being pleased.
>
> While an unmarried Christian should have his mind focused almost exclusively on how he may please the Lord, the attention of a married Christian must be focused not only on pleasing the Lord, but also on pleasing his spouse. The Bible assumes that all married persons will have their interests divided between pleasing Christ, which is always top priority, and pleasing their spouses.[7]

5. It is right to please people to the extent that you are to *become all things to all men* whom you are attempting to save for Christ. It is sometimes necessary to go outside our comfort zone and even

6. Not that there is no emotional attachment to their parents, but the emotional dependence is now exclusively on the Lord and on one's spouse.

7. *The Complete Husband* (Amityville, NY: Calvary Press Publishing, 1999), 144–45.

inconvenience ourselves, becoming whatever is biblically legitimate to accommodate others for the purpose of winning them to Christ.

> For though I am free from all men, I have made myself a *slave* to all, so that I may *win* more. To the Jews I became as a Jew, so that I might win Jews; to those who are under the Law, as under the Law though not being myself under the Law, so that I might win those who are under the Law; to those who are without law, as without law, though not being without the law of God but under the law of Christ, so that I might win those who are without law. To the weak I became weak, that I might win the weak; I have become all things to all men, so that I may by all means *save* some. I do all things for the sake of the gospel, so that I may become a fellow partaker of it. (1 Cor. 9:19–23)

The apostle Paul was willing to make himself "a slave" to all. He twice urged slaves to please their masters (Col. 3:22; Titus 2:9–10).

"To the Jews I became as a Jew . . . ; to those who are under the Law, as under the Law" (v. 20). He was willing, within the parameters of the new covenant, to make himself as Jewish as necessary to accommodate the Jews. His motive for "pleasing" the Jews in this way was to win them to Christ.

"To those who are without law, [I became] as without law" (v. 21). Here he was willing to accommodate Gentiles who were not bound to the law, making it clear to his readers that he was still under the moral law of God for the purpose of evangelism. He did not keep a kosher house, or dress in Jewish garments, or refuse to associate with their pagan friends. He tried to please them to the extent that he was biblically able so that he might win them to Christ.

"To the weak I became weak" (v. 22). He was even willing to veil his intellectual prowess to identify with those who were not as sharp as he was. His motive once again was "to win the weak." This is the same thing he did with the Corinthians to whom he was writing:

> And when I came to you, brethren, I did not come with superiority of speech or of wisdom, proclaiming to you the testimony of God. For I

determined to know nothing among you except Jesus Christ, and Him crucified. I was with you in weakness and in fear and in much trembling, and my message and my preaching were not in persuasive words of wisdom, but in demonstration of the Spirit and of power, so that your faith would not rest on the wisdom of men, but on the power of God. (1 Cor. 2:1–5)

Without compromising the gospel, Paul tried to please others in his evangelistic efforts. Without changing his message, he condescended to all sorts of people in order to preach the gospel to them in all sorts of situations. He had biblical flexibility. To this extent, it is lawful to be a people-pleaser.

6. It is right to please people by denying yourself the use of your Christian liberty, so as not to put a stumbling block before a weaker brother. Now, it's one thing if those to whom we proclaim the gospel are offended by the message itself. It's quite another if they are offended by our conduct or activities. Paul was willing to limit his freedoms in order to not set a stumbling block before those who were not yet set free from bondage to their religious laws and traditions through the gospel of grace he was preaching. He tells us to follow his example:

If one of the *unbelievers* invites you and you want to go, eat anything that is set before you without asking questions for conscience' sake. But if anyone says to you, "This is meat sacrificed to idols," do not eat it, for the sake of the one who informed you, and for conscience' sake; I mean not your own conscience, but the other man's; for why is my freedom judged by another's conscience? If I partake with thankfulness, why am I slandered concerning that for which I give thanks?

Whether, then, you eat or drink or whatever you do, do all to the glory of God. Give no offense either to Jews or to Greeks or to the church of God; just as I also *please all men in all things*, not seeking my own profit but the profit of the many, so that they may be saved. *Be imitators of me*, just as I also am of Christ. (1 Cor. 10:27–11:1)

In this passage, Paul is urging the Corinthians to avoid eating meat that has been sacrificed to idols when in the presence of those whose consciences have not been biblically programmed. This principle was to be practiced toward all men (whether unconverted Jews, pagan Greeks, or uninformed Christians). The issue was not that the meat he was abstaining from was in any way defiled. Paul's concern was that those who were bound by their own weak consciences would be defiled (violated) if they ate the meat believing it was defiled.

Elsewhere in the New Testament, Paul encourages his readers to please others. The context is almost identical to the one we just observed.

> Now we who are strong ought to bear the weaknesses of those without strength and not just *please* ourselves. Each of us is to *please* his neighbor for his good, to his edification. For even Christ did not *please* Himself . . . (Rom. 15:1–3)

These three verses (in which the word *please* appears three times) serve as a summary statement for what Paul said in the previous chapter. Romans 14 may be subtitled: "How to Handle Disputable Issues" or "How to Respond to a Weaker Brother." Again we see the same theme: Don't do anything that would cause your brother to sin—even if it means that you are inconvenienced.

> Therefore let us not judge one another anymore, but rather determine this—not to put an obstacle or a stumbling block in a brother's way. I know and am convinced in the Lord Jesus that nothing is unclean in itself; but to him who thinks anything to be unclean, to him it is unclean. For if because of food your brother is hurt, you are no longer walking according to love. Do not destroy with your food him for whom Christ died . . . Do not tear down the work of God for the sake of food. All things indeed are clean, but they are evil for the man who eats and gives offense. It is good not to eat meat or to drink wine, or to do anything by which your brother stumbles. (Rom. 14:13–15, 20–21)

The thrust of Paul's argument is: "Let each of us *please* his neighbor for his good, to his edification." He asks, "Who are you wanting to please?" We as Christians are often called upon to "please others," putting up with their scruples and notions that have no basis in Scripture. Occasionally, we have to do so with greater frequency than we think is fair. This is what it means "to bear the weaknesses of those without strength" (Rom. 15:1). It is to this extent that we are commanded to "*please* [our] neighbor for his good" (Rom. 15:2).

THE DISTINCTION

Let me close this chapter with another citation from Dr. Hugh Blair in which he distinguishes between appropriate and inappropriate attempts to please man:

> Even in cases where there is no direct competition between our duty and our fancied honor, between the praise of men and the praise of God, the passion for applause may become criminal, by occupying the place of a better principle. When vain-glory usurps the throne of virtue; when ostentation produces actions which conscience ought to have dictated, such actions, however outwardly genuine they may seem, have no claim to moral or religious praise. We know that good deeds, done merely *to be seen of men*, lose their reward with God. If, on the occasion of some trying set of circumstances, which causes us to question our course of action, the first question that comes to our mind be, not whether an action is right in itself, and such as a good man ought to perform, but whether it is such as will find acceptance with the world, and be favorable to our fame, the conclusion is too evident, that the desire of applause has obtained an inordinate position of dominance.[8]

8. *Sermons by Hugh Blair*, 187–88.

So there is a time and a place to please all (sorts of) men. It is our motive that dictates the rightness or wrongness of such people-pleasing. The questions to ask yourself are these: "Do I do it for selfish reasons to cause them to think better of me? Or do I do it out of love, not seeking my own profit, but the profit of the many?"

Three

THE DANGERS OF BEING
A PEOPLE-PLEASER

In this chapter and the next, we will look at some of the pitfalls associated with trying too hard to please people. If you still need more motivation to dethrone this idol in your life, the next two chapters should provide it. By the time we get through, you'll have a much greater appreciation for the miserable consequences that await you as long as you love "the approval of men rather than the approval of God" (John 12:43).

1. **Inordinate people-pleasing brings you into bondage by enslaving you to everyone whom you desire to please.** The Bible has much to say about so-called addictive behavior. Of course, if you look up the word *addiction* in a Bible concordance, you won't find too many citations. To understand this problem from God's point of view, you must train yourself to think outside of the box—man's box.

Perhaps you have seen the little brainteaser below. The goal is to connect the dots in the diagram, using only four straight lines that are connected end to end. Take a moment to figure it out (if you don't already know the solution).

Most people struggle to solve this puzzle because, in their minds, they draw a box around the nine dots. By limiting the solution to the space inside the box, it is impossible to solve the problem. So it is with man's trying to solve problems in living by limiting his scope of vision to "general revelation." In order to solve our puzzle, we must think outside of the box. Only then can we see the solution:

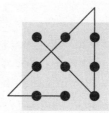

To solve life's problems God's way, we must look beyond human insight and interpretations of reality (outside the box of man's thinking) to God's insight and interpretation of reality. We must look to "special revelation." We must think in biblical terminology.

The Bible often speaks in terms of "slavery" or "bondage" when addressing addictive behaviors. Peter put it this way: "By what a man is overcome, by this he is *enslaved*" (2 Pet. 2:19). Using a different form of the same word, Paul develops the construct more fully for us:

> Do you not know that when you present yourselves to someone as *slaves* for obedience, you are *slaves* of the one whom you obey, either of sin resulting in death, or of obedience resulting in righteousness? But thanks be to God that though you were *slaves* of sin, you became obedient from the heart to that form of teaching to

which you were committed, and having been *freed* from sin, you
became *slaves* of righteousness. (Rom. 6:16–18)

Another psychological term that we hear a lot about today is *addictive personalities*. According to the passage above, we all have addictive personalities. Either we are going to be obedient to sin, and as
a result become its slave and experience death, or we're going to be
obedient to righteousness, and as a result become its slave and experience life. We have only two choices: slavery to sin (which produces
bondage) and slavery to righteousness (which produces freedom).

Now, let me point out that we are told not to become slaves to man.
"You were bought with a price; do not become slaves of men" (1 Cor.
7:23). Yet in an informal sort of way, you are making yourself the slave
of everyone whom you are wrongly trying to please. Think about it. You
have as many masters as you have observers. Every person you try to
please above and beyond what is allowed by the Scriptures becomes
your captain and your conqueror.

Being a people-pleaser is like having a little handle on your back
that others can grab hold of to push you and pull you in all directions.
Ironically, most of the time, they are unaware that they have such control over you. That's because it is you yourself who gives them this power.
By God's grace, you can break off that handle and set yourself free from
the control of others. Oh, to be sure, God wants you to serve others. But
such God-pleasing service is to be done out of a love for your neighbor
(a love that gives to his real needs), not out of a self-love that can't see
his real needs because it is too concerned about its own wants.

Richard Baxter ties in this slavery with Christ's warning about
man's inability to serve more than one master and with James's warning about becoming God's enemy if we choose to be the world's friend:

What a task have men-pleasers! They have as many masters as be-
holders! No wonder it takes them away from the service of God; for
the "friendship of the world is enmity to God;" and he that will thus
be "a friend of the world, is an enemy to God" (James 4:4). They

cannot serve two masters, God and the world. You know men will condemn you if you are true to God: if, therefore, you "must" have the favor of men, you must take it alone without God's favor. A man-pleaser cannot be true to God because he is a servant to the enemies of His service; the wind of a man's mouth will drive him about as the chaff, away from his duty, and towards his sin. How servile a person is a man-pleaser! How many masters he has, and how many mean ones at that! Man-pleasing perverts the course of your hearts and lives, and turns all from God to this unprofitable way of life.[1]

People-pleasers may become such slaves in at least two ways. First, the intense desire for man's praise and approbation puts them in bondage to man by tempting them to make decisions based on what others will think of them rather than on what God will think of them.

Consider, for example, a young woman who purchases a rather revealing dress in the hope that it will draw the eyes of certain fellows without considering whether or not such a garment conforms to the standards of biblical modesty. She is serving those fellows (and her own desire for their approval) more than she is serving Christ. Or perhaps a businessman purchases a new sports car in the hope that it will impress his friends (male and female), not taking into account whether he can biblically justify the extra expense. This man has made himself the servant of those he's trying to impress rather than the servant of Christ.

Several years ago, I had the opportunity to speak at a family conference. During my visit, I interviewed the pastor who invited me. It soon became apparent that this brother was making certain decisions based not on what the Bible says, but rather on how certain powerful and influential persons in his denomination might view him. On one hand, he was trying to please them; on the other hand, he was afraid of the consequences of displeasing them, since it was commonly reported in this denomination that people who didn't follow "company lines"

1. Richard Baxter, *Baxter's Practical Works*, vol. 1, *A Christian Directory* (Ligonier, PA: Soli Deo Gloria Publications, 1990), 186.

were treated rather severely. I was struck both with a sense of pity for this poor brother who, because of his approval problem, had become an unwitting marionette in the hands of a few bullying puppeteers, and with a sense of repulsion at the way he had allowed himself to become such a victim of abuse. As the images of that pathetic pastor haunted me in the days that followed, I recommitted myself to dealing with any vestiges of people-pleasing in my own heart lest I, too, become such a slave to man.

The inordinate fear of rejection also puts people-pleasers in bondage to man by so paralyzing them that they are diverted from fulfilling certain biblical responsibilities. I have counseled many women married to professing Christian husbands (and church members); yet these men were involved in various continual, life-dominating sins. These wives chose to live with the sins and their consequences rather than to put biblical pressure on their husbands to repent. Why did they do this? They did it because they were fearful of their husbands' rejection. They preferred to cover up their husbands' sins rather than follow the mandates of Matthew 18:15–18 (and many other similar passages) because fundamentally they were people-pleasers.[2] They were enslaved not only to their fear but to their husbands as well.

Several pastors I know believe what the Bible says about disciplining church members who continue in sin. Yet because of the fear of offending some in the church or, worse, for fear of losing their jobs, they make dismal excuses for not confronting those in the congregation who need to be rescued and restored. Thus, like the rulers in the twelfth chapter of John who would not confess him for fear of being put out of the synagogue because "they loved the approval of men rather than the approval of God" (John 12:43), these pastors have been brought into bondage because of their fear.

2. Many women probably tolerate such things not because they are people-pleasers but because they have been wrongly taught that being a "submissive wife" forbids them from helping their believing husbands overcome their sins. The local church is just one of the resources God has given to assist wives in being "suitable helpers" to their husbands. For more information, see my audiotape recording *Resources for a Wife's Protection*, available from Sound Word Associates, (219) 548–0933, http://www.soundword.com/index.html.

2. **The excessive love of praise takes from you the honor you so eagerly seek.** The very thing you long for (the esteem of others) will be subverted by your inordinate desire for man's approval. Those from whom you long to receive honor and those whom you desire to impress will eventually be offended (if not repulsed) by the pride that generates your lust.

Let's do a little experiment. Think for a moment of the proudest person you know. Who comes to mind? Do you not find it rather difficult to respect that person? Why is that? It's because the sin of pride is so obnoxious to most of us that it triggers an angry response. Perhaps that's because we know how proud we are and hate the fact that this sin still has such a stronghold in our own lives (cf. Rom. 2:1). But regardless of the reason, seeing pride in others is repulsive to most of us. So, if seeing pride in others turns you off, don't you think that others will be turned off to you when they perceive your pride? And as you now know, pride is the root sin out of which people-pleasing flows.

In warning against the dangers of seeking to gain honor by exalting oneself, Solomon illustrates how pride can backfire:

> Do not claim honor in the presence of the king, and do not stand in the place of great men; for it is better that it be said to you, "Come up here," than for you to be placed lower in the presence of the prince. (Prov. 25:6–7)

Jesus broadens Solomon's proverb by applying it to social settings:

> When you are invited by someone to a wedding feast, do not take the place of honor, for someone more distinguished than you may have been invited by him, and he who invited you both will come and say to you, "Give your place to this man," *and then in disgrace you proceed to occupy the last place.* But when you are invited, go and recline at the last place, so that when the one who has invited you comes, he may say to you, "Friend, move up higher"; then you will have honor in the sight of all who are at the table with you." (Luke 14:8–10)

On at least two different occasions, I was cured (at least temporarily) of the desire to exalt myself in the presence of others when God brought an individual into my life whose pride was so obvious, I thought to myself, *If my pride is half as obnoxious and repugnant as what I see in him, I repent from the depth of my soul.* All of us abhor that pride in others which we cherish in ourselves.

3. Immoderate people-pleasing causes you to lose eternal rewards. Jesus warns us that when we do things for the purpose of being seen by men, we forfeit the rewards that we would otherwise have had in heaven had our motives been right.

> Beware of practicing your righteousness before men to be noticed by them; otherwise you have no reward with your Father who is in heaven.
>
> So when you give to the poor, do not sound a trumpet before you, as the hypocrites do in the synagogues and in the streets, so that they may be honored by men. Truly I say to you, *they have their reward in full.* But when you give to the poor, do not let your left hand know what your right hand is doing, so that your giving will be in secret; and your Father who sees what is done in secret will reward you.
>
> When you pray, you are not to be like the hypocrites; for they love to stand and pray in the synagogues and on the street corners so that they may be seen by men. Truly I say to you, *they have their reward in full.* But you, when you pray, go into your inner room, close your door and pray to your Father who is in secret, and your Father who sees what is done in secret will reward you . . .
>
> Whenever you fast, do not put on a gloomy face as the hypocrites do, for they neglect their appearance so that they will be noticed by men when they are fasting. Truly I say to you, *they have their reward in full.* But you, when you fast, anoint your head and wash your face so that your fasting will not be noticed by men, but by your Father who is in secret; and your Father who sees what is done in secret will reward you. (Matt. 6:1–6, 16–18)

Suppose I hire you to do some work in my home for an afternoon. When you are finished, to reward you for your labor, I take you into my garage and set before you two huge piles of money. The first pile consists of one-and five-dollar bills. The second pile contains hundred-dollar bills. I hand you a large basket and tell you that you have thirty seconds to fill the basket with money from either pile. I then explain, "You may keep all the bills you are able to cram into your basket in the allotted time."

From which pile would you collect your wages?

"Why, I would choose the hundred-dollar pile, of course! I would be a fool to choose the lesser reward."

Exactly! But you make the same kind of foolish choice when you do things for man's approval rather than God's.

The person who "practic[es his] righteousness before men to be noticed by them" is doing so to please them. The man or woman who gives money for the purpose of being "honored by men" is doing so to please them. Those who "love to stand and pray in the synagogues and on the street corners, in order to be seen by men," are doing so to please men because they love the approval of men. Those who "neglect their appearance in order to be seen fasting by men" do so to please men, not God.

And so it is with you. Whether or not you do so consciously, when your motives are to please man rather than God, you are longing not to be rewarded by your Father in heaven, but to be seen (and rewarded) by men. You are not only playing the fool but being a hypocrite[3] as well.

When I lived in Atlanta, I had the privilege of counseling a good number of airline pilots. Many of them were away from home several days a week. While away from home, they were making money that they intended to spend not in another city hundreds or thousands of miles away, but in Atlanta where they live. They took only enough money with them to cover the necessities of life when in a foreign city

---

3. The meaning of the word *hypocrite* in Matthew 6:5 is "play-actor." The word for *notice* in verse 1 ("to be noticed by them") is *thea´omai*, from which we get the word *theater*. The question to ask yourself is, "On whose stage am I performing, God's or man's?"

or country. So it should be with us. We earn our wages (our rewards, if you will) down here, but we will spend them in heaven.

4. The inordinate desire for approval blinds you to your own sin. Like the virus that causes AIDS (Acquired Immune Deficiency Syndrome), which blinds the eyes of its victim's autoimmune system, the sin of pride blinds us to our sin. In Matthew 23:16–26, Jesus accused the scribes and Pharisees of being blind no less than five times. He also pointed out that their motives were infected with pride.

> Then Jesus spoke to the crowds and to His disciples, saying: "The scribes and the Pharisees have seated themselves in the chair of Moses; therefore all that they tell you, do and observe, but do not do according to their deeds; for they say things and do not do them. They tie up heavy burdens and lay them on men's shoulders, but they themselves are unwilling to move them with so much as a finger. *But they do all their deeds to be noticed by men*; for they broaden their phylacteries and lengthen the tassels of their garments. They *love* the place of honor at banquets and the chief seats in the synagogues, and respectful greetings in the market places, and being called Rabbi by men. (Matt. 23:1–7)

What motivated these religious leaders? It was the desire to be noticed and admired by others. They weren't satisfied with an occasional compliment and failed to realize that anything praiseworthy in them had been given to them by God and should be used for His honor and glory. They *loved* the places of honor at banquets. They *loved* the chief seats in the synagogues. They *loved* respectful greetings in the marketplaces. They *loved* being called "Rabbi" by men. They *loved* the approval of man rather than the approval of God and consequently lost their ability to see.

> Woe to you, *blind guides*, who say, "Whoever swears by the temple, that is nothing; but whoever swears by the gold of the temple is obligated."

You fools and *blind men*! Which is more important, the gold or the temple that sanctified the gold? And, "Whoever swears by the altar, that is nothing, but whoever swears by the offering on it, he is obligated." You *blind men*, which is more important, the offering, or the altar that sanctifies the offering? Therefore, whoever swears by the altar, swears both by the altar and by everything on it. And whoever swears by the temple, swears both by the temple and by Him who dwells within it. And whoever swears by heaven, swears both by the throne of God and by Him who sits upon it.

Woe to you, scribes and Pharisees, hypocrites! For you tithe mint and dill and cummin, and have neglected the weightier provisions of the law: justice and mercy and faithfulness; but these are the things you should have done without neglecting the others. You *blind guides*, who strain out a gnat and swallow a camel!

Woe to you, scribes and Pharisees, hypocrites! For you clean the outside of the cup and of the dish, but inside they are full of robbery and self-indulgence. You *blind Pharisee*, first clean the inside of the cup and of the dish, so that the outside of it may become clean also. (Matt. 23:16–26)

Jesus called them "blind men," "blind guides," and "blind Pharisee." What was the exact nature of their blindness? To be spiritually blind is to be ignorant, stupid, or slow of understanding (cf. Isa. 42:16, 18–19; 43:8; Matt. 15:14; Luke 4:18; John 9:39–41; Rom. 2:19; 2 Pet. 1:9; Rev. 3:17). The irony, of course, is that they believed themselves to see so well as to guide others out of darkness.[4]

The first context in which Christ categorized these religious leaders as "blind" deals with the deceptive practice of evading responsibility by taking false oaths (making promises with little or no intention of keeping them, or writing into the promises deceptive little loopholes—sort of like crossing one's fingers behind one's back).

The second context Jesus presented to convict these men of their hypocritical blindness had to do with straining at gnats and swallowing

---

4. Spiros Zodhiates, *The Complete Word Study Dictionary: New Testament*, electronic ed. (Chattanooga, TN: AMG Publishers, 2000).

camels. They would pay tithes on the leaves and seeds of ordinary house-plants but would omit the weightier matters of the law, such as justice and mercy and faithfulness. Their pride, selfishness, hypocrisy, greed, injustice, and dishonesty mattered less to them than their meticulous tithing.

The third case Jesus made against them had to do with cleaning the outside of their lives but ignoring the filth and corruption on the inside. Outwardly, the scribes and the Pharisees appeared to be righteous, but inwardly they were self-gratifying thieves. The picture Jesus paints is of an eye-catching entrée being served on the finest and most ceremonially clean platter, but when placed in one's mouth, the food turns out to be rancid. The clean platter was defiled by the rotten food.

In their religious fervor, these spiritual leaders couldn't see the essence of true worship because they were so focused on the details. They were blinded by their pride—their love of approval. They were not worshiping God but rather their own desires for esteem. They thought they could see the sin in others, but they couldn't see the sin and darkness in their own hearts. Proud people are often so focused on the external sins in others that they can't see the attitudes that generate the external sins they hold in such contempt. They spend most of their time trying to put out small fires of sin on the surface of their lives while being totally unaware that there are shrewd and significant arsonists in their hearts setting new fires faster than the existing ones can be extinguished.

HOW LUST FOR MAN'S APPROVAL BLINDS YOU TO SIN

There are at least six ways in which pride (the desire for man's approval) may blind you to your sin.

1. **Pride tempts you to exaggerate your virtues.** A proud person is likely to overvalue the knowledge, wisdom, gifts, abilities, character,

and maturity that God has given to him. He often forgets that every good and perfect thing he has was given to him by God (James 1:17) and that without God, he can do nothing (John 15:5). The proud king Nebuchadnezzar boasted (to himself, if not to others) about God's accomplishments as though they were the result of his own genius and skillfulness when he asked, "Is this not Babylon the great, which I myself have built as a royal residence by the might of my power and for the glory of my majesty?" (Dan. 4:30). As Baxter points out:

> Self-idolizing pride causes men to glory in their supposed greatness, when the greatness of God should show them their contemptible vileness. It causes them to magnify themselves when they ought to magnify their Maker. It makes the strong man glory in his strength, and the rich man in his wealth, and the conqueror in his victories, and princes and lords and rulers of the earth in their dominions and dignities, and abilities to do harm or good to others.[5]

2. **Pride tempts you to minimize your flaws.** A proud person may minimize the terribleness of his sin because of an exaggerated view of his own virtues. *So I'm not perfect*, he thinks to himself, *but I've got so many redeeming qualities, surely God will overlook this little habit of mine.* David said, "For in his own eyes he flatters himself too much to detect or hate his sin" (Ps. 36:2 NIV). The humble Christian is well aware of his weaknesses, sinfulness, lack of faith, and need of God's forgiveness and grace, but the proud person flatters himself too much to detect and hate his sin.

3. **Pride tempts you to distort and magnify the seriousness of your flaws.** On the other hand, pride can cause a person to overreact to the sins and imperfections in his life. Such a response is not motivated by a genuine concern that one has sinned against God, but rather by a selfish desire to be perfect. Perfectionist tendencies usually flow out of an inordinate desire to win the approval of others or fear of

---

5. Baxter, *A Christian Directory*, 195.

being rejected by them.[6] The conscience of a perfectionist has often been programmed not by the Word of God but by his inordinate desire for approval.

4. **Pride tempts you to change things in your life according to man's priorities rather than the agenda of the Holy Spirit.** The proud person is concerned about changing things in his or her life that really don't matter to God. Rather than looking into the Bible to see what things God wants one to put off and put on, the proud person makes a top priority of correcting things that may displease others, even though such changes matter little to God. In so doing, he puts more trust in the reasonings of his own heart than in the Scriptures. "He who trusts in his own heart is a fool, but he who walks wisely will be delivered" (Prov. 28:26). Because he is more concerned with pleasing man than with pleasing God, his spiritual guidance system is out of kilter.

5. **Pride focuses your attention on changing the outer man more than the inner man.** The changes made by the approval addict are often external issues having little to do with character. The proud person wants to clean the outside of the cup and of the dish to make him appear to be worthy or respectable. Those things (clothing, personal appearance, athletic ability, intelligence, the type of car driven, the kind of home owned, job title, amount of personal wealth), when placed on God's scale and held over against character, don't really weigh anything. God gives them all, and He expects us to use them for His glory. He does not give us things to use for our own selfish interests and agenda. They are temporal. Character is eternal. Paul reminded Timothy, "Discipline yourself for the purpose of godliness; for bodily discipline is only of little

6. Many people who believe they have a problem with "low self-esteem" actually esteem themselves too highly. The Bible says nothing about "self-esteem" but does command us to "in lowliness [humility] of mind . . . esteem others better than [ourselves]" (Phil. 2:3 NKJV). For more on this subject, see my audiotape *A Biblical View of Self-Image*, available from Sound Word Associates, (219) 548–0933, http://www.soundword.com/index.html.

profit, but godliness is profitable for all things, *since it holds promise for the present life and also for the life to come*" (1 Tim. 4:7b–8).

When the people-pleaser *is* concerned about changing his character, he is frequently motivated to be "godly," not primarily from a desire to please God, but rather from a desire to win friends and influence people.

6. An excessive love of praise tempts you to believe man's opinion of yourself over God's opinion. Jesus attributed one of the causes of unbelief to seeking honor from man instead of God. Speaking to certain Jews who were looking to kill him "because He not only was breaking the Sabbath, but also was calling God His own Father, making Himself equal with God,"[7] the Lord said:

> How can you believe, who receive honor from one another, and do not seek the honor that comes from the only God? (John 5:44 NKJV)

These proud, ambitious men sought to receive honor from one another rather than from God. They held Christ in low esteem because they held themselves in such high esteem. They didn't value the things He said because they placed too much value on their own opinions.

To the extent that you are seeking to please others more than God, you will value the opinion of fallible men more than the opinion of the infallible God. If others perceive you to be better than you are, you will trust their judgment over that of your own conscience. If they perceive you to be inadequate in an area of your life that God says is not a biblical inadequacy (not a sin), you will hasten to change it at any expense, though you know the Lord would rather have you invest your time and effort in changing those things that are offensive to Him.

When you seek to please man more than God, you will be tempted to focus your attention on "fixing" such outward things as your appearance,

7. John 5:18; see also John 5:16; 10:33; 19:7.

the impressiveness of your possessions, or your religious activities. Like the scribes and Pharisees, you will make sure that the outsides of the cups and platters are clean, but you will neglect the insides. You, like they, will strain at a gnat and swallow a camel because you place too much value on the opinion of man. You will forget that the best way to win the approval of good men is to develop, by God's grace, the character of Christ. And even if you do not forget to work on your character, you will do so for the wrong motives and thus lose your rewards. If you perform your ministries for the purpose of being seen by men, your efforts will be tainted by your pride. God will resist you even in your attempts to serve Him because you are, at heart, a people-pleaser.

"Can we please take a break now? I don't know how much more of this I can handle. This stuff is really convicting me. Besides, I feel like I'm taking a drink of water from a fire hydrant!"

Sure, we can take a break. There's too much to put into one chapter anyway. Hope to see you back here again soon. And while you are catching your breath, remember: the more we see how much we miss the mark, the more we see our need to repent (and our inability to do so apart from dependence upon Christ).

Four

MORE DANGERS OF BEING A PEOPLE-PLEASER

Good to see you again! I hope you're well rested and in a contemplative mood. New adventures and dangers lie ahead.

7. The inordinate desire for approval makes you susceptible to flattery and renders you more vulnerable to deception and manipulation from others. Flattery is trying to influence or gain an advantage over someone by praising (or pleasing) him above and beyond that which his character (or position) merits. The word *flattery* often appears in the Bible juxtaposed to such terms as *mouth*, *lips*, *tongue*, *words*, and *speech*. Flattery is a verbal snare. It is a cunning and deceitful kind of praise intended to trap and hurt the unsuspecting and to benefit the one who laid it. Flattery makes the good about you seem better than it is, and the bad about you seem less than it is. Over three hundred years ago, Henry Hurst identified several different types of flattery.[1]

▤ **A devilish flattery:**[2] This category of cajoling is the kind that comes as a part of the "temptation to sin" package. "My son, if

1. Henry Hurst, *Puritan Sermons 1659–1689*, vol. 3, *How We May Best Cure the Love of Being Flattered* (Wheaton, IL: Richard Owen Roberts, reprint, Original, London: 1661), 187–88. Much of the material in this section has been adapted and expanded from this helpful sermon.
2. Hurst's original term: *A hellish flattery*.

sinners entice you, do not consent" (Prov. 1:10). It is what Satan used against Eve in the garden of Eden ("you will be like God, knowing good and evil," Gen. 3:5) and, by perverting Scripture, tried to use against Jesus in the wilderness ("He will command His angels concerning You" and "on their hands they will bear You up, so that You will not strike Your foot against a stone," Matt. 4:6).

▤ **A revengeful flattery:** This form of flattery is motivated by a desire to get even.

> He who hates disguises it with his lips, but he lays up deceit in his heart. When he speaks graciously, do not believe him, for there are seven abominations in his heart. (Prov. 26:24–25)

Sometimes one's enemies cover their hatred with gracious words. "Deceitful are the kisses of an enemy" (Prov. 27:6). Simeon and Levi seemed reasonable and even friendly to the Shechemites in Genesis 34, convincing them to get circumcised in order to intermarry with the children of Israel. But the whole thing was a setup. After the men were incapacitated as a result of being circumcised, these two sons of Jacob not only took revenge on the men who had sexually assaulted their sister but killed every other male in the city as well.

▤ **A slavish flattery:**[3] This brand of blarney is produced by the lusts to which the flatterer is in bondage. "For such men are slaves, not of our Lord Christ but of their own appetites; and by their smooth and flattering speech they deceive the hearts of the unsuspecting" (Rom. 16:18; see also Jude 16). Perhaps the flattery of a sexual predator to his victim may be illustrative of this form of flattery.

▤ **A cowardly flattery:** This style of sweet-talking happens when the flatterer doesn't have the courage to confront others with the truth.

3. Hurst's original term: *A servile, hungry flattery.*

Such a sycophant is oblivious to the truth contained in Proverbs 28:23: "He who rebukes a man will afterward find *more* favor than he who flatters with the tongue."

▤ **A covetous flattery:** Increase in personal wealth is the impetus for this form of blandishment.

> For neither at any time did we use flattering words, as you know, nor a cloak for covetousness—God *is* witness. Nor did we seek glory from men, either from you or from others, when we might have made demands as apostles of Christ. (1 Thess. 2:5–6 NKJV)

▤ **An emulous flattery:** This is the form of flattery that extols and magnifies the good, virtuous, and praiseworthy qualities of those in our own company (or social group) above all measure. Some in the church of Corinth were boasting of their favorite teachers. By doing this, they exalted their own little clique over those in the church who wanted to follow other leaders. Of course, the teachers flattered themselves in their own eyes by exaggerating their own accomplishments. The mind-set of Paul and his companions was quite different:

> But we will not boast beyond our measure, but within the measure of the sphere which God apportioned to us as a measure, to reach even as far as you. For we are not overextending ourselves, as if we did not reach to you, for we were the first to come even as far as you in the gospel of Christ; not boasting beyond our measure, that is, in other men's labors . . . (2 Cor. 10:13–15a)

There is a logical sequence, a process, through which the approval junkie may find himself going that renders him more and more susceptible to flattery.

Step 1: A desire for man's subjective approval.[4] The people-pleaser secretly wishes that his best be seen as better than it is and his worst be seen as nobler than it is.

Step 2: An eagerness to hear exaggerated accounts of one's character and achievements. A longing soon develops to hear flatterers give glowing accounts of things that never happened, or were done in a manner greatly inferior to the way in which they were reported. Unlike Paul, who didn't want to be thought of more highly than anyone could see in him or hear from him (2 Cor. 12:6), the people-pleaser delights to hear others embellish his character and minimize his weaknesses (cf. 2 Cor. 12:10).

Step 3: A tendency to believe the interpretation of the flatterer. Although he knows that the flatterer is being less than accurate with his sugar-coated commendations and excessive excuses, the people-pleaser places more credence in these embellishments than he does in the truth. He seeks out these reports rather than looking into the mirror of God's Word. He listens to the voice of the flatterer rather than the voice of conscience.

Step 4: A setting of one's heart on that flattering interpretation. The value we place on something is inseparable from the love we bestow on it. To the extent that the people-pleaser *loves* the approval of men more than the approval of God, he *values* their opinion more than God's. Consequently, when the flatterer tells us of our own virtues, making them appear to be the product of our own innate goodness or the result of our own doing, we love and prize his opinion so much that we set our proud heart upon it, convinced that these things must be so.

Step 5: A seeking of opportunities for others to flatter. Sometimes the people-pleaser will look for opportunities to be flattered. This is

---

4. "Unconditional acceptance" is a term that we hear much about these days. Its roots also grow quickly in the soil of the heart of the people-pleaser.

more than merely fishing for compliments. Rather, it is creating opportunities to have his person, actions, or qualifications showcased before others. He does not understand the reality of Proverbs 25:27:

> It is not good to eat much honey,
> Nor is it glory to search out one's own glory.

Step 6: A choosing of friends who are willing to lie about the people-pleaser to others. The choice of friends is no little consideration in the heart of the people-pleaser. Indeed, the desire for friends is a deadly snare for many. Here are Henry Hurst's own words on this matter:

> Many thousands among great ones and rich ones cannot live without such extravagant applauders of their persons and conduct: and we justly wonder how they bear with patience the extravagant, notorious, and incredible falsities of these parasites.[5]

Such individuals tacitly or explicitly license others to lie for them. Even men in the ministry will often seek to surround themselves with and employ those who naively overlook their character flaws, seeing only the fruit of their labor. A people-pleaser is not interested in the Proverbs 27:6 kind of faithful friend who loves him enough to occasionally wound him with the truth.

In the final analysis, the act of flattery is an act of deceit. It is a lie that many are willing to believe because they excessively long for approval of others. Once they believe the first lie, they find it hard not to believe subsequent ones. They do not see the flatterer as a liar whose company should not be tolerated. "He who works deceit shall not dwell within my house; he who tells lies shall not continue in my presence" (Ps. 101:7 NKJV). Neither do they see him as a manipulator who is able to grab hold of that people-pleasing handle that protrudes from their back to push and pull them in any direction he chooses.

---

5. Hurst, *How We May Best Cure the Love of Being Flattered*, 190.

8. The inordinate desire for approval makes the people-pleaser susceptible to many other sinful temptations. Like a largemouth bass that is lured away from the safety of its covering into captivity by a flashy new artificial bait, our inordinate desires can draw us away from the safety of obedience to Christ into many different captivating sins.

> When tempted, no one should say, "God is tempting me." For God cannot be tempted by evil, nor does he tempt anyone; but each one is tempted when, *by his own evil desire*, he is *dragged away and enticed.* Then, after desire has conceived, it gives birth to sin; and sin, when it is full-grown, gives birth to death. Don't be deceived, my dear brothers. (James 1:13–16 NIV)

The two Greek New Testament words for *dragged away* and *enticed* are both borrowed from the word for *hunting*[6] and *fishing.* What is it that your evil desires do to you? They entice you to sin. From inside your heart, they carry you away toward danger.

The phrase *evil desire* in the NIV is a bit misleading because in the original, the word *evil* does not appear. The term *epithumia* speaks of desire (craving, longing, or lust) in a general sense. It may be an inherently evil desire, or it may be a good one.[7] In fact, you may even have half a dozen proof texts to substantiate the righteousness of your desire. Maybe it's a desire for your parents to trust you, or for your husband to communicate with you, or for your wife to respect you, or for your children to obey.

Now, as we've already seen, a desire for man's approval is *not* necessarily wrong. But when it becomes inordinate—that is, when we step over the line from wanting man's approval to wanting it more than we want God's approval (or when we go from simply enjoying the approval of man to "loving the approval of man")—we have stepped into the sin of idolatry. The more frequently we cross that line, the greater the likelihood that one day we will step into any number of other satanic snares.

6. In most American hunting, hunters stalk their prey, but in biblical times, hunters were more prone to entice their prey so as to tempt the animals to come to them.
7. Context is usually the best indicator of how the word is to be understood.

"To what kinds of snares are you referring?"

Let's begin with one of the most familiar ones.

The love of approval tempts the people-pleaser to say "yes" when he ought to say "no." "I can't believe I agreed to do this thing. Why didn't I say 'no' when I was asked to participate?" Ever ask yourself this question? You may now know the answer. Chances are, you said "yes" when you should have said "no" because you wanted to please someone or you didn't want to displease someone—or both.

"But what's wrong with that?"

Nothing, as long as pleasing that someone doesn't cause you to displease Someone else.

One of the most common issues in my counseling office is dealing with the Christian whose priorities have become out of whack. He has allowed saying "yes" to good things to keep him from doing other things that should have been considered more biblically necessary. Like Martha, who because she was bothered and troubled about so many things that she neglected to do the one necessary thing (to sit at Christ's feet and hear his Word), many of my counselees forget that the good things in life are often the enemies of the best things in life. They say "yes" to the good but "no" to the necessary.

Allow me to ask you a few probing questions.

How often does saying "yes" to someone keep you from daily time in the Word and prayer?

How often does saying "yes" to someone keep you from being a faithful housekeeper, employee, or student?

How often does saying "yes" to someone keep you from fulfilling your other domestic responsibilities (e.g., teaching the Scriptures to your children, disciplining them, or doing the household chores established for you by your parents)?

How often does saying "yes" to someone keep you from communicating with those closest to you (those to whom you have a biblical responsibility to communicate regularly, such as your spouse, children, or parents)?

The person who loves the approval of God more than he does the approval of man knows what God expects of him. He knows that God will be displeased with a decision based on misplaced priorities. So with all sincerity (and a clear conscience), he says to those who ask for lower-priority commitments, "I would really love to be able to do that, but I have another more pressing commitment to keep." The person who loves the approval of man more than the approval of God doesn't consider (or care) how displeased God would be if he were to overcommit to the exclusion of his other biblical responsibilities. Thus, his desire for approval lures and entices him into further sin.

The love of approval tempts the people-pleaser to be a respecter of persons (to show partiality). "My brethren, do not hold your faith in our glorious Lord Jesus Christ with an attitude of personal favoritism" (James 2:1). James lays down for us a general principle forbidding Christians from showing partiality (cf. Prov. 28:21; 1 Tim. 5:21). The context in which he condemns this attitude of personal favoritism is wealth. To put it more vividly, the golden setting around which James displays this beautiful gem (this universal code of conduct) is the milieu of kowtowing to wealthy people: showing favoritism toward a rich man is a sin.

> For if a man comes into your assembly with a gold ring and dressed in fine clothes, and there also comes in a poor man in dirty clothes, and you pay special attention to the one who is wearing the fine clothes, and say, "You sit here in a good place," and you say to the poor man, "You stand over there, or sit down by my footstool," have you not made distinctions among yourselves, and become judges with evil motives? Listen, my beloved brethren: did not God choose the poor of this world to be rich in faith and heirs of the kingdom which He promised to those who love Him? But you have dishonored the poor man. Is it not the rich who oppress you and personally drag you into court? Do they not blaspheme the fair name by which you have been called?

If, however, you are fulfilling the royal law according to the Scripture, "You shall love your neighbor as yourself," you are doing well. *But if you show partiality, you are committing sin and are convicted by the law as transgressors.* (James 2:2–9)

But we can be tempted to show personal favoritism not only to the rich, but also to the famous, the beautiful, the one in position of authority, and even the godly. If our idol of choice is wealth (if we are a lover of money), we will be tempted to show favoritism toward those whom we believe will give us wealth. But when the idol of our heart is the love of approval, we might well be tempted to show more respect to the one who will somehow give us a greater reputation. (Of course, to many, having a rich friend would be a great reputation-enhancer.)

The love of approval tempts the people-pleaser to give in to peer pressure. What is the *pressure* in *peer pressure*? It is the constraint one feels to conform to the conduct of his peers. But what if that conduct violates God's holy standards? Christians are commanded:

> *Do not be conformed* to this world, but be transformed by the renewing of your mind, so that you may prove what the will of God is, that which is good and acceptable and perfect. (Rom. 12:2)

To not conform to the crowd is to risk rejection along with all of its cruel consequences. The only thing more powerful than external peer pressure is the internal pleasure that comes from pleasing God (knowing and doing the good and acceptable and perfect will of God).

Can you imagine how impervious to influence our children would be if they feared God more than they feared the rejection of their peers? I am persuaded that the *single* best way for Christian parents to insulate their children against peer pressure is to teach them how to identify and dethrone the idol of man's approval and to replace it with an intense desire for God's approval.

The love of approval tempts the people-pleaser to be indecisive. Decisiveness is the ability to finalize decisions according to biblical principles and directives without undue delay. The people-pleaser struggles to bring a decision to a conclusion for two reasons. First, his conscience has been programmed more by what will please others than by what will please God, so that God's principles are not in the forefront of his mind when he makes decisions. Second, he is typically so concerned about how the decision will be seen by others that he spends inordinate amounts of time trying to look at the decision from every conceivable point of view. He has to fine-tune it in one way so as not to displease "this one," and tweak it another way so as not to upset "that one." He hesitates to finalize his decisions because he is petrified of making a mistake. To make a wrong decision might cause him to lose a friend—and his earthly friendships are often more valuable to him than his fellowship with Christ.

The love of approval tempts the people-pleaser to choose the wrong kinds of friends for the wrong reasons. On what basis do you choose your friends? You may have never given it much thought, but this is a very important question. The Bible repeatedly warns about the dangers of having wrong friends:

> He who walks with wise men will be wise, but the companion of fools will suffer harm. (Prov. 13:20)

> Do not be deceived: "Bad company corrupts good morals." (1 Cor. 15:33)

Many choose their friends carefully but for the wrong reasons. Some seek rich friends whose generosity they hope to "cash in on." Others go after fun-loving friends with whom they can party. Still others select as friends those whose vices are similar to their own (alcohol abuse, drug use, homosexuality, fornication) so that their vice will not stick out as unusual.

Now, let's consider the friends of the person who loves man's approval more than God's. Some men want successful businessmen to be their buddies so that they themselves will be seen as successful. Women sometimes look for friends who will not compete with them or show them up in certain areas (physical beauty, homemaking, or parenting skills). Many teenagers like to hang out only with those at school who are generally considered "cool." You see, the people-pleaser's tendency is to select as friends those who will be least likely to confront him (remember, those who love man's approval typically run away from conflict), those whom he believes will enhance his reputation, those whom he believes will be easy to please, or those whose admiration he is certain to receive.

Do not be deceived. One of the most subtly blinding effects of being a people-pleaser is that it diminishes our ability to discern potentially dangerous character flaws in our admirers. Hence we develop friendships with those whom we would otherwise avoid. Richard Baxter puts it well:

> No man is taken for so great a friend to the proud as their admirers; it doesn't matter what else they may be, they love those best who esteem them highest. The faults of these admirers can be extenuated and easily forgiven. They can be drunkards, or fornicators, or swearers, or otherwise ungodly, the proud man loves them according to the measure they honor him. If you would have his favor, let him hear that you have magnified him behind his back and that you honor him above all other men.[8]

People-pleasers will go to amazing lengths to gain a friend or to keep from losing one. They will boast, bribe, flatter, manipulate, lower their standards, live above their means, play the hypocrite, violate their convictions, change their doctrinal positions, or even lie. They crave friends not primarily for the sake of glorifying God through the friendships or for the sake of being a blessing to the friends, but for lesser,

8. Richard Baxter, *Baxter's Practical Works*, vol. 1, *A Christian Directory* (Ligonier, PA: Soli Deo Gloria Publications, 1990), 203.

more selfish motives (e.g., how such friends will make them look in the eyes of others—how they will enhance their reputation or standing or sense of belonging in the community). They are more loyal to people (for the sake of maintaining a friendship) than they are to the truth—especially if standing up for the truth might cost the friendship. Friendships with people are more important to them than friendship with God. They have never really considered that friendships with worldly people might place them at enmity with God (cf. James 4:4).

TOO TEDIOUS A TOPIC TO TACKLE

There are *many* other temptations and snares into which the people-pleaser's proud heart may lead him. For the sake of brevity (and so that reading this book will not become a tedious experience for you), I would like to *briefly* mention five more.[9]

The love of approval tempts the people-pleaser to discontentment and greed. Contentment is realizing that true satisfaction can come only from building our lives around those things that cannot be taken away or destroyed. "Do not store up for yourselves treasures on earth, where moth and rust destroy, and where thieves break in and steal. But store up for yourselves treasures in heaven, where neither moth nor rust destroys, and where thieves do not break in or steal" (Matt. 6:19–20). The temporal focus of the people-pleaser makes it all but impossible for him to lay up treasure in heaven. He spends his time collecting cheap, unstable earthly rewards, thus forfeiting eternal treasures and the security that comes with them (cf. Matt. 6:1–18). Moreover, in order for the approval junkie to keep his habit of pleasing and impressing others going, more funds are required. Rather than seeking first God's kingdom and righteousness, he seeks what the pagans seek and for the same purpose—that they might expend it upon their idolatrous lusts (cf. Matt. 6:33; James 4:3).

9. If you really haven't had enough and are truly a glutton for punishment, check out Baxter's section on people-pleasing and pride for yourself: ibid., 183–213.

The love of approval tempts the people-pleaser to be timid about sharing his faith. People-pleasers are often too embarrassed to be seen publicly giving thanks for their food, or to stand up for the truth, or to let it be known that they go to a "very conservative church." Perhaps most serious, though, is their inclination to be ashamed of the gospel. They don't want to be seen as "too pushy" or "overly zealous" or "fanatical." They don't want to be stuck with some unflattering label or religious nickname, so they keep the good news about Jesus Christ to themselves.

The love of approval tempts the people-pleaser to hypocrisy. Hypocrisy is professing (or pretending) to be or do one thing while being or doing another thing. It is invariably rooted in pride (specifically, in the idolatrous desire to please man rather than God).

> Hypocrisy largely consists of overvaluing man, and making too much of his opinions and words. The hypocrite's religion is divine in name but human in deed. It is man that he serves and observes the most. The embarrassment of the world is the evil that he most studiously avoids. The high esteem and commendation of the world is his reward.[10]

The love of approval tempts the people-pleaser to respond defensively when reproved by others.

> When a proud man is justly reproved, he immediately studies to deny or extenuate his fault (this shows you that he is more concerned with his honor than with his honesty). It is a hard thing to bring him to a voluntary confession, and to thank you for your love and faithfulness, and to commit to be more vigilant in the future. The humble man, on the other hand, is prompt to believe that he is much more guilty than he is innocent, and to say even more against himself than you do.[11]

10. Ibid., 178.
11. Ibid., 204.

The love of approval tempts the people-pleaser to loquaciousness. Be it boasting, or flattering, or fishing for compliments, the inordinate desire for approval tempts the idolater to open his mouth before engaging his brain. Solomon says, "When there are many words, transgression is unavoidable, but he who restrains his lips is wise" (Prov. 10:19), and "a fool's voice is known by his many words" (Eccl. 5:3b NKJV).

9. **Immoderate people-pleasing robs the approval-seeker of his peace and joy.** Can you think of an Old Testament character whose intense pride and desire for man's approval cost him everything he had? How about Haman in the book of Esther? I love it when the Bible gives us a glimpse into a person's heart by revealing the way he spoke to himself.

> So Haman came in and the king said to him, "What is to be done for the man whom the king desires to honor?" And Haman said to himself, "Whom would the king desire to honor more than me?" (Esth. 6:6)

Haman's pride turned him into a monster. His desire for and addiction to approval enticed him to many other sins, including anger, discontentment, self-pity, bitterness, jealousy, and ultimately murder (attempted genocide).

> When Haman saw that Mordecai neither bowed down nor paid homage to him, Haman was filled with rage . . .
> Then Haman went out that day glad and pleased of heart; but when Haman saw Mordecai in the king's gate and that he did not stand up or tremble before him, Haman was *filled with anger* against Mordecai. Haman controlled himself, however, went to his house and sent for his friends and his wife Zeresh. Then Haman recounted to them the glory of his riches, and the number of his sons, and every instance where the king had magnified him and how he had promoted him above the princes and servants of the king. Haman also said, "Even Esther the queen let no one but me come with the king to the banquet which she had prepared; and tomorrow also I am

invited by her with the king. *Yet all of this does not satisfy me every time I see Mordecai the Jew sitting at the king's gate.*" (Esth. 3:5; 5:9–13)

Haman's pride and jealousy destroyed any happiness he may have known. His extreme disappointment over not receiving approbation from Mordecai also made it impossible for him to enjoy his own family, his wealth, and the tremendous honor he had already received. That's what being a people-pleaser can do for you, too.

Early in my own ministry, after delivering a message that was below my expectations, I would sometimes allow myself to be robbed of the joy that comes from knowing that the Lord was pleased to use me and bless others. Why? Because I was more concerned with man's approval than I was with God's. Almost invariably, I knew that the content of what I was presenting was sound, practical, useful, and necessary to my audience. Yet because my delivery was not as smooth and polished as I had hoped, I would be angry and depressed for hours. Whom was I really trying to please? Not God, but men.

Another sin that flows from an inordinate desire for man's approval deserves mention here. By seeking to please man rather than God, you set yourself up to be plagued by anxiety. Anxiety (or worry) will steal the peace and joy that are part of your birthright as a Christian. How much time do you spend thinking about how to avoid displeasing others? May I suggest that most of these thoughts that you believe are simply a matter of not wanting to displease others fall more accurately into the arena of anxiety. When you are overly concerned about displeasing others, you are worrying about what they will think of you or how they might reject you or how they might cause you grief in some other way. And worry is a sin.

The Holy Spirit commands us in Philippians 4:6 to "be anxious for nothing." Jesus said in Matthew 6:34, "Do not worry about tomorrow." Worry is also a lack of faith in God (cf. Matt. 6:28–30). Moreover, worry damages the body: "Do you not know that you are a temple of God and that the Spirit of God dwells in you? If any man destroys the temple of

God, God will destroy him, for the temple of God is holy, and that is what you are" (1 Cor. 3:16–17). Finally, worrying consumes an inordinate amount of time that could be better spent thinking about and doing those things that are eternally profitable. The Bible commands us to "walk circumspectly, not as fools but as wise, redeeming the time, because the days are evil" (Eph. 5:15–16 NKJV).

To spend your time thinking about what you can do to keep from disappointing *him*, or what might happen if you were to displease *her*, or how it might look if you did *this*, or how you might be rejected if you didn't do *that*, rather than simply thinking about how you can please God, is not only worry, but stupidity. By filling your mind with such anxiety-producing thoughts, you short-circuit the peace and joy that the Holy Spirit gives to those who love Christ and his Word. "Great peace have those who love Your law, and nothing causes them to stumble" (Ps. 119:165 NKJV).

Add to this anxiety the perpetual disappointment and frustration that will inevitably result when you make it one of your chief goals to do something that is not even possible and you have a formula that is guaranteed to rob you of your joy and peace. As we will see in the next chapter, investing so much of your time, effort, and thought in trying to please people rather than God is truly an exasperating exercise in futility.

Five

YOU CAN'T PLEASE
ALL OF THE PEOPLE EVEN
SOME OF THE TIME

Perhaps you've thought, "I can please some of the people all of the time, and all of the people some of the time, but I can't please all of the people all of the time." I say: "You can please some of the people *some* of the time, and all of the people *none* of the time, but you can please God *most* of the time. In other words, it is more likely, from a biblical perspective, that you will be able to please God most of the time than that you will be able to please all men some of the time." It is going to take two chapters to cover both sides of this proverb, so please stay with me. Let's begin with the notion of pleasing none of the people all of the time. There may be no more powerful argument to persuade you to stop seeking the approval of man than that of the profound folly, futility, and utter impossibility of trying to please all of the people some of the time.

Suppose you have five one-dollar bills in your pocket—nothing else. Twelve homeless children walk up to you begging for money. Can you please them all? If your motive is to please man, you will be disappointed. You will end up displeasing and being reviled by more people than you are pleasing. But if your desire is to please God, you will not be disappointed regardless of just which way you choose to distribute the money.

Let's take a closer look at some of the reasons why effectively pleasing men is so inane and virtually impossible.

"Wait a minute, Lou. Not so fast! What about that verse in Corinthians you mentioned earlier where Paul says that he tries to 'please all men in all things'?"

That's a good and fair question. The exact reference is 1 Corinthians 10:31–33:

> Whether, then, you eat or drink or whatever you do, do all to the glory of God. Give no offense either to Jews or to Greeks or to the church of God; just as I also please all men in all things, not seeking my own profit but the profit of the many, so that they may be saved.

"All men" in this passage doesn't mean *every single man* but rather *all types* (or *all kinds*) *of men*. Paul wasn't trying to please every single man (he makes this clear in Galatians 1:10); but as mentioned in chapter 2, in order to not give offense to the Jews or Greeks or Christians, he was trying to please all these types of people in a variety (all kinds) of ways. Now that we've cleared up that matter, let's see why attempting to please man is such an exercise in futility.

1. **It is fruitless to try to please men because each person is different and therefore, by pleasing some, you will inevitably displease others.** Paul asks the question in 1 Corinthians 4:7 (NKJV), "Who makes you differ from another?" The obvious answer is, "God does." These inherent differences include such things as tastes, interests, intellect, gifts, and abilities. Since each of us likes and dislikes any number of things based on our unique personality, pleasing all people—even a small cross section of them—is an impossible thing to do in most cases. When you add man's sinful heart into the equation, the statistical probability of pleasing even some men all of the time is infinitesimally small.

Let's use this book for an example. If it is lengthier than some of you were expecting, I could fall into disfavor with you for being so long-winded. "He's intoxicated with the exuberance of his verbosity," some will say. On the other hand, if I cut my topic short out of deference to those who are not accustomed to reading a time-consuming tome (as I did in the previous chapter), I will deeply disappoint you (not to mention anger you for wasting your money on a book that offers such a limited treatment of the problem). I'm confident that someone somewhere is, in fact, going to find fault with me for not covering in the book some element of the people-pleasing problem or one of its biblical solutions.

If I do not use as many entertaining illustrations as some of you would like, I run the risk of losing your interest. Yet if I use frequent illustrations, I will be considered by a few to be a "storyteller" rather than a Christian writer who is to be "taken seriously."

If I tell a funny story or two, some may accuse me of using the book to display my showmanship. Others will think me too serious or stiff if I refrain from using humor. They might say, "Lou, you need to 'lighten up' and 'loosen up' more when you're writing. You're too serious." Still others who know me best would opine, "It doesn't matter what you say, Lou. You couldn't intentionally be funny if your life depended on it."

If I use the word *sin* too much, I will be labeled by some as a "legalist" or as a "Bible-thumping fundamentalist who likes to put people on guilt trips."[1] Then again, if I don't talk enough about sin and its repugnancy to God, I'll be thought of by a number of you as a "compromising, neo-evangelical psychobabbler."

If I quoted from the King James translation of the Bible, some of you would remind me that we are living in the twenty-first century. If I cited the NASB, some would brand me a modernist. And if I ever quoted from a dynamic equivalent, such as the NIV—albeit only for clarification of meaning—some might label me as a heretic.

---

1. I do consider myself to be a Bible-believing fundamentalist in the sense that there are certain fundamental Bible doctrines from which I could never be dissuaded. Of this I am not ashamed.

If I quoted dozens of verses but didn't explain them in context, believing that the Holy Spirit would use God's Word as He sees fit in your life, I would be accused of proof-texting and of not arguing my case well enough. But if I exegeted every passage quoted in the book for my readers, someone would think I come across like a college professor who needs to write books for seminary students rather than for laymen.

You may have noticed by now that I like to use contractions in my writing. Yet if I use too many of them, some will think my writing to be too casual, if not unprofessional. If I don't use any contractions, some of y'all will think that I'm a stiff, prim and proper, punctilious (Yankee) snob who needs to learn to relate better to the common man (or woman).

Now, the point is not so much who's right and who's wrong in this matter, but rather whom I am trying to please in my writing. No activity, no behavior, no attitude will please all men at all times! The only thing that seems to please most of the people most of the time and command enduring and consistent praise is true Christian character. But even genuinely Christlike character can be misunderstood and will displease some.

2. It is unrealistic to try to please people because selfishness distorts their thinking and raises their expectations above that which you can reasonably fulfill. Let's consider how the noetic effects of sin have enfeebled man's judgment. *Noetic* refers to the effects that sin has on man's thought and thinking.

> So this I say, and affirm together with the Lord, that you walk no longer just as the Gentiles also walk, in the *futility of their mind*, being *darkened* in their *understanding*, excluded from the life of God because of the ignorance that is in them, because of the *hardness* of their heart . . . (Eph. 4:17–18)

Every part of man's heart and mind has been negatively affected by sin. This means that everything—from his conscience to his sense of humor, his perceptions to his judgments—is, in varying degrees, marred by the fall. You and I are totally depraved. That sounds terrible, and—

well, it really is. "Total depravity" doesn't mean that we are as bad as we might be but rather that, among all the other parts of our human nature, our abilities to think correctly have been distorted. Sin has affected man's *entire thought process*—his perceptions, his reasoning ability, his judgments, his motives, his appetites, his desires, and his expectations. Why, then, would you trust his ability to discern your character and determine the basis on which he approves or disapproves of you? Why trust him to determine the standard by which he accepts or rejects you?

Listen also to what God says to us through the prophet Isaiah about esteeming fallen man's opinion:

> Stop regarding man, whose breath of life is in his nostrils; for why should he be esteemed? (Isa. 2:22)

Richard Baxter had some insightful things to say about the self-centered nature of man's expectations:

> Remember that men are so selfish that their expectations will be greater than you will be able to satisfy. They will not consider those things that might prevent you from giving them what they desire, such as your ministry to others, or your job, or your necessary diversionary activities. They want you all to themselves as though you had no one else to care for but them. Frequently, when I was under tremendous time pressure, a multitude of people each thought that I should have spent all of my time with them. When I visited with one, there were ten offended that I was not visiting them at that very moment. When I was speaking with one, many more were offended that I was not rather talking with them. If those with whom I am speaking consider me to be courteous and attentive, those with whom I could not converse—except maybe for a brief moment or two—consider me to be discourteous and inattentive. How many have been upset with me because God and conscience commanded me to spend my time on greater and more important things.[2]

2. Richard Baxter, *Baxter's Practical Works*, vol. 1, *A Christian Directory* (Ligonier, PA: Soli Deo Gloria Publications, 1990), 187.

3. It is futile to try to please people because most of them are un-regenerate and believe you to be "foolish" and "strange." You will be profoundly disappointed if you, as a Christian, try to please unregen-erate men, expecting them to approve of those things in your life that convict them of their sin, or expecting them to understand the things in your life that they have not the capacity to understand.

First, consider the issue of unduly seeking to please those who are likely to be convicted by your words and actions. The Scriptures are filled with examples of unregenerate men and women who were furious at God's servants because their obedience was such a rebuke to them.

Take the apostles, for example. After being miraculously released from prison by an angel, they were dragged from the temple before the Sanhedrin to stand trial.

> But Peter and the other apostles answered and said: "We ought to obey God rather than men. The God of our fathers raised up Jesus whom you murdered by hanging on a tree. Him God has exalted to His right hand to be Prince and Savior, to give repentance to Israel and for-giveness of sins. And we are His witnesses to these things, and so also is the Holy Spirit whom God has given to those who obey Him."
>
> When they heard this, they were furious and plotted to kill them. (Acts 5:29–33 NKJV)

And then there was Stephen:

> When they heard this, they were furious and gnashed their teeth at him. But Stephen, full of the Holy Spirit, looked up to heaven and saw the glory of God, and Jesus standing at the right hand of God. "Look," he said, "I see heaven open and the Son of Man standing at the right hand of God."
>
> At this they covered their ears and, yelling at the top of their voices, they all rushed at him, dragged him out of the city and began to stone him. Meanwhile, the witnesses laid their clothes at the feet of a young man named Saul. (Acts 7:54–58 NIV)

Time will not permit the mention of all the others (such as Cain vs. Abel, Saul vs. David, Haman vs. Mordecai, and of course, the scribes, Pharisees, Sadducees, High Priest, people of Nazareth, etc., vs. Jesus) whose words and actions brought such vicious disapproval from those who did not understand the things of God. So if the lives of these brought such conviction on (and elicited such wrath from) the lost, how wise an investment is it for you to spend your time, effort, and thoughts on selfishly seeking their approval?

And then consider the matter of expecting unregenerate men and women to understand your spirituality.

What would you say if I told you that right there in the room (or place) where you are reading these words, there are hundreds of other voices, and that if I were there with you, I would be able to hear them all?

"I'd say, 'I know a counselor who is in need of some serious counseling.'"

Well, it's true. Right there where you are, there are lots of voices, but you can't hear them, can you? You could if you had the right receiver. You see, I have in my possession a special radio that can pick up not only AM and FM frequencies, but television, weather, and shortwave signals as well. I can hear them all. And you could, too, if you had the right equipment. Then, of course, there are all those digital telephone and satellite radio and television waves around you that could also be received with the precise technology.

"All right, so you're not as crazy as I thought, but what does this have to do with not being able to please all of the people some of the time?"

Simply this: For a moment, you thought it was foolish and strange of me to claim that I could hear voices that you could not hear. The Bible says that people who do not have the Holy Spirit (the divine receiver that helps us understand and apply to our lives the truth of Scripture) think that our way of life is foolish and strange:

But a natural man does not accept the things of the Spirit of God, for they are foolishness to him; and he cannot understand them, because they are spiritually appraised. (1 Cor. 2:14)

For we have spent enough of our past lifetime in doing the will of the Gentiles—when we walked in lewdness, lusts, drunkenness, revelries, drinking parties, and abominable idolatries. In regard to these, they think it *strange* that you do not run with them in the same flood of dissipation, *speaking evil of you.* (1 Peter 4:3–4 NKJV)

There will always be those around you who, because they do not know Christ, will necessarily be displeased with your way of life. You'll never be able to please them as long as you obey the Lord.

4. It is unreasonable to try to please people because even among Christians, judgmental attitudes and critical spirits are all too prevalent. I'm going to ask you to be brutally honest about something. On a scale of 1 to 10 (1 being "I regularly make very unloving critical comments about others," and 10 being "I hardly ever make uncharitable judgments in my heart about others"), how critical are you of others? Before you answer, read this:

Also do not take to heart everything people say, lest you hear your servant cursing you. For *many times*, also, your own heart has known that *even you* have cursed others. (Eccl. 7:21–22 NKJV)

But no one can tame the tongue; it is a restless evil and full of deadly poison. With it we bless our Lord and Father, and with it we curse men, who have been made in the likeness of God; *from the same mouth come both blessing and cursing.* My brethren, these things ought not to be this way. (James 3:8–10)

So how would you rate yourself? The truth is, even though we know it's wrong, and even though we do not want others to do it to us, most of us regularly make very unloving judgments about others. Often the judgments of our hearts gush out of our mouths.

> The mouth speaks out of that which fills the heart. The good man brings out of his good treasure what is good; and the evil man brings out of his evil treasure what is evil. (Matt. 12: 34b–35)

I like the way Baxter sees it:

> Few people know the circumstances and reasons for what you do. They will presume to criticize you before they hear what you have to say. Had they done so, they would have absolved you of all charges in their own mind. It is rare to meet, even among professing believers who are sincerely committed [to Christ], those who are fearful and sensitive about sinning in this area of rash, ungrounded judging.[3]

Now, if even we Christians struggle to one degree or another with being too critical, why should you waste your resources by trying so hard to please such critical creatures as we are? God is the only one who evaluates us righteously. "Many seek the ruler's favor, but justice for man comes from the LORD" (Prov. 29:26).

Some time ago, one of my friends began to criticize another one of my friends to me. I looked friend number one straight in the eyes and, with a smile on my face, said, "That's all right. I know something bad about *everybody* I know."

5. It is futile to try to please people because even Jesus Christ, the Perfect Man, did not please everyone. You and I are far (light-years) from perfect. But even if we were perfect, we still wouldn't be able to please everyone. Listen to what some of Jesus Christ's critics had to say about Him:

> The Son of Man has come eating and drinking, and you say, "Behold, a gluttonous man and a drunkard, a friend of tax collectors and sinners!" (Luke 7:34)

3. Ibid., 188.

Both the Pharisees and the scribes began to grumble, saying, "This man receives sinners and eats with them." (Luke 15:2)

When Jesus came to the place, He looked up and said to him, "Zaccheus, hurry and come down, for today I must stay at your house." And he hurried and came down and received Him gladly. When they saw it, they all began to grumble, saying, "He has gone to be the guest of a man who is a sinner." (Luke 19:5–7)

"But because I speak the truth, you do not believe Me. Which one of you convicts Me of sin? If I speak truth, why do you not believe Me? He who is of God hears the words of God; for this reason you do not hear them, because you are not of God."

The Jews answered and said to Him, "Do we not say rightly that You are a Samaritan and have a demon?" (John 8:45–48)

Even with all His virtues—His blamelessness, His ability to heal, His love, His goodness, His wisdom, His lack of partiality, His compassion, His sincerity, and all the rest of His perfections—He did not prevent everyone from speaking evil against Him and rejecting Him. Neither did He try to do so. Why, then, should you? "If they have called the head of the house Beelzebul, how much more will they malign the members of his household!" (Matt. 10:25b)

6. It is useless to try to please people because they are fundamentally incapable of being pleased by anyone or anything other than Christ. To be sure, man can look to virtually anything for pleasure and satisfaction. But in the final analysis, nothing pleases and satisfies man the way God does.

Sheol [hell] and Abaddon [destruction] are never satisfied, nor are the eyes of man ever satisfied. (Prov. 27:20)

The eye is not satisfied with seeing, nor is the ear filled with hearing. (Eccl. 1:8b)

"And My people will be satisfied with My goodness," declares the LORD. (Jer. 31:14b)

The only hope you and I have of pleasing people is by introducing them to the only One who can truly please and satisfy them—the Lord Jesus Christ. Yet even that has one difficulty—especially if you are a people-pleaser: by introducing them to the Savior, you face a greater likelihood of being rejected by them yourself. Are you ashamed of the gospel of Christ? If so, as I alluded to earlier, it could be another indication that you love the approval of man more than the approval of God. Or can you say with Paul, "I am not ashamed of the gospel, for it is the power of God for salvation to everyone who believes . . ." (Rom. 1:16)? Jesus said, "For whoever is ashamed of Me and My words, the Son of Man will be ashamed of him when He comes in His glory, and the glory of the Father and of the holy angels" (Luke 9:26).

I hope I've persuaded you (not that I'm trying to impress you) that "you can please some of the people *some* of the time, and all of the people *none* of the time . . ." In the next chapter, we'll examine the more important segment of the proverb, "You can please God *most* of the time."

Six

BUT YOU CAN PLEASE GOD

You are about to read what is probably the most important chapter in this book. I mention that not because you are going to learn here some of the many practical things you can do to overcome the love of approval (as you will in the final segments of *Pleasing People*), but because, in principle, learning to please God instead of man is the single greatest remedy to the problem of pleasing man. So if you comprehend and apply nothing else in this book but what you are about to learn, you will be well on your way to freedom.

It's not enough for you to simply stop being a people-pleaser. The biblical process of change (putting off and putting on, cf. Eph. 4:22ff.) requires not only that you break your unbiblical patterns of thinking, but also that you replace them with their proper alternatives. The fear of man is to be replaced with fear of God. The desire to please man above all else is to be replaced with the desire to please God above all else. The fear of displeasing man (or of falling into his disfavor) is to be replaced with the fear of displeasing God (or of falling into His disfavor). The love of man's approval is to be replaced with the love of God's approval. Remember, the people-pleasing problem does not lie in the *liking* of man's approval but rather in the *loving* of man's approval *above and beyond* God's approval. "For they *loved* the approval of men rather than the approval of God" (John 12:43).

To eliminate the lust for man's approval, you'll have to replace it with a lust for God's approval. The best way to dethrone this approval idol is to prayerfully develop a desire (cultivate an appetite) for the approval of the One who righteously judges not only your words, actions, and attitudes, but also the thoughts and intentions of your heart. This must be your highest goal—your number-one priority.

Jim Elliot used to speak of earning his AUG degree. *AUG* stood for the King James English rendition of the phrase in 2 Timothy 2:15, *Approved Unto God*: "Study to shew thyself approved unto God, a workman that needeth not to be ashamed, rightly dividing the word of truth." Based on his biography, I doubt that Jim Elliot was the kind of man who struggled much with being a people-pleaser. As we've seen, neither was the apostle Paul. Why? For the same reason: he was more concerned about pleasing God than pleasing man.

> Therefore we also have as our *ambition* [make it our aim], whether at home or absent, to be *pleasing* to Him. (2 Cor. 5:9)

Is it your ambition to please God? Have you really made it your aim to do so? If you want to overcome the sin of people-pleasing, you've got to aspire to nothing less.

Imagine what it will be like to long for God's approval more than the approval of all men. Think of the day when you long to please God so much that you no longer worry about what others think of you. "There goes [insert your name]," they'll say of you. "He's the most objective, impartial, and God-fearing person I know. He doesn't seem to care what others think of him." And when you stand before the Lord, you'll hear Him say, "Well done, thou good and faithful servant." Moreover, that little "love of approval" handle that protrudes from your back by which others now control you will be broken. The strings that others now use to manipulate and intimidate you will be cut, and you will experience a new freedom to serve God without fearing man. Fix your hope on these goals until they become a reality.

BENEFITS OF PLEASING GOD RATHER THAN PEOPLE

In the last chapter, we explored the futility of trying to please man. Let's now look at (and compare) the advantages of pleasing God over the disadvantages of trying to please man.

1. You have only one Master to please rather than many. To begin with, having only one boss is much easier than having many. Years ago, I was the front-end manager of a large grocery store in a prominent chain of supermarkets in the New York City area. My duties included being responsible for the cashiers and shopping-cart retrievers, and for making sure that every item that lcft the store was rung up properly and paid for. It was one of the most exasperating jobs I've ever had. (I was only twenty years old at the time, so I'm sure my youth and immaturity played a large part in my frustration.) But the greatest external contribution to the problem was the fact that I had more than a dozen bosses. Not only was I accountable to (and required to follow the directives of) the store manager, but I was also accountable to the assistant manager, the department managers (grocery, dairy, produce, meat, and frozen foods), the district manager and his assistants, the district chief of security and his assistant, and the family who owned the chain and who were really the top bosses. At any given time, I could and would get orders from any number of them. My frustration, as you can imagine, had to do with the fact that their instructions would sometimes conflict. So to please one, I would have to displease another. In my mind, I had to sort out the pecking order so that I would always follow the instructions of the boss with the greatest authority.

So how many bosses are you trying to please? If you are seeking to please man, you have many masters to serve. Or as Richard Baxter put it, "If you seek first to please God and are satisfied with that, you have but one to please instead of multitudes; and a multitude of masters are harder to please than one."[1]

1. Richard Baxter, *Baxter's Practical Works*, vol. 1, *A Christian Directory* (Ligonier, PA: Soli Deo Gloria Publications, 1990), 191.

2. The One you please is wiser than man and will neither misunderstand you nor treat you unreasonably. How many times have you been misunderstood by others? How often have your words, actions, attitudes, thoughts, and motives been misjudged by those closest to you? Yet how many times has the Lord misunderstood you? He has *never* misread, misjudged, misunderstood, or misconstrued *anything* about you.

How many times have others been unreasonable with you? How often have they taken advantage of you and mistreated you? How frequently has man criticized you and falsely accused you? How many times have you been robbed of justice and equity by your fellow man? Can you say such things about Almighty God? "Does God pervert justice? Or does the Almighty pervert what is right?" (Job 8:3). Of course not! The Lord knows when you sit down and when you rise up. He understands your thoughts afar off. He comprehends your going out and your lying down. He is acquainted with all your ways. In fact, there is not a word on your tongue that He does not totally know (cf. Ps. 139:2).

Even "the foolishness of God is wiser than men, and the weakness of God is stronger than men" (1 Cor. 1:25). Why, then, would you choose to court the favor of your fickle fellows over that of your wise and merciful heavenly Father? Why would you stoop to serve such an unjust master as a multitude of unreasonable men when you could serve the most understanding and reasonable Master, the Creator and Sustainer of the universe?

3. The One you please will judge you not on outward appearance, but on that which is in your heart. Unlike your fellow man, God sees not only your words, actions, and attitudes, but also your thoughts and motives.

> But the LORD said to Samuel, "Do not look at his appearance or at the height of his stature, because I have rejected him; for God sees not as man sees, for man looks at the outward appearance, but the LORD looks at the heart." (1 Sam. 16:7)

Look for a moment at the diagram below. You and I are able to see with some degree of accuracy our own words, actions, attitudes, thoughts, and motives. The further into our hearts we look, however, the more difficult it becomes for us to evaluate things accurately. In other words, because they are more readily apparent to our view, our words and actions are much easier to detect than our attitudes, thoughts, and motives. As the arrows in the diagram extend downward into the hidden areas of the heart, they become darker to represent the greater difficulty we have in seeing things clearly.

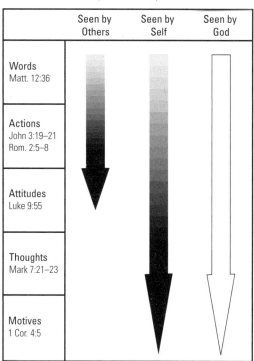

Things That Proceed Out of the Heart
(Mark 7:20–23)

	Seen by Others	Seen by Self	Seen by God
Words Matt. 12:36			
Actions John 3:19–21 Rom. 2:5–8			
Attitudes Luke 9:55			
Thoughts Mark 7:21–23			
Motives 1 Cor. 4:5			

Now, when it comes to evaluating others, it is a different matter. Since we cannot see the thoughts and motives of others, we cannot accurately judge them. Indeed, we are actually forbidden to do so:

"Therefore do not go on passing judgment before the time, but wait until the Lord comes who will both bring to light the things hidden in the darkness and disclose the motives of men's hearts; and then each man's praise will come to him from God" (1 Cor. 4:5). Sadly, this biblical prohibition does not prevent many from making such judgments and using such "inadmissible evidence" against us. Consequently, not only are our words, actions, and attitudes subject to the uncharitable scrutiny of man (love is supposed to put the best interpretation on these external observations according to 1 Corinthians 13:7), but our thoughts and motives come under fire as well.

God is the only one who can see and rightly evaluate all our external and internal behavior. And He assesses these things in our lives even better than we can.[2] His ability to judge these areas is at once more severe and more merciful than our own sin-tainted capacity to discern ourselves. Hugh Blair explains the depth of God's ability to evaluate our conduct:

> God is the only unerring judge of what is excellent. His approval alone is the substance of honor; all other praise is but the shadow of honor. But the Sovereign of the world sees you in every light in which you can be seen . . . From Him you may receive the praise of good actions that you had no opportunity of performing. For he sees them through your motives; he judges you by your intentions; he knows what you would have done if you but had the opportunity. You may be in his eyes a hero or a martyr, without undergoing the labors of the one, or the sufferings of the other. His inspection, therefore, opens a much wider field for praise than what the world can offer you . . .[3]

Something else to consider before moving on to the next point is God's sovereignty over your life. It is God, and God alone, who possesses the assets and abilities to order the circumstances of your

---

2. We should judge our own thoughts, words, attitudes, and motives (cf. 1 Cor. 11:27–34) using the Word of God, which is "able to judge the thoughts and intentions of the heart" (Heb. 4:12).

3. *Sermons by Hugh Blair, D.D.* (London: T. Cadell; C & J Rivington, 1827), 189.

life so as to bring you either happiness or misery. He is the one who can make you or break you in every area. Why, then, do you seek with such enthusiasm to influence man, who is himself unable apart from God's authorization to do anything for you? "Who is there who speaks and it comes to pass, unless the LORD has commanded it?" (Lam. 3:37)

Is it not an exercise in futility to seek to please man *more* than the living God, who is the blessed controller of all things and who has promised to sovereignly work all things together for good to those who love him? By pleasing God and seeking His approbation above that of your fellow man, you can demonstrate your love for Him and thus secure your claim to this precious promise of Romans 8:28:

> And we know that God causes all things to work together for good to those who love God, to those who are called according to His purpose.

4. The One you please is not a respecter of persons. According to William Barclay, University of Glasgow lecturer, "*respect of persons* is the New Testament phrase for undue and unfair partiality; it means pandering to someone because he is rich or influential or popular."[4] The literal meaning of the Greek phrase "to lift up the face of" is an exact translation of a Hebrew idiom found several times in the Old Testament. Originally, "to lift up the countenance of someone" meant "to regard him favorably." It soon metamorphosed into "showing favoritism." John MacArthur describes the kind of partiality that God is incapable of showing:

> That exact idea is seen in the popular symbolic statue of justice as a woman blindfolded, signifying that she is unable to see who is before her to be judged and therefore is not tempted to be partial either for or against the accused. Sometimes she is also pictured with her hands tied, suggesting she cannot receive a bribe.

4. William Barclay, ed., *The Letters of James and Peter*, in *The Daily Study Bible Series*, rev. ed. (James 2:1) (Philadelphia: Westminster Press, 2000), electronic edition.

Unfortunately, there is partiality even in the best of human courts, but there will be none in God's day of judgment. Because of His perfect knowledge of every detail and because of His perfect righteousness, it is not possible for His justice to be anything but perfectly impartial. Such things as position, education, influence, popularity, or physical appearance will have absolutely no bearing on God's decision concerning a person's eternal destiny.[5]

Following are a few New Testament Scripture passages that confirm this truth.

Acts 10:34   Opening his mouth, Peter said: "I most certainly understand now that God is not one to show partiality . . ."

Romans 2:11   For there is no partiality with God.

Galatians 2:6   But from those who were of high reputation (what they were makes no difference to me; God shows no partiality)—well, those who were of reputation contributed nothing to me."

Ephesians 6:9   And masters, do the same things to them, and give up threatening, knowing that both their Master and yours is in heaven, and there is no partiality with Him.

Colossians 3:25   But he who does wrong will be repaid for what he has done, and there is no partiality. (NKJV)

1 Peter 1:17   And if you call on the Father, who without partiality judges according to each one's work, conduct yourselves throughout the time of your stay here in fear . . . (NKJV)

God is the kind of judge whose opinion cannot be bought, prejudiced, or unduly influenced.

5. John MacArthur, *Romans* (Rom. 2:11) (Chicago: Moody Press, 1996).

5. The One you please is immutable. Unlike man, whose mind often changes with the minutest bit of "new information," God's mind doesn't change. "Jesus Christ is the same yesterday, today, and forever" (Heb. 13:8 NKJV).

For I am the LORD, I do not change . . . (Mal. 3:6 NKJV)

Also the Glory of Israel will not lie or change His mind; for He is not a man that He should change His mind. (1 Sam. 15:29)

How often has God told you to do one thing and then reversed His decision, requiring you to do another? When was the last time you read something in the Bible, only to discover the next time you read it that it had been revised? How many times has pleasing God one day involved doing something that would displease Him the next?

The things that please man today may very well displease him tomorrow. Even in marriage, people change their minds, as illustrated in one of my previous books:

When my wife Kim and I were on a trip in our first year of marriage, I stopped at a local convenience store to fill the car with gasoline. She asked me if I would please get her something to drink. I remembered she had told me several times previously that her favorite soft drink was Diet Pepsi.™ As I opened the glass door to the refrigerator, I spied a Tab™ and remembered her telling me that she hated Tab.™ "I've got to find a Diet Pepsi,™" I thought to myself. "She hates Tab.™" After locating the Diet Pepsi™ and paying for it and the gas, I confidently walked up to her side of the car with "her favorite soft drink" in my hand, expecting her to be so pleased that I had remembered.

"Diet Pepsi,™" she said, with disappointment in her voice. "I really wanted a Tab.™"

"But you told me that you *absolutely hate* Tab!™" I said with profound incredulity!

"I know, but today I want a Tab™, and I think I'm starting to prefer Tab™ to Diet Pepsi.™ "[6]

Now, if pleasing one's spouse is hard to do because of the tendency
to change our mind, how much more difficult is it to please those with
whom we are not so well acquainted? Man changes his mind regularly.
God doesn't change His.

"But what about those verses that say God repented?"

Sure, a number of verses (e.g., Gen. 6:6; Exod. 32:14; Jer. 18:8; Amos
7:3, 6; Jonah 3:10) say that God repented (or relented). But as R. A. Torrey
explains in his book *Difficulties in the Bible: Alleged Errors and Contradictions*:

> If God does remain the same in character, infinitely hating sin and
> absolutely unchangeable in His purpose to visit sin with judgment,
> then if any city or any person changes in attitude toward sin, God must
> necessarily change in His attitude toward that person or city. If God
> remains the same, if His attitude toward sin and righteousness is un-
> changing, then His dealings with men must change as they turn from
> sin to repentance. His character remains ever the same, but His deal-
> ings with men change as they change from the position that is hate-
> ful to His unchanging hatred of sin to one that is pleasing to His
> unchanging love of righteousness.[7]

The God of the Bible is stable, unwavering, consistent, and un-
changeable. As Baxter put it, "He is not pleased with one thing today,
and another . . . tomorrow; nor with one person this year, whom He will
be weary of the next."[8]

**6. The One you please does not require you to harm yourself in
order to please him, but is pleased only with those things that will ultimately lead to your own happiness.** God does not delight in taking

6. Lou Priolo, *The Complete Husband* (Amityville, NY: Calvary Press, 1999), 28.

7. R. A. Torrey, *Difficulties in the Bible: Alleged Errors and Contradictions* (Willow Grove, PA:
Woodlawn Electronic Publishing, 1998), electronic edition.

8. Baxter, *A Christian Directory*, 192.

away from His servants everything that brings them happiness, satisfaction, or pleasure. Neither is He a harsh taskmaster who delights in seeing His servants harmed. Some people view God as an uncaring, callous, cosmic-killjoy who is ready to pounce on any of His subjects who start enjoying themselves too much.

"Well, I certainly don't see God *that* way."

Good! But let me ask about your view of the Bible. How do you regard all those commands that God has placed in there? Do you see them as a burden or as a blessing? A proper view of God sees His commands not as toilsome, pleasure-stealing burdens to be lugged around, but rather as divine invitations to health, happiness, and (to a certain degree) prosperity. "Blessed are those who hear the word of God and observe it." (Luke 11:28)

God is pleased with those things that will eventually lead to our happiness. Yes, it is true that God often expects us to forfeit short-term happiness for the sake of long-term happiness. Sometimes we are called to sacrifice temporal happiness so that we might experience a greater measure of eternal bliss. But He never asks of us that which is not in our own best interest and for our own ultimate happiness.

Man's expectations of us are often quite different, aren't they? We are often called on or expected to do immoral and dangerous things by those we are trying to please.

> "If you really want to please me:
>   go into debt to buy me what I want,
>   or do whatever it takes to lose 10 pounds,
>   or go to bed with me,
>   or get drunk with me,
>   or get high with me,
>   or lie for me,
>   or let me cheat on this test by peeking over your shoulder,
>   or break the law for me,
>   or look the other way when I break the law,
>   or stay home from church with me."

In the final analysis, God is much more merciful with what it takes to please Him than man could ever be. For even when man is merciful, his shortsightedness rarely takes into account either the blessedness of having godly character or the bliss of eternal rewards.

7. The One you please will not be influenced by talebearers, gossips, or false accusers. Neither will he be misled by misinformation. Let's face it. You and I live among talebearing, troublemaking tattlers whose natural bent it is to exalt themselves by criticizing others (cf. Eccl. 7:22; Matt. 5:19; James 3:9). Of course, all tales about you will be told behind your back when you are incapable of answering your accusers face to face (cf. Prov. 18:17; John 7:51; Acts 25:16).

Most men will believe the bad they hear about you secondhand and allow it to influence their opinion of you more readily than they will believe and be influenced by a good report about you. Sadly, this happens all too often among Christians, even among Christians who claim to be friends. Baxter explains:

> And if the men who hear, think well of the one who accuses or backbites you, they think it lawful to believe him. And if they are friends or associates of the talebearer, his honesty (and accuracy) will be assumed and his credibility will not be questioned. It is not unusual for even a learned, ingenious or even a godly man to be too forward in uttering, from the mouth of others, an evil report. In such cases, the hearer thinks himself fully justified for believing it and reporting it to others.[9]

MISLED BY MISINFORMATION

Suppose you and I are members of the same church. It's Sunday morning before worship, and we are standing around reminiscing with our mutual friends about the great time we had at the football game last evening. In the course of our conversation, I am called away by the

9. Ibid., 188 (loose paraphrase).

pastor. You then exclaim, "Lou and I sat together for every play, and he was sober for the entire game!" You would have spoken the truth. You would also have seriously misled our friends by implying things about me that were erroneous. Misinformation takes many forms. The truth isn't plural, but lies come in all shapes and sizes.

When it comes to misinformation, people are gullible—especially God's people. Most of the lies that were perpetrated in the Bible successfully duped their victims. When lies were detected, it usually took a special act of God to expose them (e.g., the two harlots who stood before Solomon; Ananias and Sapphira).[10] Only God knows who is telling the truth and who is lying. He cannot be misled by any variety of falsehood, no matter how cleverly disguised. His opinion of you is totally unaffected by misinformation that others are prone to believe about you.

Speaking of Christ, Isaiah prophesied, "He will not judge by what His eyes see, nor make a decision by what His ears hear; but with righteousness He will judge the poor, and decide with fairness for the afflicted of the earth" (Isa. 11:3b–4a). Unlike man, God is impervious to the influence of erroneous reports (and is therefore much easier to please).

Your primary calling in life is to please and glorify God in all that you do. The knowledge that you are walking worthy of the Lord, pleasing Him in all respects (cf. Col. 1:10), should be a source of peace, security, joy, and contentment that will prevail over any fear of man's disapproval. If God is pleased with your life, what does it matter if man is displeased? God's approval and favor is a sufficient reward.

---

10. For more information about liars, see my recording *Dealing with Deception*, available from Sound Word Associates, (219) 548–0933, http://www.soundword.com/index.html.

Seven

SOME POINTS ABOUT PRIDE

We have learned a lot, up to this point, about particular manifestations of pride in the heart of the people-pleaser. But before we look at God's answers to this problem, I'd like to zoom out in order to examine the sin of pride with more of a wide-angle lens. It is quite necessary to do so because the fibers of pride are so interwoven into the fabric of our lives that they affect each other more than tangentially.

What exactly is pride? As we proceed with this chapter, I'll be giving you four working definitions of the sin of pride and then discuss some of its more common manifestations in our lives. We will take a look at some of the antidotes to the sin of pride in Part Two.

1. **Pride is the delusion that our achievements are primarily the results of our own doing.** A delusion is an erroneous belief or opinion. The dictionary defines it as a false belief strongly held in spite of invalidating evidence, especially as a symptom of mental illness. (By this definition, our mental hospitals are filled with people who are crazy . . . *about themselves!*)

Since I've covered this material previously, I will not belabor the point here other than to remind you again of 1 Corinthians 4:7, which asks, "What do you have that you did not receive?"[1]

2. Pride is esteeming ourselves above and beyond the condition and proportion that God has appointed for us. To refresh your memory, *condition* is our state of being—everything from the state of our health to our IQ to our social standing. In other words, our condition would be the situation or circumstances in which the Lord has chosen to place us. *Proportion* is the relative magnitude, quantity, or degree of those conditions (or circumstances) chosen for us by God.

Let's take a look again at someone in Scripture who esteemed himself above and beyond the condition and proportion appointed for him—that "wicked Haman" (Esth. 7:6):

> During that night the king could not sleep so he gave an order to bring the book of records, the chronicles, and they were read before the king. It was found written what Mordecai had reported concerning Bigthana and Teresh, two of the king's eunuchs who were door-keepers, that they had sought to lay hands on King Ahasuerus. The king said, "What honor or dignity has been bestowed on Mordecai for this?" Then the king's servants who attended him said, "Nothing has been done for him." So the king said, "Who is in the court?" Now Haman had just entered the outer court of the king's palace in order to speak to the king about hanging Mordecai on the gallows which he had prepared for him. The king's servants said to him, "Behold, Haman is standing in the court." And the king said, "Let him come in." So Haman came in and the king said to him, "What is to be done for the man whom the king desires to honor?" And *Haman said to himself, "Whom would the king desire to honor more than me?"* (Esth. 6:1–6)

1. Richard Baxter has an interesting section in his directory that really develops this theme. "If you have anything to be proud of," he says, "remember what it is, and that it is not your own, but has been given or lent to you by God, who especially hates pride." Richard Baxter, *Baxter's Practical Works*, vol. 1, *A Christian Directory* (Ligonier, PA: Soli Deo Gloria Publications, 1990), 111–12.

Haman esteemed himself *above* and *beyond* the condition and proportion God had appointed for him. He is a prime example of the fool Paul spoke of in Galatians 6:3: "For if anyone thinks he is something when he is nothing, he deceives himself." Haman's pride deceived him into thinking that he was the man most worthy of honor in the king's court. Boy, was he in for a surprise!

> Then Haman said to the king, "For the man whom the king desires to honor, let them bring a royal robe which the king has worn, and the horse on which the king has ridden, and on whose head a royal crown has been placed; and let the robe and the horse be handed over to one of the king's most noble princes and let them array the man whom the king desires to honor and lead him on horseback through the city square, and proclaim before him, 'Thus it shall be done to the man whom the king desires to honor.'"
>
> Then the king said to Haman, "Take quickly the robes and the horse as you have said, and do so for Mordecai the Jew, who is sitting at the king's gate; do not fall short in anything of all that you have said." So Haman took the robe and the horse, and arrayed Mordecai, and led him on horseback through the city square, and proclaimed before him, "Thus it shall be done to the man whom the king desires to honor."
>
> Then Mordecai returned to the king's gate. But Haman hurried home, mourning, with his head covered. (Esth. 6:7–12)

Can you imagine the humiliation Haman faced? The very man toward whom he was so bitter—the man who refused to bow down to him—not only was chosen by the king to receive the honor Haman thought belonged to him, but had the best seat in the house to watch Haman cry out Mordecai's accolades before the people. Pride is the one sin that is the most swiftly and the most severely judged by God. "Everyone who is proud in heart is an abomination to the LORD; assuredly, he will not be unpunished." (Prov. 16:5).

3. Pride is the desire to be *esteemed by others* above and beyond the condition and proportion that God has appointed for us. It's bad enough to esteem yourself above and beyond the condition and proportion appointed to you by God. It's *worse* to want others to do so.

Do you remember the account of that married couple in the book of Acts who were snuffed out by God within hours of each other because of something they said? A cursory reading of the text might lead you to believe that Ananias and Sapphira were judged for their deception. But if you really look, you will see that it was their *pride* that motivated them to lie!

> But a man named Ananias, with his wife Sapphira, sold a piece of property, and kept back some of the price for himself, with his wife's full knowledge, and bringing a portion of it, he laid it at the apostles' feet. But Peter said, "Ananias, why has Satan filled your heart to lie to the Holy Spirit and to keep back some of the price of the land? While it remained unsold, did it not remain your own? And after it was sold, was it not under your control? Why is it that you have conceived this deed in your heart? You have not lied to men but to God." And as he heard these words, Ananias fell down and breathed his last; and great fear came over all who heard of it. (Acts 5:1–5)

How and why did Ananias and Sapphira lie? They lied by leading the church to believe that they had given the entire portion (of the proceeds from the sale of their property) to the Lord. They were free to give only a portion of the sale to the church. It was under their control. They lied because they wanted the church to esteem them proportionately above and beyond the honor they were due. In Part Two of this book, we'll look briefly at another man who had an inordinate desire for others to esteem him above and beyond what he had been given. The Bible says of him that he "love[d] to be first." Do you know his name?

4. Pride is the desire to *exalt ourselves* above and beyond the condition and proportion that God has appointed for us. This is the pinnacle of pride: to exalt yourself to a higher position than you deserve. It's what the devil did that got him thrown out of heaven. It's what

Eve and Adam did to get them thrown out of the garden. As we've seen, it's what Ananias and Sapphira did to get thrown out of the church and out of this life! It's bad enough to esteem yourself above and beyond the condition and proportion appointed to you by God. It's even worse to want others to do so. And it's worse yet to exalt ourselves above and beyond the condition and proportion that God has appointed for us.

> Do not claim honor in the presence of the king, and do not stand in the place of great men; for it is better that it be said to you, "Come up here," than for you to be placed lower in the presence of the prince, whom your eyes have seen. (Prov. 25:6–7)

Pride is an insidious thing. Just when you are convinced that you have one of its tentacles under control, another one snakes out to grab you. Oh, it has probably been there all along, but you never saw it before. So off you go to try to bring it under the Spirit's control, and in time, by God's grace, you do. Then, just as you're thinking you've got it under control, out wriggles another one. Pride is like a garment with a million secret pockets that you're constantly discovering.

Since you are interested in dealing with one manifestation of pride (the problem of desiring approval), you also should be interested in learning the extent to which pride has wrapped its ugly tentacles around other areas of your heart. So, with the help of Richard Baxter, I've put together a list of some general manifestations of pride in the lives of believers. You will recognize some of them from previous chapters. Some of them are new. I've also included a few pertinent Scripture quotations for your consideration. As you read through them, put a check (☑) next to the evidences of pride in your own life.

☐ **Boasting about and taking credit for your wisdom, abilities, and gifts as though they were acquired primarily by self-effort.** The desire to *exalt ourselves* above and beyond the condition and proportion that

God has appointed for us is most often expressed in boasting. A proud person fails to connect the dots between his achievements and God's grace. He is perhaps most blinded to the fact that even his desire, wisdom, and strength to accomplish his goals (his "self-effort") are gifts from God.

> Every good thing given and every perfect gift is from above, coming down from the Father of lights, with whom there is no variation or shifting shadow. (James 1:17)

> For who regards you as superior? What do you have that you did not receive? And if you did receive it, why do you boast as if you had not received it? (1 Cor. 4:7)

☐ **Selfishly using for your own glory and benefit the wisdom, abilities, and gifts that God has given you for His glory and the benefit of others.** It is easy for the people-pleaser to exploit the things with which God has blessed him for personal advantage. Displaying your wisdom, gifts, and abilities so that you will receive more glory, power, and praise than God is devilish and proud. To excessively profit financially from these things can even be wrong—especially if one doesn't invest his earnings back into God's kingdom.

> I am the LORD, that is My name; and My glory I will not give to another, nor My praise to carved images. (Isa. 42:8 NKJV)

☐ **Viewing God in such a way as to think He was made[2] for your pleasure rather than vice versa (making God a means to an end rather than worshiping Him as the sovereign Creator and Sustainer of the universe).** Some people view God as a cosmic bellhop. "I just snap my fingers and He gives me what I want." Others think of Him as they would a vending machine. "I just put in my coins, push the button, and 'presto,' out comes my order." Of course, when they don't get what they wanted,

2. For the record: God is eternal and therefore was not "made."

they treat God as they would the machine—they complain, and pound, and kick like a child throwing a tantrum. The truth is, we live, serve, breathe, and have our very being at God's pleasure.

> Therefore we also have as our ambition, whether at home or absent, to be pleasing to Him. (2 Cor. 5:9)

> For not one of us lives for himself, and not one dies for himself; for if we live, we live for the Lord, or if we die, we die for the Lord; therefore whether we live or die, we are the Lord's. (Rom. 14:7–8)

☐ **Having a greater desire to be loved by others than for others to love God (wanting others to love you more than they love God).** Not only do the proud desire men's approval more than God's, they expect people to love them more than God. Baxter explains:

> Pride makes men more desirous to be over loved themselves, than that God be loved by themselves or others. They would gladly have the eyes and hearts of all men turned on them, as if they were as the sun, to be admired and loved by all who see them.[3]

When others choose to obey God rather than please him, the proud person takes it personally. If someone declines his invitation or request for the purpose of fulfilling another, more pressing biblical responsibility, the haughty man takes it personally, "gets his feelings hurt," becomes jealous, pouts, sulks, worries, or takes any number of other selfish actions. Why? Because at some level (consciously or otherwise), he wants to be loved more than God.

> How can you believe, when you receive glory from one another and you do not seek the glory that is from the one and only God? (John 5:44; see also Matt. 6:2ff.; 23:5–7; John 12:42–43)

3. Baxter, *A Christian Directory*, 196.

Hear, O Israel! The LORD is our God, the LORD is one! You shall love the LORD your God with all your heart and with all your soul and with all your might. (Deut. 6:4–5)

☐ **Having a greater dependence on self than on God's grace and provision.** The people-pleaser depends on his own efforts to win friends and influence people. He doesn't consider that God is the one who provides him with the ability to do so.

Trust in the LORD with all your heart and do not lean on your own understanding. In all your ways acknowledge Him, and He will make your paths straight. (Prov. 3:5–6)

He who trusts in his own heart is a fool, but he who walks wisely will be delivered. (Prov. 28:26)

Thus says the LORD, "Let not a wise man boast of his wisdom, and let not the mighty man boast of his might, let not a rich man boast of his riches; but let him who boasts boast of this, that he understands and knows Me, that I am the LORD who exercises lovingkindness, justice and righteousness on earth; for I delight in these things," declares the LORD. (Jer. 9:23–24)

☐ **Resorting to defensiveness, blame-shifting, justification, or anger when lawfully reproved by another.** The proud person is unteachable. He foolishly loathes reproof and correction. The thought that someone might see him as a sinner is, to him, an embarrassment of tremendous proportions. Consequently, he learns to be quite adept at protecting himself by using these clever and calculated distractions. It never crosses his mind that by humbling himself in such circumstances, he would gain the honor he so selfishly craves. He doesn't understand the dynamics of Proverbs 15:33 and 18:12, "before honor comes humility."

The fear of the LORD is the beginning of knowledge; fools despise wisdom and instruction. (Prov. 1:7)

> Do not reprove a scoffer, or he will hate you, reprove a wise man and
> he will love you. (Prov. 9:8; cf. Prov. 15:2)

> He is on the path of life who heeds instruction, but he who ignores re-
> proof goes astray. (Prov. 10:17)

> Whoever loves discipline loves knowledge, but he who hates reproof
> is stupid. (Prov. 12:1)

☐ **Having a censorious, critical, condemning, accusing, judgmental attitude toward others, especially those in positions of authority.** The people-pleaser uses any and all means to minimize the
competition. He detracts from the good name of others so that he himself might have a better name in the eyes of his audience. Those in positions of authority are especially threatening because they, by virtue of
those positions, have greater ability to gain approval for themselves as
well as greater power to influence others against the proud dissembler.

> Be merciful, just as your Father is merciful. Do not judge, and you will
> not be judged; and do not condemn, and you will not be condemned;
> pardon, and you will be pardoned. (Luke 6:36–37)

> Do not speak against one another, brethren. He who speaks against
> a brother or judges his brother, speaks against the law and judges the
> law; but if you judge the law, you are not a doer of the law but a judge
> of it. (James 4:11)

☐ **Being more prone to command than to obey, to teach than to be
taught, to speak than to listen.** The proud person loves to gives orders
and hates to obey them—especially from those he perceives as inferior.
For him, it's generally much easier to give directions than to follow them.
The people-pleaser may long for the honor associated with being a teacher
without wanting to invest the hard work necessary to do first what he is
telling others they must do. Pride is at the heart of his hypocrisy.

> Then Jesus spoke to the crowds and to His disciples, saying: "The scribes and the Pharisees have seated themselves in the chair of Moses; therefore all that they tell you, do and observe, but do not do according to their deeds; for they say things and do not do them. They tie up heavy burdens and lay them on men's shoulders, but they themselves are unwilling to move them with so much as a finger. But they do all their deeds to be noticed by men . . . They love the place of honor at banquets and the chief seats in the synagogues, and respectful greetings in the market places, and being called Rabbi by men. But do not be called Rabbi; for One is your Teacher, and you are all brothers . . . Do not be called leaders; for One is your Leader, that is, Christ. But the greatest among you shall be your servant." (Matt. 23:1–11)

☐ **Having little or no respect for authority in general.** Like the tyrant Diotrephes, who thought little of the apostle John's ecclesiastical authority because he loved to be first among his peers, proud people struggle to respect those who have the power to put and keep them in their place.

> I wrote something to the church; but Diotrephes, who loves to be first among them, does not accept what we say. For this reason, if I come, I will call attention to his deeds which he does, unjustly accusing us with wicked words; and not satisfied with this, he himself does not receive the brethren, either, and he forbids those who desire to do so and puts them out of the church. (3 John 9–10)

☐ **Becoming impatient or upset when contradicted in speech, especially publicly.** Rather than being grateful for the gift of counsel he received, a proud person despises both the correction and the corrector. Unlike the wise man of Proverbs 25:12, whose ear welcomes rebuke as a piece of jewelry ("Like an earring of gold and an ornament of fine gold is a wise reprover to a listening ear"), he sees it as something that will mar his appearance and so cause him to become unattractive in the eyes of the one he longs to impress. And if the contradiction is public, he will act as though someone had poured salt into an open wound. Perhaps that's just the medicine he needs.

> A scoffer does not love one who reproves him, he will not go to the wise. (Prov. 15:12)

☐ **When wronged, being unwilling to forgive an offender who has not demonstrated extreme submission or repentance.** Proud people struggle to grant forgiveness to those who are not wallowing in sorrow over their offenses. They want not a simple "I repent," as the Scriptures require (Luke 17:4), but the great proof of repentance. If you're having a hard time connecting the dots between pride and lack of forgiveness, imagine asking forgiveness from someone who responds like this: "I'm not ready to extend my forgiveness to you. You haven't offended just any ole person; you've offended *ME*! And I don't grant people forgiveness simply on the basis of their word without their somehow otherwise propitiating my anger." (Of course, when it comes time for him to confess his own sin, the arrogant individual expects those he has offended to overlook his "little mistakes.")

A humble believer recognizes the enormity of his own debt of sin that Christ has forgiven and considers any offenses that he himself must forgive as minutiae in comparison (cf. Matt. 18:21–35). He willingly grants forgiveness to those who sincerely ask for it. (In the absence of hard evidence to the contrary, he takes the repentant brother at his word.)

> Be on your guard! If your brother sins, rebuke him; and if he repents, forgive him. And if he sins against you seven times a day, and returns to you seven times, saying, "I repent," forgive him. (Luke 17:3–4)

☐ **Investing more resources to establish your own honor than to establish God's honor.** A proud person uses his resources to promote his own glory more than God's glory. His checkbook is under the influence more of his pride than of the Holy Spirit. Even when he does give to God, he often does so with a motive to improve or maintain his standing in the eyes of those he wants to impress with his generosity. Any benefit that others might receive from his gifts is secondary to the benefit of his reputation. He would rather skimp on secret acts of benevolence than on "apparel, and appearance, and the entertaining of friends, or anything else that is for ostentation, or for himself."[4]

> It is not good to eat much honey, nor is it glory to search out one's own glory. (Prov. 25:27)

> Do not store up for yourselves treasures on earth, where moth and rust destroy, and where thieves break in and steal. But store up for yourselves treasures in heaven, where neither moth nor rust destroys, and where thieves do not break in or steal; for where your treasure is, there your heart will be also. (Matt. 6:19–21)

> How can you believe, when you receive glory from one another and you do not seek the glory that is from the one and only God? (John 5:44)

☐ **Being unwilling to admit when you are wrong.** This is the one manifestation of pride that is common to most of us. It's the one sin that marriage counselors are forced to confront most often. Conflicts often occur when one person sins against another.[5] Such conflicts cannot be effectively resolved short of confession (and repentance) on the part of the sinning party. That takes humility. But a proud person is slow to see and acknowledge his fault. His immediate response to the mere hint of wrongdoing is not to consider the sinfulness of his own heart and the likelihood of his own culpability, but rather to dispute or extenuate the allegation. So what prevents most conflicts from being resolved is usually pride. Perhaps that's why Solomon said, "By pride comes nothing but strife" (Prov. 13:10a NKJV).

---

4. Ibid., 197.
5. Sin is not the only cause of conflict. Sometimes conflicts can occur when (nonsinful) differences in people's views, values, lifestyles, or approaches to problems cause them to disagree.

Then the LORD said to Cain, "Where is Abel your brother?" And he said, "I do not know. Am I my brother's keeper?" (Gen. 4:9)

□ **Being inordinately curious about those things that you do not have a biblical need to know.** A proud person presumes to have authority that he has not been granted. God doesn't give everyone the right to conduct an investigation into the lives of everyone else: "It is the glory of God to conceal a matter, but the glory of kings is to search out a matter" (Prov. 25:2). The hunt for unnecessary information (the desire to get "the scoop" on someone or about something) is often little more than an attempt to puff oneself up through the misuse of knowledge. "Knowledge makes arrogant, but love edifies" (1 Cor. 8:1).

When the woman saw that the tree was good for food, and that it was a delight to the eyes, and that the tree was desirable to make one wise, she took from its fruit and ate; and she gave also to her husband with her, and he ate. (Gen. 3:6; see also 1 Sam. 6:19)

O LORD, my heart is not proud, nor my eyes haughty; nor do I involve myself in great matters, or in things too difficult for me. (Ps. 131:1)

□ **Being discontented with your position in life.** Proud people are not content with their allotment of praise-producing assets. They deserve better—better pay, better friends, better toys, more clout, more commendations, more respect. Rather than willingly submitting to and delighting in God's wise and loving disposal in every condition of life, they murmur and complain against Him for not giving them more. No matter how much they acquire, they will never be content. They will always want just a little bit more. Like Satan, whose pride led to his fall, their pride, if left unchecked, would drive them to "aspire to all the prerogatives of God, and to depose Him, and to dethrone Him of His Godhead and majesty that they might have His place."[6]

6. Baxter, *A Christian Directory*, 198.

Then Haman recounted to them the glory of his riches, and the number of his sons, and every instance where the king had magnified him and how he had promoted him above the princes and servants of the king. Haman also said, "Even Esther the queen let no one but me come with the king to the banquet which she had prepared; and tomorrow also I am invited by her with the king. Yet all of this does not satisfy me every time I see Mordecai the Jew sitting at the king's gate." (Esth. 5:11–13)

☐ **Being ungrateful for God's mercies.** Proud people tend to be ungrateful because they believe they are responsible for their own achievements and blessings. As Baxter puts it:

Pride causes men to return the thanks to themselves, which is due to God for the mercies they have received. They thank God only as a courtesy; but they seriously ascribe it to their own care, or will, or industry, or power.[7]

The king reflected and said, "Is this not Babylon the great, which I myself have built as a royal residence by the might of my power and for the glory of my majesty?" (Dan. 4:30)

For men will be lovers of self, lovers of money, boastful, arrogant, revilers, disobedient to parents, ungrateful, unholy . . . (2 Tim. 3:2)

☐ **Failing to pray.** A proud person doesn't like to ask others for what he needs. He sees it as too much like begging. "I can provide for my own needs, thank you very much," is his attitude. Prayer to him is an unnecessary activity—he has more important things to do with his time. The humble soul, on the other hand, sees his need to depend on God for everything—life, breath, food, shelter, grace, health, fellowship, and every other good and perfect gift. He accepts the fact that prayer is the ordained means of securing what he needs and wants from the hand of God and thankfully welcomes this dependent relationship.

7. Ibid., 196.

The wicked, in the haughtiness of his countenance, does not seek Him. All his thoughts are, "There is no God." (Ps. 10:4)

☐ **Being insensible to the dangers of temptation (being self-confident about handling temptation).** Since the proud person is prone to depend on himself rather than on the Lord's power, he believes that he is capable of detecting all sorts of spiritual danger. But because his pride blinds him to the sinful desires in his heart ("each one is tempted when, by his own evil desire, he is dragged away and enticed," James 1:14 NIV), he cannot see how susceptible to temptation he actually is. Consequently, he thinks little of going places, participating in activities, and associating with people who might entice him to sin. The humble, on the other hand, are keenly aware of their dependence on God in all areas of life, suspicious of their sinful hearts, very mindful of the dangers they face, and diligent to avoid stepping into sin's trap.[8]

The prudent sees the evil and hides himself, but the naive go on, and are punished for it. (Prov. 22:3)

Therefore let him who thinks he stands take heed that he does not fall. (1 Cor. 10:12)

☐ **Being oversensitive to correction.** That which causes a person to overreact to criticism (to feel a pinprick as though he were being knifed in the back) is pride. Being easily offended over reproof (especially if the reproof is given in jest) is a sure sign that one has made an idol of his reputation.

A scoffer does not love one who reproves him, he will not go to the wise. (Prov. 15:12)

☐ **Having difficulty in being pleased (because of excessively high expectations).** Because he wants to show off his achievements, a proud

8. See ibid., 199.

person often has high expectations of himself. He also likes to raise the bar even higher than God does for others, who never quite seem to measure up. Moreover, because he longs to be seen and respected and honored from those around him, no one (except perhaps another people-pleaser) can afford to invest the time to do everything his insatiable appetite for approval requires. There will always be something that doesn't quite measure up to his expectation—some word, or inflection, or facial expression, or gesture, or attitude, or omission that will displease him. Baxter again says it well:

> As godly, humble men rightly amplify their sins in light of the greatness and excellency of God whom they offend; so the proud man foolishly amplifies every little wrong that is done to him, and every word that is said against him, and every supposed omission or neglect of him, because of the high estimation he has of himself.[9]

> So the taskmasters of the people and their foremen went out and spoke to the people, saying, "Thus says Pharaoh, 'I am not going to give you any straw. You go and get straw for yourselves wherever you can find it, but none of your labor will be reduced.'" So the people scattered through all the land of Egypt to gather stubble for straw. The taskmasters pressed them, saying, "Complete your work quota, your daily amount, just as when you had straw." (Exod. 5:10–13)

Obviously, there is enough material about the subject of pride to fill a book. It can't all be unpacked in one chapter. I pray that what I have included here will convince you that the degree of pride in your life is greater than you probably realize and that it will require much grace and humility (God gives grace to the humble) to subdue it. If you would like to learn more, let me urge you to get a copy of Baxter's book and read it for yourself. At the time of this writing, a helpful portion of this work entitled *Directions Against Man-Pleasing* can be found online and downloaded in PDF format from http://www.puritansermons.com.

9. Ibid., 203.

Part Two

GOD'S SOLUTION

Oh what a mercy is an upright heart!—That renounces the world and everything in it that stands in competition with his God. And who takes God to be his God indeed; and to be his Lord, his Judge, his Portion, and his All: who in temptation remembers that God is watching, and in all his duty is motivated and ruled by the will and pleasure of his Judge; and considers the observation and thoughts of man as he would the presence of a bird or beast (unless piety, justice or love requires him to have respect for man as God may require); who when men applaud him as a person of exceptional godliness or holiness is apprehensive and fearful lest the all-knowing God should think otherwise of him than his applauders: and who when under all the criticisms, reproaches and slanders of men (even though good men might be tempted to thus abuse him) can live in peace, resting upon the approbation of his God alone, and can rejoice in his justification by his righteous Judge and gracious Redeemer, though the insignificant criticisms of man condemn him.

Truly I cannot understand how any other man than this can live a life of true and solid peace and joy. If God's approbation and favor don't give you peace, nothing can rationally give it to you. If the pleasing of God doesn't satisfy you, though men, though *good* men, though *all* men should be displeased with you, I don't know how or when you will ever be satisfied.

—RICHARD BAXTER, *Baxter's Practical Works*, vol. 1, *A Christian Directory* (Ligonier, PA: Soli Deo Gloria Publications, 1990), 191.

Eight

CHARACTERISTICS OF A GOD-PLEASER

As I tried to make clear in chapter 6, the single most important thing you can do to stop being a people-pleaser is to become a God-pleaser. If you want to be cured of the spiritual disorder of people-pleasing, you must develop a desire (cultivate an appetite) for the approval of the One who righteously judges not only your words, actions, and attitudes, but also the thoughts and intentions of your heart. "Therefore we also have as our ambition [we make it our aim], whether at home or absent, to be pleasing to Him" (2 Cor. 5:9). As a Christian, your chief mandate, your number-one priority, your ultimate ambition, your main purpose for living is to please God. What could be more important to you than that?

If you are familiar with the *Westminster Shorter Catechism*, you know the very first question and its answer:

> Question: What is the chief end of man?
> Answer: Man's chief end is to glorify God, and to enjoy him forever.

God is pleased when we glorify Him.

When you please God, you have everything you need (security, happiness, peace, comfort, contentment, and freedom)—even if the whole world is displeased with you.

"So what does a God-pleaser look like?"

He looks, talks, acts, reasons, and is motivated quite differently from his foil. In chapter 1, we looked at some of the criteria for diagnosing the "spiritual disorder" of a people-pleaser. Let's now examine the characteristics of his counterpart.

CHARACTERISTICS OF A GOD-PLEASER

1. **He realizes that he cannot please God apart from being a Christian.** The Bible makes it emphatically clear that no man is, in and of himself, capable of pleasing God:

> Those who are in the flesh cannot please God.
> However, you are not in the flesh but in the Spirit, if indeed the Spirit of God dwells in you. But if anyone does not have the Spirit of Christ, he does not belong to Him. (Rom. 8:8–9)

Those who are in the flesh, that is, those who have not been regenerated by the Spirit of God, cannot do *anything* to bring pleasure to God, no matter how hard they try. He is so righteous and holy that even the daily chores (the plowing, planting, harvesting) of the wicked are seen through His eyes as sinful: "A haughty look, a proud heart, and the plowing of the wicked are sin" (Prov. 21:4 NKJV). In fact, the attempts that unregenerate men and women make at righteousness are repugnant to God: "And all our righteous deeds are like a filthy garment" (Isa. 64:6).

God, who Himself is perfect, can be pleased only with perfection. Man is not just imperfect—he suffers from total depravity.

> To be totally depraved is to suffer from corruption that pervades the whole person. Sin affects every aspect of our being: the body, the soul, the mind, the will, and so forth. The total or whole person is corrupted

by sin. No vestigial "island of righteousness" escapes the influence of the fall. Sin reaches into every aspect of our lives, finding no shelter of isolated virtue.[1]

In order for God to be pleased, something must take place to deal with man's corruption by sin—something that will change his standing before the Holy King. He must be made righteous.

"But how does all this happen?"

When Christ, God's Son, the Perfect Man, died on the cross, He did so to take the punishment for sinners, as well as to give them credit for His righteousness. His death actually accomplishes *two* things for repentant sinners: the believer's sin is transferred to Christ, whom God punishes in his place; and Christ's righteousness is transferred to the believer's account, changing his legal standing and making him perfect. Theologians sometimes refer to this twofold transaction as *double imputation*. It becomes binding only when a person, by faith, puts his trust in Christ—not simply as a historical figure, or as a good example, or as a righteous man, or even as God, but as the Son of God who died in the Christian's place (as his substitute).

Only then can God be pleased. Only then does the Holy Spirit indwell individuals and fit them (from within) to a life of service that is pleasing to God. Therefore, only those who are born again by the Spirit of God are capable of pleasing God. For a more thorough explanation about how to be born again, please refer to Appendix A.

The unregenerate man cannot please God for at least three other reasons. The first has to do with his *lack of understanding.* Do you remember the illustration in chapter 5 about all those voices in the room with you that you could hear only with the right receiver? The point I made there was that unregenerate man cannot hear God's voice because he doesn't have the receiver. Without the ability to hear, he cannot understand.

1. R. C. Sproul, *Grace Unknown: The Heart of Reformed Theology* (Grand Rapids: Baker Books, 2000), 118.

> But a natural man does not accept the things of the Spirit of God, for
> they are foolishness to him; and he cannot understand them, because
> they are spiritually appraised. (1 Cor. 2:14)

Without the ability to comprehend the things of God, the unsaved person cannot really understand what it takes to please Him.

Second, the natural man cannot please God because of his *lack of ability*. The Bible tells us what pleases God. It contains many directives that are very difficult, if not impossible, to follow—especially on a regular basis. Paul asks in Galatians 3:3, "Are you so foolish? Having begun by the Spirit, are you now being perfected by the flesh?" The obvious implied answer is, "Of course not." Man cannot grow spiritually in his own strength. Without the Holy Spirit's enabling power, man simply doesn't have what it takes to please God.

The third reason has to do with natural man's *lack of proper motives*. Remember, total depravity means that every part of man is corrupt—even his motives. He does what he does selfishly, often with ulterior motives. What did Jesus say is the first commandment? "You shall love the Lord your God with all your heart, and with all your soul, and with all your mind" (Matt. 22:37). But we can't love God until we comprehend His love for us through the Spirit. "We love, because He first loved us" (1 John 4:19). Since the love of God has not been poured out in his heart by the Holy Spirit (Rom. 5:5), the unbeliever cannot please God, even if he tries, because his selfish (unloving) motives disqualify him before he even gets started.

2. He studies the Scriptures to understand exactly what it takes to please God. The God-pleaser is serious about "trying to learn what is pleasing to the Lord" (Eph. 5:10). Unlike the people-pleaser, who spends his time studying the interests, aversions, words, inflections, and body language of people, this man invests his time studying those things that please God. This means that he spends plenty of time in the Word and plenty of time getting the Word into his heart.

I delight to do Your will, O my God; Your Law is within my heart. (Ps. 40:8)

Pleasing God requires doing His will. But you can't do His will unless you first know it. The God-pleaser wants to understand what the will of his Lord is (cf. Eph. 5:17).

The person who delights (seeks his happiness) in the Lord delights (seeks his happiness) in the Scriptures. He reads them, studies them, memorizes them, meditates on them, runs to them when he has questions to answer, decisions to make, passions to quell, and crises to face. He loves them because they show him how to live a full, rewarding, exciting life that pleases God.

I shall *delight* in Your commandments, which I *love*. And I shall lift up my hands to Your commandments, which I *love*; and I will meditate on Your statutes. (Ps. 119:47–48)

O how I *love* Your law! It is my meditation all the day. Your commandments make me wiser than my enemies, for they are ever mine. I have more insight than all my teachers, for Your testimonies are my meditation. I understand more than the aged, because I have observed Your precepts. (Ps. 119:97–100)

Therefore I *love* Your commandments above gold, yes, above fine gold. Therefore I esteem right all Your precepts concerning everything, I hate every false way. (Ps. 119:127–28)

Your word is very pure, therefore Your servant *loves* it. (Ps. 119:140)

Consider how I *love* Your precepts; revive me, O LORD, according to Your lovingkindness. The sum of Your word is truth, and every one of Your righteous ordinances is everlasting. (Ps. 119:159–60)

I hate and despise falsehood, but I *love* Your law. Seven times a day I praise You, because of Your righteous ordinances. Those who *love* Your

law have great peace, and nothing causes them to stumble. I hope for
Your salvation, O LORD, and do Your commandments. My soul keeps
Your testimonies, and I *love* them exceedingly. I keep Your precepts and
Your testimonies, for all my ways are before You. (Ps. 119:163–68)

At this point, you may be wondering, "What exactly *does* the Bible
say about how to please God?" This question is so vital to overcoming
the love of man's approval that we will devote the entire next chapter
to laying the foundation for its answer.

3. In everything he does, he is conscious of pleasing God. The mind
of the God-pleaser is set "on the things above, not on the things that
are on earth" (Col. 3:2). Therefore, it doesn't matter much to him what
men on earth think of him because he is much more cognizant of
heaven's evaluation and approbation. In every decision he makes, he
knows that he is choosing either to please God or to displease Him.

I used to read some of the Old Testament laws (such as Leviticus 19:19:
"You are to keep My statutes. You shall not breed together two kinds of your
cattle; you shall not sow your field with two kinds of seed, nor wear a garment upon you of two kinds of material mixed together") and wonder,
"Why does the Lord possibly care about such things? What sanctifying
value, what righteous purpose did such commands have for His children?"
"I don't know," I would answer, "but I'm sure glad I live under the new
covenant and don't have to concern myself with those pesky little laws."

But I could never square that answer with 2 Timothy 3:16:

All Scripture is inspired by God and profitable for teaching, for reproof, for correction, for training in righteousness . . .

That is, until someone helped me realize the profitability (usefulness)
of such directives to New Testament saints.

God wanted His people to know that in every decision they made
(even down to their food and clothing), they would be choosing either for
Him or against Him. "There is My way to prepare your food," He says,

"and there's the wrong way." "There's My way to make your clothing, and there's the wrong way." "There's My way to conduct your business and the wrong way."[2] This antithetical way of thinking seems utterly foreign to the pluralistic, twenty-first–century man, who sees everything on a relativistic continuum, not in black or white but in 256 shades of gray.

The very questions he asks himself before committing to a particular course of action are much different from those of his counterpart.

People-Pleaser	God-Pleaser
What will others think if I do this?	What will God think if I do this?
Will I fail?	How will God be glorified if I fail?
How can I make him love me?	How can I show Christ's love to him?
Am I as pretty as she?	Am I as godly as Christ?
Will being his friend improve my image?	Will being his friend glorify God?
How can I keep him from rejecting me?	How can I minister to him?
Will I embarrass myself?	Will I sin against God?
What do my friends expect me to do?	What does the Bible say I should do?

4. When he pleases people, he does so out of loving motives, not selfish ones. The God-pleaser is well aware not only of the first Great Commandment, but also that "the second is like it, 'You shall love your neighbor as yourself'" (Matt. 22:39).

2. It's not that we must pray about and ask for guidance on every little decision (Lord, which tie should I wear today?). But there are guiding directives and principles that, once internalized, help us make wise decisions.

He knows that love involves giving.

For God so loved the world, that He *gave* His only begotten Son, that whoever believes in Him shall not perish, but have eternal life. (John 3:16)

I have been crucified with Christ; it is no longer I who live, but Christ lives in me; and the life which I now live in the flesh I live by faith in the Son of God, who loved me and *gave* Himself for me. (Gal. 2:20 NKJV)

Walk in love, just as Christ also loved you and *gave* Himself up for us, an offering and a sacrifice to God as a fragrant aroma. (Eph. 5:2)

Husbands, love your wives, just as Christ also loved the church and *gave* Himself up for her . . . (Eph. 5:25)

And the God-pleaser knows that love gives people what they *need*, not necessarily what they *want*.

Now as they were traveling along, He entered a village; and a woman named Martha welcomed Him into her home. She had a sister called Mary, who was seated at the Lord's feet, listening to His word. But Martha was distracted with all her preparations; and she came up to Him and said, "Lord, do You not care that my sister has left me to do all the serving alone? Then tell her to help me." But the Lord answered and said to her, "Martha, Martha, you are worried and bothered about so many things; *but only one thing is necessary*, for Mary has chosen the good part, which shall not be taken away from her." (Luke 10:38–42)

Martha was behaving as though she had a *need* for her sister to help in the kitchen. As it turns out, her perceived need was only a *want*. What she needed was to sit at the feet of Christ and hear His Word.

But most of all, the God-pleaser realizes that unless his motives are right, he can give away all he has and is, but he still won't exemplify biblical love.

If I speak with the tongues of men and of angels, but do not have love, I have become a noisy gong or a clanging cymbal. If I have the gift of prophecy, and know all mysteries and all knowledge; and if I have all faith, so as to remove mountains, but do not have love, I am nothing. And if I *give* all *my possessions* to feed the poor, and if I *surrender* [*give*] *my body to be burned*, but do not have love, it profits me nothing. (1 Cor. 13:1–3)

Let's again contrast the people-pleaser with the God-pleaser, this time looking at some of their possible motives for giving.

People-Pleaser	God-Pleaser
To boost his reputation	To obey God, to show love to God
To be commended	To glorify God
To be seen differently than he really is	To minister to others
To gain some other temporal reward	To gain eternal rewards
To avoid conflict	To bring about peace
To avoid rejection	To show love to others
To receive honor	To worship God
To receive praise	To express gratitude to God
To edify himself	To edify another

5. He knows that "it is more blessed to give than to receive."[3] Because the man who loves to please God is not consumed by selfishness or fear, his focus is on what he can *give*, not on what he can *get*.

The Bible contains an interesting corollary between sinful fear and selfishness. People who are selfish *tend* to be fearful. People who are

3. Acts 20:35.

135

fearful are *necessarily* selfish. Perhaps the best way to demonstrate this principle is by studying the antithesis of both sins. According to the Scriptures, the opposite of (and remedy for) sinful fear is *love*. First John 4:18 explains, "There is no fear in love; but perfect love casts out fear, because fear involves punishment, and the one who fears is not perfected in love."

And love is also antithetical to (as well as the antidote for) the sin of selfishness. According to 1 Corinthians 13:5, love "does not seek its own." It is not selfish. Try looking at it as an equation:

Love is the opposite of **Fear**

Love is the opposite of **Selfishness**

Now see what remains when you "factor out" love from the equation.

Fear

Selfishness

Fear and selfishness are corollaries. We can also grammatically demonstrate the same biblical relationship between fear and selfishness. Consider these definitions:

Love is being more concerned with what I can *give* than with what I can *get*.

Selfishness is being more concerned with what I can *get* than with what I can *give*.

Fear is being more concerned with what I *might lose* than with what I can *give*.

The people-pleaser's self-focus predisposes him to be fearful. That fear affects the way he relates to others. ("What if I get rejected? What if I embarrass myself?") The God-pleaser, on the other hand, because he is motivated by love, is free to focus on meeting his neighbor's needs. He's more concerned about giving to his neighbor than he is about getting. Let's contrast the selfish (taking) thoughts of the people-pleaser with the loving (giving) thoughts of the God-pleaser.

People-Pleaser	God-Pleaser
"I wonder what he'll think of me."	" I wonder what his needs are."
"I'd better not let him get too close to me."	"Maybe I can be a good influence on him."
"If he gets too close, he'll realize I'm not perfect and then he'll reject me."	"What matters is not what he thinks of me but how I can minister to him."
"I've got to keep him from finding out about my problems."	"I wonder if he has any problem that I can help him solve God's way?"
"I'll probably make a fool of myself."	"If I make a fool of myself, so be it. I'm more concerned about meeting his needs than I am about what he thinks of me."

A God-pleaser is more concerned about fulfilling his God-given responsibilities or meeting the needs of others than about the potential consequences of a particular action. He doesn't allow the thought of unpleasant consequences to keep him (paralyze him) from loving God and loving others.

6. He considers amending not only his actions, but also his thoughts and motives. Unlike the people-pleaser, who's primarily concerned about external appearances, the God-pleaser is more concerned about what's on the inside. He knows that who he is in his heart is who he *really* is as a person. He recognizes not only that God sees what is in his heart, but also that God evaluates not as man does (on the basis of appearance), but on the basis of what's on the inside. "Man looks at the outward appearance, but the LORD looks at the heart" (1 Sam. 16:7b). He understands the meaning of Christ's words in Luke 6:45:

> The good man out of the good treasure of his heart brings forth what is good; and the evil man out of the evil treasure brings forth what is evil; for his mouth speaks from that which fills his heart.

Sanctifying this inner man, whom no one but the Lord sees, is the ambition of this God-fearing Christian.

He realizes that his "heart is more deceitful than all else and is desperately sick" (Jer. 17:9), that in his inner being there are "evil thoughts, fornications, thefts, murders, adulteries, deeds of coveting and wickedness, as well as deceit, sensuality, envy, slander, pride and foolishness," and that "all these evil things proceed from within and defile the man" (Mark 7:21–23). Consequently, he cleanses himself "from all defilement of flesh *and spirit*, perfecting holiness *in the fear of God*" (2 Cor. 7:1).

Jesus was constantly confronting religious leaders with their foolish and futile attempts to clean up the outside of their lives.

> But the Lord said to him, "Now you Pharisees clean the outside of the cup and of the platter; but inside of you, you are full of robbery and wickedness. You foolish ones, did not He who made the outside make the inside also?" (Luke 11:39–40)

He told them over and over again that it is the *inside* that matters most to God. This theme of Christ's can be seen in numerous places throughout the Sermon on the Mount. From the internal focus of the Beatitudes to the "you have heard that it was said [keep these rules] . . . but I say unto you [what matters to God is the heart's attitude]," to His warnings about giving and praying and fasting so as to be seen by men rather than "in secret," Christ taught that God demands not just righteous acts but also righteous attitudes.

Let's contrast the people-pleaser's external focus with the God-pleaser's internal focus.

People-Pleaser	God-Pleaser
"What can I wear to the party that will not make me look fat?"	"To whom can I minister at this party?"
"I don't smoke, drink, chew, or go with girls who do."	"My goal is to do nothing that will harm my body (the Holy Spirit's temple) or bring reproach to the name of Christ."
"My pastor will be disappointed if he finds out that I went to that movie."	"I will not go to any movie that will violate my conscience."
"I've got to do my homework if I don't want to be embarrassed."	"I've got to do my homework if I want to be a faithful steward."
"I've got to go read my Bible now because it's late and my parents expect me to read it every day."	"I'm going to try to read my Bible every day because it's so vital to my spiritual growth."
"I've got to learn how to stop putting my foot in my mouth."	"What is it in my heart that tempts me to say such foolish things?" Or: "What can I say that will edify others or bring glory to God?"

7. He is concerned about fulfilling not only his public duties but also his private ones. The person who loves God's approval does not put all his spiritual energies into doing public duties (corporate worship, teaching, Sunday school, Bible studies, evangelistic outreach, showing hospitality, etc.). He budgets his time so as to discharge his private obligations as well.

Behind closed doors, he worships God, thanking Him for who He is and for all He has done. He confesses his sin to God, and repents of it. He agonizes in intercessory prayer. He gives of his money and material possessions in secret (if not anonymously). When he fasts, he does so in such a way that no one will know what he's up to. He prepares his heart for worship *before* he goes to church. He reads and studies his Bible regularly. He meditates on Scripture. He cooperates with the Holy Spirit in the sanctification process. He cares for his soul and for the souls of those for whom he is responsible. And if anyone tries to pressure him into additional public service, he will not accept it if, in his heart, he knows it will keep him from fulfilling his private obligations.

Moreover, he behaves in an upright way when he is in his own home. His attitude is, "I will walk within my house in the integrity of my heart" (Ps. 101:2b). He flees temptation, resists the devil, and controls his temper and his appetites when no one is around just as he does when people are looking.

8. He is more concerned with what God sees in his heart than what man sees in his appearance. The God-pleaser is keenly aware that God sees and judges not only what he does and says, but also what he thinks and wants. He is concerned not primarily with the external flaws that men might see, but with internal "mental attitude" sins. He knows that from God's point of view, thoughts and motives are (mental) *actions*. The God-pleaser understands that the law is designed to point man to the sins deep within the recesses of his heart and that no matter how well he tries to keeps the law externally, his heart is so wicked that he must depend on God's grace for forgiveness. And not only does he depend on grace for forgiveness, but he also depends on it for the supernatural power needed to mortify the sinful beast within—the beast that he knows will never be *fully* tamed this side of glory. Yet he struggles to subdue it because he wants to please the One who called him to glory and virtue.

Even though he knows that the plans he is making wouldn't be condemned by most God-fearing men, and might even be praised, he doesn't proceed with them until he has examined his heart to make sure that he is doing the right thing for the right reason *in the sight of God*. He is performing on God's stage for an audience of One. Though many others may be watching, he considers the applause of God to be better and sweeter, more thunderous and more glorious than the applause of all the kings and rulers, celebrities, and dignitaries he will ever hope to meet. He knows that mere humans can evaluate him only subjectively and superficially by what they see with their eyes, but that God will evaluate him righteously by what he sees in his heart.

9. He programs his conscience by the Bible rather than by the culture. Both the English and Greek words for *conscience* have the same etiological meaning. The Greek word *suneidesis* means "with knowledge." So does *conscience* (*con* is Latin for "with"; *science*, of course, means "knowledge"). Our consciences can be programmed with either correct or inaccurate data. The Bible speaks of a weak conscience (1 Cor. 8:7, 10, 12), a seared (or branded) conscience (1 Tim. 4:2), a defiled conscience (Titus 1:15), a conscience that is in need of cleansing from dead works (useless acts, Heb. 9:14), and an evil conscience (Heb. 10:22). We do not, therefore, come into this world with a conscience that is perfectly programmed according to the Bible. We must cooperate with the Holy Spirit (the Master Programmer) by placing into our hearts the knowledge of God's Word that He will use to write the program. "But solid food is for the mature, who because of practice have their senses trained to discern good and evil" (Heb. 5:14).

So if we're not careful, we can develop scruples about things that the Bible says nothing about. In fact, we can even have a conscience that is programmed *contrary to* Scripture: "Woe to those who call evil good, and good evil" (Isa. 5:20). I have counseled people who thought it was necessarily wrong to "hurt someone's feelings," to not send their children to a certain prestigious school, to confront those in positions of authority, to say no to requests from their friends, and even to step on bugs. Where did they get these ideas? Not from a systematic study of God's Word, but from their culture: their family, friends, and acquaintances. I recently made a trip to the West Coast to speak to a dear congregation whose members were predominantly from one ethnic background. On this trip, it became apparent to me that in some Asian families, respect for parents and extended family[4] was expected to outweigh respect for the truth—even to the point of obeying one's parents before one's spouse, not confronting habitual sin, or even lying in order to not "offend" a family member. The pressure to be more loyal to people than to the truth was staggering.

People-pleasers are especially prone to imbibing these unbiblical scruples because rather than wanting to please God, they are focused on pleasing their families, friends, classmates, working associates, Bible study leaders, hunting, fishing, and golfing buddies, country-club pals, and even people they've never met before. They experience more distress over man's disapproval than over God's displeasure. They have a greater consciousness of the former than of the latter because their consciences are pricked more deeply by man's dissatisfaction with them than by God's.

10. **He does not shy away from necessary conflict or confrontation.** A God-pleaser is a true peacemaker. He is willing to confront sin when it is biblically necessary—even if it results in conflict, rejection, the loss of a friendship, or even persecution. His decision to confront is not made on the basis of pragmatism but on biblical directives and precepts. He knows when to confront because he knows what the Bible

4. The sad irony here is that we, in Western culture, have lost the biblical concept of "respect" for others that many in the East thankfully still hold as sacred.

says about sin. He knows that if he does not confront when God says he must confront, he will be sinning. As much as he may dread the confrontation, he dreads the thought of displeasing God even more. He is driven not by fear of man, but by a love for God and a conscience that sustains him even in the face of rejection.

Just this morning, I received a telephone call from a friend who had driven all night to confront his father about a long-standing sin. He called to tell me that his father had erupted at the confrontation and to ask for prayer. Of course, I wasn't there to hear whether or not the confrontation was conducted according to biblical principle, or whether or not my friend provoked his father to anger by a sinful response, but I do know that this man went into the confrontation knowing that such an angry response from his father was very possible and that he did it because he loved God and loved his parents. It is indeed rare to find such courage. My friend is a true God-pleaser.

In my book *Teach Them Diligently*, I've written about an imaginary plaque that hangs on the back wall of my office right between (and ten feet beyond) the two chairs in front of my desk.

> This make-believe work of art has embroidered upon it in big bold letters the words of Proverbs 28:23: "He who rebukes a man will afterward find more favor than he who flatters with the tongue." It's there to remind me that I must not get discouraged or distracted with the uncomfortable tension that often accompanies reproof—tension in my own heart and tension which I perceive in the voices and on the faces of those I reprove. It's there to give me hope that later on (if not at present), after the reproof has been given and the restoration has occurred, God will be most glorified,[5] and I will find favor in the eyes of my repentant counselee.[6]

A God-pleaser has armed himself with the mind of Christ, and after seeking wise counsel, he marches off into battle with the confidence that

5. God will ultimately be glorified even if no repentance takes place when He executes judgment on the unrepentant.

6. Lou Priolo, *Teach Them Diligently* (Woodroff, SC: Timeless Texts, 2000), 48.

he is serving at the pleasure of his Commander in Chief. He is courageous and is not paralyzed with the fear that he might be wounded in the line of duty.

11. He does not worry or fret when he displeases people if, by so doing, he pleases God. We've already established the fact that people-pleasers are largely motivated by fear. As I've said, fear is *often* sinful. And worry, fear's little cousin, is *always* sinful. Both Jesus and Paul gave us instructions not to worry.

> For this reason I say to you, *do not be worried* about your life, as to what you will eat or what you will drink; nor for your body, as to what you will put on. Is not life more than food, and the body more than cloth-ing? Look at the birds of the air, that they do not sow, nor reap nor gather into barns, and yet your heavenly Father feeds them. Are you not worth much more than they? And who of you *by being worried* can add a single hour to his life? And *why are you worried* about clothing? Observe how the lilies of the field grow; they do not toil nor do they spin, yet I say to you that not even Solomon in all his glory clothed himself like one of these. But if God so clothes the grass of the field, which is alive today and tomorrow is thrown into the furnace, will He not much more clothe you? You of little faith! *Do not worry* then, say-ing, "What will we eat?" or "What will we drink?" or "What will we wear for clothing?" For the Gentiles eagerly seek all these things; for your heavenly Father knows that you need all these things. But seek first His kingdom and His righteousness, and all these things will be added to you.
>
> So *do not worry* about tomorrow; for tomorrow will care for it-self. Each day has enough trouble of its own. (Matt. 6:25–34)

> *Be anxious for nothing*, but in everything by prayer and supplication with thanksgiving let your requests be made known to God. (Phil. 4:6)

Unlike the people-pleaser, who worries himself sick when he senses that he may have displeased someone by his words (or actions), the person who pleases God knows how to dismiss such anxiety with the assurance that he has, in fact, said (or done) that which pleases God. Now, it's not that the God-pleaser never wonders whether he could have said things better, or that he never ponders a more biblical course of action than the one he took, or that he doesn't listen to valid criticism and ask for forgiveness when he knows that he has sinned in the process of trying to please God, but if he knows *that he hasn't sinned*, he does not worry or fret about the consequences of his actions. He trusts God to use what he has said or done for His glory, and he knows that God is causing all things to work together for his own good (Rom. 8:28–29).

Although this chapter has been far from an exhaustive representation of the characteristics of a God-pleaser, it should give you something to aim for as you begin to change your focus from pleasing people to pleasing God.

I sometimes try to paint a vivid picture of the twofold process of change (sometimes referred to as the put-off/put-on dynamic) in the minds of my counselees with the help of a visual aid that usually sits on my desk.

Taking hold of a small glass, I say, "This glass represents your heart." Then, picking up the pitcher of cold water next to it, I fill the glass about halfway.

"If I wanted to empty this glass so as to make it difficult for someone to come along and refill it, what could I do? If I simply emptied the glass, someone could easily come along and fill it up again. To make the glass more difficult to be refilled, I would start pouring into the glass something heavier than the water—perhaps little grains of sand, or maybe a dense fluid (like one of those liquid drain openers whose commercials you've probably seen on TV). As the heavier substance entered the glass, it would penetrate the water and descend to the bottom of the glass.

"As the glass begins to fill from the bottom, what do you think will happen to the water?" I ask the counselee.

"It will be displaced and eventually spill out over the top of the glass."

"Exactly! The water in this glass is like the sin in our hearts. We *dis*place the sin by *re*placing it with something better (or biblically heavier)."

In dependence upon the Holy Spirit, we must learn to replace corrupt words with edifying words (Eph. 4:29), ungodly behavior with godly behavior, sinful thoughts with righteous thoughts, selfish motives with loving motives, bad attitudes with good ones. We must make it our goal to become proficient in whatever the biblical alternative is for what we are trying to change in our lives. So you, as a former people-pleaser, must now set your mind on becoming the kind of person who seeks to please God first and foremost and to please man only as a fruit of your intense desire to please God.

Nine

SO WHAT EXACTLY DOES IT TAKE TO PLEASE GOD?

Have you ever wondered what it really takes to please God? If you want to stop inordinately pleasing man, you will have to know how to answer this question. (Being a people-pleaser is contrasted in Ephesians 6:6 with "doing the *will of God* from the heart.") Of course, the short answer is that to please God, you must obey His will as revealed in the Bible.

But what's the long answer? What *exactly* and *specifically* does the Bible say it takes to please the Lord? That's what I will begin to answer in this chapter. I say "begin" because the answer I provide in the next few pages will not be the *long* answer (an exhaustive answer couldn't fit within the pages of one book—let alone one chapter). What I hope to give you here is the long*er* answer—at least longer than the one that you as a recuperating people-pleaser probably have now.

Oh, and did I mention (to those of you who just might be tempted to skip over this chapter) that you are commanded to know the answer to my question? That's right; the Bible instructs you to study this matter of pleasing God: "Walk as children of Light . . . , *trying to learn* what is pleasing to the Lord" (Eph. 5:8–10). So please stay with me. The eight truths that will be unpacked in the next few pages are important to every believer—especially to those for whom pleasing people has been more important than pleasing God.

Let's begin with the most essential thing: faith.

1. Pleasing God requires faith.

> By faith Enoch was taken up so that he would not see death; and he was not found because God took him up; for he obtained the witness that before his being taken up *he was pleasing to God. And without faith it is impossible to please Him*, for he who comes to God must believe that He is and that He is a rewarder of those who seek Him. (Heb. 11:5–6)

The kind of faith that pleases God is more than mere intellectual assent to the existence of a supreme being. The God of the Bible wants to be acknowledged as the one true God. But while just believing that Jesus is God may qualify you to be "a Christian" in the eyes of many so-called Christians, it does not in the eyes of Him to whom you will someday have to give an account. Even the belief that Christ died on the cross to pay the penalty for hell-deserving sinners is not the kind of faith that saves. The devil knows this to be true—and he knows it with more certainty than any mortal being—yet his faith won't save him.

The faith that pleases God is a dependent faith—a faith that doesn't just believe the truth of Scripture, but depends on the Truth-Giver to make good His promises, and it commits itself to following that truth. This sort of faith is supernatural—it is a gift from God. "For by grace you have been saved through faith; and that not of yourselves, it is the gift of God; not as a result of works, so that no one may boast" (Eph. 2:8–9).

Without saving faith, no one can please God. The Bible plainly declares in Romans 8:8 that "those who are in the flesh *cannot please God*." The reason for this can be seen in the following verse:

> However, you are not in the flesh but in the Spirit, if indeed the Spirit of God dwells in you. But if anyone does not have the Spirit of Christ, he does not belong to Him. (Rom. 8:9)

Before we can do anything that will please God, His Spirit must be operating in our lives. As we saw in the last chapter, you and I simply do not have the ability to consistently do what the Bible says will please Him until we are saved (cf. Prov. 15:9; 21:4). The attempts we do make to reform our lives before we are saved are characterized by wrong motives and superficiality. Changes that truly please God are internal: they are made in our hearts. Biblical change requires a transformation of our thoughts and motives (cf. Rom. 12:2; Eph. 4:23; Heb. 4:12). For more about saving faith in Christ, let me refer you to Appendix A.

But the faith that pleases God goes well beyond salvation. God is pleased by a vigorous faith that is operational moment by moment. God-pleasing faith lives life with the conviction that God keeps His promises—both in this life and in the next. The one whose faith pleases God does not just "believe that He is," but also believes "that He is a *rewarder* of those who *seek* Him" (Heb. 11:6). As John MacArthur puts it:

> It is not enough simply to believe that God exists. In order to please Him it is also necessary to believe that He is moral and just, that He will reward faith in Him. We must recognize God as a personal, loving, gracious God to those who seek Him. Enoch believed this within the revelation he had. He did not believe God was merely a great impersonal cosmic force. He believed in and knew God in a personal, loving way . . . For three hundred years Enoch had fellowship with the true God, a God whom he knew to be just, merciful, forgiving, caring, and very personal.[1]

The life of Enoch points us to another important element of pleasing God: walking the walk.

2. Pleasing God requires walking with Him. What did Enoch do that was so pleasing to God? He walked with God.

1. John MacArthur, *Hebrews* (Chicago: Moody Press, 1996), electronic edition.

> Then Enoch *walked with God* three hundred years after he became the father of Methuselah, and he had other sons and daughters. So all the days of Enoch were three hundred and sixty-five years. Enoch *walked with God*; and he was not, for God took him. (Gen. 5:22–24)

The word *walked* appears twice in this passage. In the Septuagint (the Greek translation of the Old Testament), the word *walked* is translated with the phrase "was pleasing." It is the same Greek word translated twice as *please* in Hebrews 11:5–6: "before his being taken up he *was pleasing to* God. And without faith it is impossible *to please* Him . . ." So to walk with God is to please him (cf. 1 Thess. 4:1).

Another key passage of Scripture that relates your walk to your ability to please God is Colossians 1:9–10:

> For this reason also, since the day we heard of it, we have not ceased to pray for you and to ask that you may be filled with the knowledge of His will in all spiritual wisdom and understanding, *so that you will walk in a manner worthy of the Lord, to please Him in all respects*, bearing fruit in every good work and increasing in the knowledge of God . . .

Your walk refers to your daily pattern of conduct[2]—the way you conduct your inner and outer life. You are to conduct your affairs in a manner that is *worthy* of (deserving of or appropriate to) the Lord—in a way that *pleases* Him. And you are to please Him in *all respects* (in all things)—in every area of your life (with every step of your walk), pleasing God is to be your ambition.

To walk with God is also to have communion with Him. When I speak of communion (or fellowship) with God, I do not mean a mystical intimacy wherein the Holy Spirit whispers words of comfort and assurance into our ears.[3] Rather, I'm referring to the assurance that comes

---

2. The word *walk* is often metaphorically used in the Bible to denote the course or path that one chooses to follow. Specific qualifying characteristics of the "Christian way of walking" are given in the Bible to make it clear that the walk of the believer is to be noticeably different from the walk of unbelievers. Indeed, Christians should be identifiable by the way they walk.

3. Of course, our communication with God *does* go both ways. We speak to God in prayer. He speaks to us through the words of the Bible (cf. Heb. 1:1–2; 1 Peter 1:16–21).

from confessing and forsaking all known sin and the sense of close-
ness to God that comes from having a clean conscience and drawing
near to Him through Bible study and prayer.

Further, to walk with God is to advance or make progress in one's
godliness—to become more like Christ. As George Whitefield said in
his sermon *Walking with God*:

> Walking, in the very first sense of the word, seems to suppose a pro-
> gressive motion. A person that walks, though he moves slowly, goes
> forward—he does not continue in one place. And so it is with those
> that walk with God. They go on, as the Psalmist says, "from strength
> to strength" or, in the language of the apostle Paul, "they pass from
> glory to glory, even by the Spirit of the Lord."[4]

Theologians sometimes refer to this advancement as progressive
sanctification. Sanctification is a work of God whereby the Holy Spirit
conforms those whom He has regenerated into the image of Christ. But
unlike justification (an act of God whereby He declares sinners justified
who have trusted in Christ), sanctification requires our cooperation.

3. Pleasing God requires sanctification (holiness). The word *walk*
is closely associated with the word *sanctification*.

> Finally then, brethren, we request and exhort you in the Lord Jesus,
> that as you received from us instruction as to how you ought *to walk
> and please God* (just as you actually do walk), that you excel still more.
> For you know what commandments we gave you by the authority of
> the Lord Jesus. For this is the will of God, your sanctification; that *is*,
> that you abstain from sexual immorality . . . (1 Thess. 4:1–3)

Do you see your Christian walk as merely a matter of obeying certain rules and avoiding certain sins because that is what God requires?
Or do you see your walk as an opportunity to bring pleasure to God in

4. This sermon may be read in its entirety at: http://www.reformed.org/documents/Whitefield/
WITF_002.html.

expression of your love for Him? The Christian walk is not simply a matter of keeping your life relatively free from sin—it's a matter of your heart motives.

God's will for your life (and therefore that which is pleasing to Him) is for you to be holy. To be precise, it is the Lord's will that you become increasingly set apart (dedicated) to Him—that you become progressively freer from sin,[5] and increasingly characterized by love for God and neighbor. It pleases God when you work together with the Holy Spirit as He, through the Word, transforms you into the image of Christ.

As we have already seen, to walk is not to remain stationary but to make progress in a particular direction. So it is with our sanctification. Step by step, we move a little closer to the goal of becoming like Christ. God is the one who sanctifies, but we must cooperate with the Spirit's work as "our inner man is being renewed day by day" (2 Cor. 4:16). And since the Word of God is a necessary ingredient in this process, it stands to reason that the best way to work together with the Spirit is to spend time "day by day" in the Book that He wrote to help us accomplish our goal.

Sometimes people confuse the means of sanctification with the goal of sanctification. R. C. Sproul makes an important distinction between spirituality (or piety) and righteousness:

> Over the years I've had many young Christians ask me how to be more spiritual or more pious. Rare has been the earnest student who said, "Teach me how to be righteous." Why, I wondered, does anybody want to be spiritual? What is the purpose of spirituality? What use is there in piety?
>
> Spirituality and piety are not ends in themselves. In fact they are worthless *unless* they are means to a higher goal. The goal must go beyond spirituality to righteousness.
>
> Spiritual disciplines are vitally necessary to achieve righteousness. Bible study, prayer, church attendance, evangelism, are necessary for Christian growth, but they cannot be the final goal. I cannot

5. The particular sin that Paul was encouraging the Thessalonians to abstain from in their attempts to please God was fornication (sexual sin).

achieve righteousness without spirituality. But it is possible to be "spiritual," at least on the surface, without attaining righteousness.[6]

In your attempts to please God—as you do those things that foster spiritual growth (the things that you can do to cooperate with the Holy Spirit's sanctifying work in your life), don't lose sight of the goal: becoming more like Christ. And don't think that you are *necessarily* pleasing God just because you are engaging in these activities on a regular basis. If your motive is wrong—if you think, for example, that these sanctifying activities are themselves the goal (and barometer) of your spirituality—God will not be pleased with your efforts. As you will recall, the scribes and Pharisees were very adept at doing these things; yet Christ saw them as hypocrites. Why? They were considered hypocrites largely because they did these religious things for the approval of men.

Another element of sanctification deserves mention. It has to do with the purpose of the thing that has been sanctified. According to the *Evangelical Dictionary of Biblical Theology*:

> To sanctify someone or something is to set that person or thing apart for the use intended by its designer. A pen is "sanctified" when used to write. Eyeglasses are "sanctified" when used to improve sight. In the theological sense, things are sanctified when they are used for the purpose God intends. A human being is sanctified, therefore, when he or she lives according to God's design and purpose.[7]

You have been set apart for God's purposes. One of those purposes is for His glory and pleasure. God's pleasure, as we will see in the next requirement, is what pleasing Him is all about.

4. Pleasing God requires your cooperation. You may be wondering why I am belaboring this point. It's not just because I want to be

6. R. C. Sproul, *Pleasing God* (Wheaton, IL: Tyndale House Publishers, 1988), electronic edition.

7. Walter Elwell and Walter A. Elwell, *Evangelical Dictionary of Biblical Theology*, electronic ed. (Grand Rapids: Baker Book House, 1997), electronic edition.

sure you get it. I also want to open up to you another vital yet often over-looked passage of Scripture that deals with pleasing God:

> So then, my beloved, just as you have always obeyed, not as in my pres-ence only, but now much more in my absence, *work out* your salvation with fear and trembling; for it is God who is at work in you, both to will and to work for His *good pleasure*. (Phil. 2:12–13)

The salvation we are commanded to work out in this passage is obviously not the state of the soul after death. God has already worked that out for us (technically, according to verse 13, it has been worked in us), through Christ's work on the cross. The directive to work out our salvation (bring it to completion) addresses our responsibility to ac-tively participate in the work of progressive sanctification. So to please God, you must (by faith) do what the Bible says is necessary to grow as a Christian.

At the risk of overstating my case, let me suggest that it is not *usu-ally* necessary to wait for the Spirit to "move you" before you obey the Bible. Sure, you should pray, asking God for wisdom to do what the Bible says—and the grace to do it. You should also be sure that your mo-tives are right. And there are times when seeking counsel on how to proceed may be beneficial. But waiting for God to zap you with an in-fusion of grace from heaven rather than acting in faith (which, you will remember, is our first requirement for pleasing God) and doing what God has already given you the wisdom to do often amounts to delayed obedience.

It is often only *after* we step out in faith and do the things the Bible requires, having first been given the wisdom of God, that this grace "to will and to work" (this supernatural desire and ability to obey God) be-comes operative in our lives.

But the main point I want to emphasize from this passage (v. 13) has to do with the phrase "for His good pleasure." The single original word from which the term *good pleasure* is derived is not found in clas-sical Greek literature. It was almost completely restricted to Jewish and

Christian literature and occurs for the first time in the Greek Bible.[8] The verbal form of this word means "to please" or "to be well pleased." It was spoken by the "voice out of the heavens" after Jesus was baptized by John: "This is My beloved Son, in whom I am well-pleased" (Matt. 3:17). The English dictionary defines the verb *to please* as "to give enjoyment, pleasure or satisfaction to."

So when we "work out" our own salvation—when we do those things that the Bible says cause us to grow as Christians—we are pleasing God. Think of that: your spiritual growth and the things you do to cooperate with the Holy Spirit in the process of growth delight and bring pleasure to God. In light of this, shouldn't you invest more of your "thought time" thinking about pleasing Him than about pleasing people?

5. Pleasing God requires doing good works. We must return again to Colossians 1:9–10, for it contains two more essentials for pleasing God. The first is fruitfulness:

> For this reason also, since the day we heard of it, we have not ceased to pray for you and to ask that you may be filled with the knowledge of His will in all spiritual wisdom and understanding, so that you will walk in a manner worthy of the Lord, to please Him in all respects, *bearing fruit in every good work* and increasing in the knowledge of God . . .

Fruit is important to God. He is pleased when our lives manifest an abundance of it. Jesus said, "My Father is glorified by this, that you bear much fruit, and so prove to be My disciples" (John 15:8). Although the Bible speaks of many varieties of fruit (e.g., a person who has been converted to the faith, Rom. 1:13; the praise of God's people, Heb. 13:15; the development of Christian character, Gal. 5:22–23, Heb. 12:11; and even charitable gifts, Rom. 15:26–28), the specific variety of fruitfulness that Paul has in mind here is the kind that has to do with "good

8. *Theological Dictionary of the New Testament*, 10 vols., ed. Gerhard Kittel and Gerhard Friedrich, trans. Geoffrey W. Bromiley (Grand Rapids: Eerdmans, 1976), electronic edition.

works." In fact, he tells us that God actually prepared these works for us to do long ago: "For we are His workmanship, created in Christ Jesus for good works, which God prepared beforehand so that we would walk in them" (Eph. 2:10). Good works (like all else in the sanctification process) are the result of what God is doing in our lives even though we must take the initiative to bring them to pass. He intends for us to regularly and habitually perform them. It is a big part of what we were created to do.

"But what makes my works good?" you may ask.

I like the way M. G. Easton put it:

> Works are "good" only when, (1) they spring from the principle of love to God. The moral character of an act is determined by the moral principle that prompts it. Faith and love in the heart are the essential elements of all true obedience. Hence good works only spring from a believing heart, can only be wrought by one reconciled to God (Eph. 2:10; James 2:18, 22). (2.) Good works have the glory of God as their object; and (3) they have the revealed will of God as their only rule (Deut. 12:32; Rev. 22:18–19).[9]

So godly actions motivated by a love for God and neighbor are the essence of good works. The Christian who pleases God is involved in performing a variety of useful ministries for others, be they activities of mercy, charity, prayer, or service. Of course, he does so not for the approval of man, for this would be displeasing to the Lord, but for the pleasure of God.

Another passage that ties doing good things in to pleasing God is Hebrews 13:16: "And do not neglect doing good and sharing, for with such sacrifices God is pleased." "Doing good" is closely connected to sharing. Be it your money, your home, your food, your time, your wisdom, or a seat in your car, God is pleased when you tangibly share the things he has given you with other believers.

9. M. G. Easton, *Easton's Bible Dictionary* (Oak Harbor, WA: Logos Research Systems, Inc., 1996), electronic edition.

6. Pleasing God requires knowledge and wisdom. The third essential element for pleasing God found in Colossians 1:9–10 is a growing knowledge of Him:

> For this reason also, since the day we heard of it, we have not ceased to pray for you and to ask that you may be *filled with the knowledge of His will in all spiritual wisdom and understanding*, so that you will walk in a manner worthy of the Lord, to please Him in all respects, bearing fruit in every good work *and increasing in the knowledge of God . . .*

The longer we walk with God and the harder we work for Him, the greater our knowledge of Him should be. As we are to grow in our fruitfulness for Him, so we are to grow in our *perceptiveness* of him. Knowledge is necessary for both our walk and our work.

The concept we have of knowledge today, however, is different from the knowledge of which the Bible speaks. For to the average American, knowledge is "facts to be learned." This secular notion pursues knowledge for knowledge's sake. The idea behind this view is to amass as much knowledge as one can in order to know more than the next person. Learning, in other words, is self-serving. The goal is to get as many letters after your name as possible so that you can get a well-paying job so that you can find real satisfaction in doing whatever you enjoy.

This self-oriented view of learning is antithetical to the biblical view. For the Christian, knowledge is not "facts to be learned," but rather "truth to be lived." Wisdom is not acquiring knowledge for the sake of knowledge, but rather for the sake of implementation. In the process of giving the Great Commission, Jesus didn't instruct the apostles to teach their disciples *to know* His commandments, but rather to teach them "*to observe* all that I commanded you" (Matt. 28:20). He didn't say in Luke 11:28, "Blessed are those who *know* the word of God," but rather, "Blessed are those who *hear* the word of God *and observe it*." Paul didn't say to Timothy, "The things you have heard from me in the presence of many witnesses keep to yourself and do not disclose to anyone unless you can use them to brag about how much knowledge you have acquired." The things Paul taught him he was to entrust to faithful men, who were to be able to teach others also (2 Tim. 2:2).

Why did Paul pray that the Colossians would be "filled with the knowledge of His will in all spiritual wisdom and understanding" (Col. 1:9)? Because he wanted all his disciples to know the Scriptures so well that their hearts would be repositories bursting (*filled*) with the truth necessary to determine God's will for their lives. But it didn't end there. The ultimate purpose for this knowledge was for them to *walk* in such a way that would please and glorify God.

So we grow *through* (by means of) the true knowledge of God. "But grow in the grace and knowledge of our Lord and Savior Jesus Christ" (2 Pet. 3:18). And where do we find this knowledge? We find it in the Bible. "Like newborn babies, long for the pure milk of the word, so that by it you may grow in respect to salvation" (1 Pet. 2:2).

Do you remember the prayer King Solomon prayed soon after his inauguration?

"Sure. He asked God for wisdom."

That's right. And how did God respond to Solomon's request?

"He gave him wisdom plus lots of other neat stuff."

Right again. But don't forget the most important part of God's response: He was pleased.

In Gibeon the LORD appeared to Solomon in a dream at night; and God said, "Ask what you wish me to give you." Then Solomon said, "You have shown great lovingkindness to Your servant David my father, according as he walked before You in truth and righteousness and uprightness of heart toward You; and You have reserved for him this great lovingkindness, that You have given him a son to sit on his throne, as it is this day. Now, O LORD my God, You have made Your servant king in place of my father David, yet I am but a little child; I do not know how to go out or come in. Your servant is in the midst of Your people which You have chosen, a great people who are too many to be numbered or counted. *So give Your servant an understanding heart* to judge Your people to discern between good and evil. For who is able to judge this great people of Yours?"

It was pleasing in the sight of the Lord that Solomon had asked this thing. (1 Kings 3:5–10)

How regularly do you pray for wisdom? Solomon said, "Wisdom *is* the principal thing; therefore get wisdom. And in all your getting, get understanding" (Prov. 4:7 NKJV). How often do you ask God to bless you with the things He values rather than the things you do? Such prayers are lovely in the ears of the Lord. Matthew Henry makes a point about this event that should have significance to all people-pleasers:

> By this choice Solomon made it appear that he desired to be good more than great, and to serve God's honor more than to advance his own. Those are accepted of God who prefer spiritual blessings to temporal, and are more solicitous to be found in the way of their duty than in the way to preferment.[10]

7. Pleasing God requires gratitude (worship). In requirement 5, we looked briefly at Hebrews 13:16, noting that it contained two sacrifices that we, as Christians, could make that would be pleasing to God: "And do not neglect *doing good* and *sharing*, for with such sacrifices God is pleased." In the verse that precedes it, another God-pleasing sacrifice is mentioned:

> Through Him then, let us continually offer up a sacrifice of praise to God, that is, the fruit of lips that give thanks to His name. (Heb. 13:15)

The offering up of praise (the fruit of our lips that give thanks to His name) is another "sacrifice" with which God is pleased. But expressing gratitude to God is more than a sacrificial duty. It is a service.

---

10. Matthew Henry, *Matthew Henry's Commentary on the Whole Bible: Complete and Unabridged in One Volume* (1 Kings 3:5) (Peabody, MA: Hendrickson Publishers, 1996), electronic edition.

Yes, by giving thanks to the Lord for who He is and what He has done, you actually perform a service (a good work, if you please) to God that brings Him pleasure (i.e., it pleases Him).

> Therefore, since we receive a kingdom which cannot be shaken, *let us show gratitude*, by which we may offer to God an *acceptable* service with reverence and awe . . . (Heb. 12:28)

The term *acceptable* here is an adverbial form of a word we looked at earlier that means "well-pleasing."

The word for *gratitude* is really the word commonly translated *grace* in the Bible. Here it is translated *gratitude* (in Greek, "let us have gratitude"). What's the connection between grace and gratitude? To show grace to someone is to delight him. It is to bring that person joy, happiness, and gratification. It is an expression of lovingkindness and goodwill that pleases the person who is being graced. God's grace toward us engenders these things in our hearts. When we express our thanksgiving to Him for all He has done, we delight, please, and gratify Him. We respond to God's grace, given to us in Christ, by offering back to Him gratitude (a form of grace), which is our "acceptable service."

But more than this, our gratitude becomes the basis and motivation of our worship. We worship God out of a heart filled with gratitude for who He is and what He has done for us.

To *offer service* to God is to worship Him. This broadens our understanding of what pleasing God is all about. For the Christian, life is about worship—worshiping God in ways that are acceptable (or pleasing) to Him. Our understanding of worship cannot be limited to Sunday mornings. For although God desires to be worshiped corporately, He also longs for us to please and worship Him by giving thanks (and being obedient) every day of our lives. Asaph (the psalmist) understood the connection between offering praise to God and living a godly life: "Whoever offers praise glorifies Me; and to him who orders his conduct aright I will show the salvation of God" (Ps. 50:23 NKJV).

Finally, our worship is to be offered to God "with reverence and awe," that is, with godly fear: the realization that God (much more than men, by the way) is watching and evaluating our thoughts, words, attitudes, and actions. By keeping your heart filled with thanksgiving and your mind focused on worshiping God, you will gradually weaken the grip that people-pleasing has on you.

8. Pleasing God requires godly ambition. In Philippians 2:12, we have already seen that pleasing God requires our working together with the Holy Spirit in the progressive sanctification process. But we are about to look at a verse that raises the standard even higher than "work out your own salvation with fear and trembling."

> Therefore *we also have as our ambition*, whether at home or absent, to be pleasing to Him. For we must all appear before the judgment seat of Christ, so that each one may be recompensed for his deeds in the body, according to what he has done, whether good or bad. (2 Cor. 5:9–10)

There is such a thing as righteous ambition. Paul uses the word *ambition* to describe his own desires: "It has always been my ambition to preach the gospel where Christ was not known . . ." (Rom. 15:20 NIV). He even urged the Thessalonians to be ambitious about a few things: "But we urge you, brethren, to excel still more, and to make it your *ambition* to lead a quiet life and attend to your own business and work with your hands, just as we commanded you . . ." (1 Thess. 4:10b–11)

An ambition is a strong desire to achieve something. Some people have a strong desire to achieve wealth. Some, like Diotrephes (3 John 9), are ambitious for a particular position. The ambition of the people-pleaser is to achieve man's admiration, honor, favor, and respect.

So what is this godly ambition? Some versions of the Bible translate the phrase *we have as our ambition* with expressions such as "we make it our aim," "we make it our goal," "we labor," and "our only goal is" (to please God). A person with godly ambition has such a heartfelt determination to bring pleasure to God that it penetrates everything he does—every thought, every decision, every word, every attitude. Though he may fail periodically, even regularly, the God-pleaser strives to have this ambition *rule* everything he does.

The etymology of the word *ambition* should be of special interest to you as a former people-pleaser. The term literally means "love of honor." From there it moves to being actuated (moved to action) by the love of honor. It then morphs into the idea of *striving* to bring something to pass, then to be ambitious, and finally to strive earnestly or to make it one's aim.[11] As a people-pleaser, you were ambitious for the honor of men. Now, as a God-pleaser, you make it your ambition to refocus your desires on pleasing God.

Having a godly ambition to please God is tied to eternal rewards (2 Cor. 5:10). To the extent that pleasing (and glorifying) God is the ruling motive for the things you do while "in the body," you will be recompensed at the judgment seat of Christ. And as Jesus made so clear in his Sermon on the Mount (Matt. 6:1–18), to the extent that pleasing (being seen by) people is the ruling motive in your decisions, you will lose your heavenly rewards.

I would like to briefly mention one final element of godly ambition for your consideration: the resolve to not be distracted from one's eternal purpose.

> Suffer hardship with me, as a good soldier of Christ Jesus. No soldier in active service entangles himself in the affairs of everyday life, so that he may *please* the one who enlisted him as a soldier. (2 Tim. 2:3–4)

A soldier is single-minded. He is prepared to suffer hardship. Although he may regularly participate in the daily affairs of life (i.e., side business ventures, sports, music, television, hobbies, social activities,

11. James Strong, *Enhanced Strong's Lexicon* (G5389) (Elmira, ON: Woodside Bible Fellowship, 1996), electronic edition.

and doing things that please people), he does not become entangled with them. He does not (as the original Greek implies) inextricably weave them into the fabric of his life. On the battlefield, these good things will distract him, slow him down, and prevent him from doing his job. And what motivates the soldier to minimize his distractions? The ambition to "please the one who enlisted him as a soldier."

So it is with you. You have been selected to serve in God's army. He is the one from whom you take orders. You serve at *His* pleasure. If you are serious about learning to please the Lord and Savior, Jesus Christ, you won't allow anything to become so inextricably woven into your life that it distracts you from doing what He has enlisted you to do.

As I explained at the outset of this chapter, the requirements of pleasing God that I have covered are far from exhaustive. For example, the term translated *well-pleasing* is used elsewhere in the New Testament. As Warren Wiersbe points out:

> It is well-pleasing to God when we present our bodies to Him as living sacrifices (Romans 12:1), and when we live so as to help others and avoid causing them to stumble (Romans 14:18). God is well-pleased when His children separate themselves from the evil around them (Ephesians 5:10), as well as when they bring their offerings to Him (Philippians 4:18). He is pleased with children who submit to their parents (Colossians 3:20), as well as with saints who permit Jesus Christ to work out His perfect will in their lives (Hebrews 13:20–21).[12]

Insufficient as it may be, that is my attempt at the long*er* answer to the question: What exactly does it take to please God? I hope you now have a better idea of what the Bible says about this matter. But what are you going to do with what you have learned? How specifically are you going to put off your people-pleasing attitudes and replace them with God-pleasing ambition? Here is a work sheet that will help you implement the basic truths you have just learned.

12. Warren W. Wiersbe, *The Bible Exposition Commentary* (2 Cor. 5:9) (Wheaton, IL: Victor Books, 1996), electronic edition.

PLEASING GOD WORK SHEET

After each God-pleasing requirement listed below, write down several specific ways to put into practice each principle we have studied in this chapter.

1. How can I please God with my *faith*?

2. How can I please God in my *walk* with Christ?

3. In what areas of my life would God be pleased to have me be more *sanctified (holy)*?

4. In what ways can I please God by *cooperating* with the Spirit's sanctification process?

5. What *good works* can I do to please God?

6. How can I please God by growing in my *knowledge* of Him?

7. How can I offer up to God sacrifices of *thanksgiving*?

8. How can I *make it my ambition to please God* in all things?

Ten

WHAT ARE YOU WEARING?

When you put on your shirt or blouse this morning, which way did you button it? Did you start from the bottom and work up? Did you begin at the top and work down? Or did you start somewhere in the middle and work your way up and then down? Chances are, you have to think for a moment to answer that question because you button your shirt pretty much the same way every morning.

"But I don't have buttons on my shirt today!"

OK, fine. How did you put on your buttonless blouse, T-shirt, sweatshirt, or sweater this morning? Did you put your arms through the sleeves first, and then poke your head through the opening of the garment? Or did you pull it over your head first—and then struggle to squeeze your arms into that small opening between your garment and your body as you found the sleeves by feeling your way around the inside of the thing? The same principle applies. You probably get dressed the same way every morning without much thought because you have done it the same way for years.

But do you remember when you first learned to button your shirt? Maybe you were three or four years old. Can you remember how hard it was? You had to carefully line up the buttons on one side of the shirt with the buttonholes on the other. Then you struggled to grasp a button with the thumb and forefinger of one hand, as you stuck the thumb of your other hand partway through the corresponding buttonhole to spread it open. Your chin was pressed tightly against the top of your chest as you labored to slide that little button with your thumb at least halfway through the hole so that (after grasping the underside of the shirt with the index finger of your "button hand" to see better) you could grasp part of the button with the thumb and forefinger of your "buttonhole hand" and bring it safely through the rest of the way.

But now you can perform this complex behavior quickly, easily, and unconsciously because you have practiced it over and over again. Yet how quickly, easily, and unconsciously do you put on the garment of humility?

THE GARMENT OF HUMILITY

In 1 Peter 5:5, we read, "Clothe yourselves with humility toward one another, for God is opposed to the proud, but gives grace to the humble." If the love of man's approval is rooted in the sin of pride, it follows that an important element of learning to put off the sin of people-pleasing is to put on humility. In this case, you are to put it on as you would an article of clothing.[1] And like getting dressed, it's something you probably need to do every day.

At first, you may have to make a very conscious effort to pick it up, put your arms through the sleeves, button it, tuck it in, and straighten out the collar. In time, clothing yourself with humility should require less concentration. To be sure, you'll still have to dress yourself in humility every morning. But if you practice, it probably won't require as much time, effort, and thought as it did in the beginning.

1. The meaning of the word *egkombóomai*, "to clothe" in 1 Peter 5:5, is "to gather or tie in a knot, hence to fasten a garment, to clothe, to gird oneself." There was something called an *egkómboma*, a long white apron or outer garment with strings worn by slaves, from which this word was apparently derived. Source: Spiros Zodhiates, *The Complete Word Study Dictionary: New Testament* (Chattanooga, TN: AMG Publishers, 2000), electronic edition.

THE PREREQUISITE TO HONOR

Have you learned the biblical paradox that honor comes not by exalting self but by humbling oneself?

I mentioned in chapter 6 that when I was twenty years old, I was the front-end manager of a large supermarket in New York. What I didn't mention about that position was that I had a crew of fifty or so employees who were directly answerable to me. I learned at an early age that I could not conceal my weaknesses from those who were under my authority. I learned to apply Proverbs 15:33 to the workplace:

> The fear of the LORD is the instruction of wisdom, and *before honor is humility.* (NKJV)

Here is how I reason this out in my mind:

"I am a sinner.

"Because I'm a sinner, it shouldn't surprise me when I make mistakes.

"If *I'm* not surprised by the fact that I make mistakes, others should not be, either.

"When I sin, or make a mistake, I may very well fall a notch or two in the esteem or estimation of those who saw me commit the blunder.

"If I try to cover up my sin or deny that I've done anything wrong, or in some way justify my actions, I will be likely to slip a few more notches in the approval poll." (Proverbs 28:13 says, "He who conceals his transgressions will not prosper, but he who confesses and forsakes them will find compassion.")

"If, on the other hand, I do what the Bible says and humble myself, I may regain a notch or two in the estimation of my staff and end up at least where I started before I fell. I may even end up more highly esteemed as a result of acknowledging my sin in this way.

"But most of all, whether or not I regain the approval of man, I'm going to obey God because this will meet with His approval, and His approval means more to me than the approval of anyone else."

Honor is like an elusive butterfly. If you run after it, it will almost certainly escape from you. Yet if you do not seek to capture it but sit still, it may come and rest on your shoulder. Honor may also be compared to your shadow. It runs away from you when you attempt to pursue it and follows you just as quickly as you run away from it.

Think of the many throughout history who, in their day, were considered by most to be "the scum of the world, the dregs of all things" (1 Cor. 4:13), and yet have since obtained more honor than all their contemporaries.

THE WORD OF GOD IS A TIGER

I'll never forget a bit of authoring advice I received after sending the manuscript for my first book to a friend, John Sowell. I had inserted plenty of Bible references throughout the book for my readers to look up, but not many actual quotations that they could read as they were working through the text. What was John's advice?

> "God's Word is the tiger that devours the heart set on the flesh. Unleash that tiger upon your readers' hearts."

My friend knew the convicting and life-changing power of the written Word and wanted me to expose my readers to its influence.

I'm getting ready to unleash a tiger on you. As you read the following verses, I'd like for you to notice two things common to most of the passages I quote. Look first for a cause-and-effect relationship. Observe especially the "if"/"then" association stated or implied in these passages. Second and more importantly, please take note of this vital antithetical construct: Either you humble yourself (voluntarily) or you will be humbled by God (involuntarily)!

> Moses and Aaron went to Pharaoh and said to him, "Thus says the LORD, the God of the Hebrews, 'How long will you refuse to *humble yourself* before Me? Let My people go, that they may serve Me.'" (Exod. 10:3)

Then the word of the LORD came to Elijah the Tishbite, saying, "Do you see how Ahab has *humbled himself* before Me? Because he has humbled himself before Me, I will not bring the evil in his days, but I will bring the evil upon his house in his son's days." (1 Kings 21:28–29)

"But to the king of Judah who sent you to inquire of the LORD thus shall you say to him, 'Thus says the LORD God of Israel, "Regarding the words which you have heard, because your heart was tender and you *humbled yourself* before the LORD when you heard what I spoke against this place and against its inhabitants that they should become a desolation and a curse, and you have *torn your clothes and wept before Me,* I truly have heard you," declares the LORD. "Therefore, behold, I will gather you to your fathers, and you will be gathered to your grave in peace, and your eyes will not see all the evil which I will bring on this place."'" So they brought back word to the king. (2 Kings 22:18–20)

[If] My people who are called by My name *humble themselves* and pray and seek My face and turn from their wicked ways, then I will hear from heaven, will forgive their sin and will heal their land. (2 Chron. 7:14)

So the princes of Israel and the *king humbled themselves* and said, "The LORD is righteous."
When the LORD saw that they *humbled themselves,* the word of the LORD came to Shemaiah, saying, "They have *humbled themselves* so I will not destroy them, but I will grant them some measure of deliverance, and My wrath shall not be poured out on Jerusalem . . ." (2 Chron. 12:6–7)

And when he [King Rehoboam] *humbled himself,* the anger of the LORD turned away from him, so as not to destroy him completely; and also conditions were good in Judah. (2 Chron. 12:12)

Do not be called leaders; for One is your Leader, that is, Christ. But the greatest among you shall be your servant. Whoever exalts himself shall be humbled; and whoever *humbles himself* shall be exalted. (Matt. 23:10–12)

Two men went up into the temple to pray, one a Pharisee and the other a tax collector. The Pharisee stood and was praying this to himself: "God, I thank You that I am not like other people: swindlers, unjust, adulterers, or even like this tax collector. I fast twice a week; I pay tithes of all that I get." But the tax collector, standing some distance away, was even unwilling to lift up his eyes to heaven, but was beating his breast, saying, "God, be merciful to me, the sinner!" I tell you, this man went down to his house justified rather than the other; for everyone who exalts himself will be humbled, but he who *humbles himself* will be exalted. (Luke 18:10–14)

Being found in appearance as a man, He *humbled Himself* by becoming obedient to the point of death, even death on a cross. For this reason also, God highly exalted Him, and bestowed on Him the name which is above every name, so that at the name of Jesus every knee will bow, of those who are in heaven and on earth and under the earth, and that every tongue will confess that Jesus Christ is Lord, to the glory of God the Father. (Phil. 2:8–11)

Humble yourselves in the presence of the Lord, and He will exalt you. (James 4:10)

All of you, clothe yourselves with humility toward one another, for God is opposed to the proud, but gives grace to the humble.

Therefore *humble yourselves* under the mighty hand of God, that He may exalt you at the proper time . . . (1 Pet. 5:5–6)

"OK, I get the point, but how do I *humble myself* so that God won't have to humble me?"

I'm about to tell you. But please remember: you can't put on the garment of humility in your own strength. Make these principles a matter of prayer.

LET'S GET DRESSED

To begin with, you must be quick to acknowledge when you are wrong. As I've already told you, refusing to admit wrongdoing is the greatest single manifestation of pride we see in couples who come in for marriage counseling. Confessing one's sins to God is, for most of us, rather easy. We very much want His forgiveness and know that He stands ready to forgive. Besides, we recognize that He already knows how awful we really are, and yet He still loves us. Yes, He even gave Himself for us. He won't condemn us.

But confessing our sins to people against whom we've sinned—well, that's another matter. They don't know exactly how messed up we are on the inside. They may not stand willing to forgive. If they're Christians, of course, they're supposed to forgive. But not every professing Christian does what he's supposed to do. Besides, they may not forget. They may hold a grudge. They may use it against us sometime in the future. They may lose respect for us. They may lose trust in us and not give us a chance to earn it back. Basically, they may reject us. If you want to fear God rather than man, you will not allow your apprehension of these possibilities tempt you to cover your sin. Instead, you will admit mistakes freely, and if you have sinned against someone, you will seek his forgiveness.

FORGIVENESS: WHAT DOES IT MEAN?

The Bible instructs us to forgive, "just as God in Christ also has forgiven you" (Eph. 4:32). How does God forgive us? He tells us in Isaiah 43:25 and Jeremiah 31:34: "I, even I, am the one who wipes out your transgressions for My own sake, and I will *not remember* your sins," and "I will forgive their iniquity, and their sin I will *remember no more.*"

Does God have amnesia? No—God is all-knowing. He knew about your sins before you ever thought to commit them. When the Bible speaks of God's not remembering our sins, it refers to the fact that He does not hold them against the forgiven sinner. When Christ died on the cross, He did so to pay the penalty for guilty sinners like you and me. Christ's death, therefore, was a substitution. We discussed double imputation in chapter 8: Christ died to take the blame for our sin so that we, as saved individuals, might be credited with His righteousness. Rather than charging our sins to our own account, God charges them to the account of Jesus Christ. When we truly believe the gospel (the "good news" that if we repent and place our faith in what Christ has done by substituting Himself for us on the cross and rising from the dead, God promises to forgive all our sins and give us eternal life), we claim the *promise* that God will not hold our sins against us anymore.

So forgiveness is fundamentally a *promise*. As God promises to not hold our sins against us, so we also must *promise* to not hold the sins of those we've forgiven against them. This promise can be broken down into three parts. First, you promise to not bring up the offense to the forgiven person so as to use it against him. Second, you promise to not discuss the forgiven offense with others. Finally, you promise to not dwell on the forgiven offense yourself, but remind yourself instead that you have forgiven your offender "just as God in Christ also has forgiven you" (Eph. 4:32).

When you ask for forgiveness, you secure for yourself this promise. Asking forgiveness is much better than simply apologizing. An apology (which really implies that you are explaining why you did what you did) leaves the ball up in the air.

You say, "I'm sorry." The offended brother says, "I'm sorry, too." The ball is still up in the air. No one is assuming the biblical responsibility to reconcile. You say, "I'm sorry." The other person says, "You are sorry! You are one of the *sorriest* people I know."

Now, wouldn't you rather tie up those loose ends by asking the person you offended to not hold your offense against you ever again? Let me suggest an approach for seeking forgiveness that has proved most effective. The approach typically has five steps. (This example is of a husband asking forgiveness of his wife.)

First, acknowledge that you have sinned. Let the offended party know that you realize what you did was wrong.

Example: "I was wrong for not paying attention while you were talking to me."

Second, identify your sin by its specific biblical name. Using biblical terminology, let her know that you know what you did violated Scripture and therefore was a sin against God.

Example: "That was selfish and inconsiderate of me."

Third, acknowledge the harm your offense caused.[2]

Show remorse (sympathy) for the hurt your sin may have caused.

Example: "It really grieves me that I hurt you in this way." Or: "I'm so sorry I upset you by my rudeness."

Fourth, demonstrate repentance by identifying an alternative biblical behavior. One of the best ways to demonstrate repentance (a change of mind) to the offended person is by letting her know that you have thought through a more biblical option than the one for which you are about to ask forgiveness.

Example: "I should have turned off the television when you first told me that you thought you were having a nervous breakdown."

Fifth, ask for forgiveness. This step puts the ball into the court of the offended one. (It's as if you're saying, "Are you going to do the right thing and forgive me, or aren't you?")

Example: "Will you forgive me?"

NOT SELF-ESTEEM BUT OTHERS-ESTEEM

Another thing you can do to clothe yourself with humility is to learn to esteem others better than yourself.

> Let nothing be done through selfish ambition or conceit, but in lowliness of mind let each *esteem others better than himself.* Let each of you

2. This third step is optional and may not always be appropriate.

look out not only for his own interests, but also for the interests of others. Let this mind be in you which was also in Christ Jesus, who, being in the form of God, did not consider it robbery to be equal with God, but made Himself of no reputation, taking the form of a bond-servant, and coming in the likeness of men. (Phil. 2:3–7 NKJV)

This, for me, is one of the most difficult imperatives to implement in the whole Bible. That's because I am by nature both selfish and proud. It's not that I think I'm a good person—far from it. Most of the time, I'm appalled by my own sinfulness. My problem is that I am so quick to forget that every good thing I have (especially in the way of spiritual gifts) comes from God. I have to make a *conscious* effort to esteem others better than myself because of my tendency to think too highly of myself.

For through the grace given to me I say to everyone among you not to think more highly of himself than he ought to think; but to think so as to have sound judgment, as God has allotted to each a measure of faith. (Rom. 12:3)

My wicked heart wants to take credit for the gifts and abilities God has given me. That, you will remember, is the essence of pride: believing that *I* am responsible for the things God has given me. "What do you have that you did not receive? And if you did receive it, why do you boast as if you had not received it?" (1 Cor. 4:7). The essence of humility is the recognition that God (and those He has placed in my life) is responsible for my achievements.

Every good thing given and every perfect gift is from above, coming down from the Father of lights, with whom there is no variation or shifting shadow. (James 1:17)

"So how can I esteem others better than myself?"

I'll tell you in a moment. First, I just want to point out another passage of Scripture that deals with the same issue in almost the same way. A little farther down in Romans chapter 12, we come to verse 10: "Be devoted to one another in brotherly love; give preference to one another in honor . . ." Rather than saying that we should esteem others better than ourselves, it says that we must "give preference to one another in honor." That is, "outdo one another in showing honor."[3] We are not to prefer our own importance to the importance of others, but rather show honor (sincere appreciation and admiration) to others by putting them first.

OK. Here are some practical ways you can begin the process of esteeming others better than yourself.

SPECIFIC WAYS TO ESTEEM OTHERS BETTER THAN YOURSELF

1. Don't assume that others have *exactly* the same evil motives as you find in your own heart (love "believes all things," 1 Cor. 13:7), but rather put the best possible interpretation on their actions.

2. Look for those virtuous qualities in others that you know you are most in need of yourself. Then seek their help in acquiring those qualities.

3. Don't assume that your time, money, energy, thoughts, and opinions are more valuable than your neighbor's.

4. When making a decision, consider not only how that decision will affect your own interests, but also how it will affect the interests of others.

5. Be alert not only to your own needs, but also to the needs of others.

6. Demonstrate your high estimation of others by commending them for those qualities that are biblically worthy of praise.

7. Guard your heart from developing a pattern of critical, condemnatory, accusatory, judgmental thoughts about others.

3. NASB, footnote for Romans 12:10.

175

(Such thoughts make it very difficult, if not impossible, to esteem others better than yourself.)

8. Pray for your brothers and sisters in Christ.

9. Remind yourself often that God has given to you everything you have to be proud of and that He has often used others to get you where you are. Thank God and thank those whom He has used to bless you.

PUTTING ON THE MIND OF CHRIST

Another essential (yet often neglected) article of humility with which you ought to adorn yourself is biblical meditation. J. I. Packer defines meditation in this way:

> Meditation is the activity of calling to mind, and thinking over and dwelling on, and applying to oneself, the various things that one knows about the works and ways and purposes of God.[4]

Putting on humility involves putting on the mind of Christ. When the Bible says that "we have the mind of Christ" (1 Cor. 2:16), it doesn't mean that the moment we become Christians, our spiritual IQs skyrocket through the roof. The mind of Christ is contained in Scripture. To the extent that we know Scripture, our minds will be infused with the mind of Christ.

Meditation fastens into our hearts truths we have received but have not yet assimilated into our character.[5] Meditation is perhaps the most effective and powerful means that the Spirit of God uses to permanently amalgamate into our character truth that we may previously have received only intellectually or superficially. This undigested truth becomes a part of our makeup when we are willing to invest our time in ruminating on it.

4. J. I. Packer, *Knowing God* (Downers Grove, IL: InterVarsity Press, 1993) 18.
5. Sound Word Associates, (219) 548–0933, http://www.soundword.com/index.html, carries my cassette and compact disc recording (no. LP56) entitled *How to Meditate on Scripture*, which will provide much more detailed practical assistance than I can provide here.

My library contains a reprint of an old book that addresses the issue of biblical meditation. It is entitled *The Christian's Daily Walk in Holy Security and Peace.*

> Merely reading, hearing, and having transient thoughts of biblical truths do not leave *half* that impression of goodness upon the soul, which they would do, if they might be recalled, and fixed there by *serious* thought. Without this meditation, the good food of the soul passes through the understanding, and either is quite lost, or is like *raw* and *undigested food*, which does not nourish those creatures that chew the cud, until they have retrieved it back and chewed it better. Meditation is the Christian's way of chewing the cud. All the outward means of salvation do little good in comparison, except that by meditation they are thoroughly considered, and laid up in the heart . . . Meditation digests, engrafts, and turns the spiritual knowledge gained from God's Word . . . into the very life and substance of the soul, changing and transforming you according to it, so that God's will as revealed in the Bible and your will become one, so that you choose and delight in the same things as He does.[6]

In 1666, Oliver Heywood published a book entitled *Heart Treasure*, in which he had much to say about biblical meditation:

> Christian meditation is the contemplative and earnest fixing of the mind on the great spiritual realities which the Bible has revealed to us . . . Meditation is the soul's conference with itself; the discourse which it holds with truth obtained, and impressions received, in the secret sanctuary of its own consciousness. It is the . . . solemn endeavor of the soul to bring home to itself divine things; and so to resolve, ponder, and digest them, as to work their transforming power into every element and faculty of its being . . . It is the digestive process, by which spiritual food nourishes the soul and promotes its growth in holiness.

6. Henry Scudder, *The Christian's Daily Walk in Holy Security and Peace* (Harrisonburg, VA: Sprinkle Publications, 1984), 108.

Lack of meditation is the primary reason that so many profess-ing Christians, in spite of exposure to the most excellent teaching, still remain ignorant, unstable, and unfruitful; "ever learning, but never able to come to the knowledge of the truth." Instruction flows in upon them from all sides; but their hearts and minds are like sieves, out of which everything runs as fast as it is poured in. The impressions which truth makes on their minds are as temporary as characters traced on the sands of the seashore, which the next wave erases forever. But meditation *imprints truth deeply* on the conscience, and *engraves* it on the tablets of "the inner man," as with the point of a diamond . . . It thus becomes incorporated into the soul; and forms, as it were, a part of it; and it is ever present, to regulate the heart's affections and to control and guide all of its movements.[7]

I believe that two passages really hit the bull's-eye when it comes to exposing and correcting pride in our hearts. They will both help replace a focus on self with a focus on Christ. We will look at the first passage (2 Cor. 12:2–10) in chapter 12. The second contains what is commonly known as the *kenosis* (in Greek, "to make empty") passage because it speaks of the way in which Christ laid aside His privileges:

Do nothing from selfishness or empty conceit, but with humility of mind regard one another as more important than yourselves; do not merely look out for your own personal interests, but also for the in-terests of others. Have this attitude in yourselves which was also in Christ Jesus, who, although He existed in the form of God, did not regard equality with God a thing to be grasped, but emptied Him-self, taking the form of a bond-servant, and being made in the like-ness of men. Being found in appearance as a man, He humbled Himself by becoming obedient to the point of death, even death on a cross. For this reason also, God highly exalted Him, and bestowed on Him the name which is above every name, so that at the name of Jesus every knee will bow, of those who are in heaven and on earth

7. Oliver Heywood, *Heart Treasure* (1666; repr., Beaver Falls, PA: Soli Deo Gloria, 1997), 250ff.

and under the earth, and that every tongue will confess that Jesus
Christ is Lord, to the glory of God the Father. (Phil. 2:3–11)

Our beloved Richard Baxter asked some probing questions about
the humility of Christ that are worthy of our contemplation. No doubt
they were the fruit of his own meditation.

> Can you be proud while you believe that your Savior was clothed with
> flesh, and lived in modesty, and made himself of no reputation, and
> was despised and scorned and spat upon by sinners, and shamefully
> treated and nailed as a common criminal to a cross?
>
> Did Christ take upon himself the form of a servant so that you could
> domineer and have the highest place of honor?
>
> Did Christ not have a place to lay his head so that you could insist upon
> a home with luxurious furnishings?
>
> Must you brave it out in your most fantastic outfits instead of your
> Savior's seamless coat?
>
> Did he pray for his murderers so that you could demand vengeance
> for petty words and wrongs?
>
> Did he patiently endure being spit upon and pummeled so that you
> could, with impatient pride, abuse others?[8]

If you want to put off pride and put on humility, if you want to replace
the love of man's approval with the love for God's approval, one of the
best things you can do is to learn how to meditate on God's Word.[9]

8. Richard Baxter, *Baxter's Practical Works*, vol. 1, *A Christian Directory* (Ligonier, PA: Soli
Deo Gloria Publications, 1990), 209.
9. Even the daily *reading* of Scripture can help fight against the sin of pride. One of the
reasons God commanded each king of Israel to read his own handwritten copy of the Scriptures
"*all the days of his life*" was so "*that his heart may not be lifted up above his countrymen*"(Deut.
17:19–20).

MORE ACCESSORIES TO HUMILITY

As you think about how to clothe yourself with humility, don't forget the accessories: the neckties, hats, purses, jewelry, and gloves. You are not fully dressed without them. Here are a few to get you started.

1. **Give your reputation to God.** Several pages back, I quoted the New King James translation of Philippians 2:3–7. I did so because of the way this rendition translates a word that is so full, it has no exact English equivalent. It is a word that in context has perplexed theologians for centuries. The Greek word, *kinosis*, means "to make empty." The question is, "Of what exactly did Christ empty Himself?" The Authorized and the New King James translations focus on Christ's reputation, saying of Him that He "made Himself of no reputation." Of course, Christ gave up much more than his reputation when he took on human form, but He was willing to humble Himself, giving up the glory he had previously had with God the Father.

A proud person is one who has made an idol of his own reputation. Now, even a humble person may desire to do lawful things that will establish for himself "a good name" for the cause of Christ. But he gives his reputation to the Lord, knowing that he may choose, for a season, to blemish that reputation so that, in the long run, the cause of Christ may be advanced. The pain involved with having your reputation tarnished can be excruciating, but God will use such an experience for His glory and for your good if you wait for Him to rebuild it in His time.

"How can a tarnished reputation rebound for God's glory or my good?"

Perhaps God intends the humbling experience to be an avenue to more of God's grace—twice it says that He "gives grace to the humble" (James 4:6 and 1 Pet. 5:5). It may be that the character you develop as a result of having your reputation damaged will bring praise to God as people see more of Jesus Christ in you now than they ever could before. If your reputation is damaged as a result of false accusations, it may be that you will be vindicated when people see your character and find it difficult to believe that the things they heard about you are true. It may be that those who gave an untrue report about you will be found out.

Then, of course, there is the impact on your ministry. Several years ago, I went through a severe trial in which my reputation was brought into question by an individual who tried to discredit me. He called together some of my friends and got them to testify against me for "offenses" committed years before. It was one of the most humiliating experiences of my life. But the Lord used the brokenness of that experience to make me examine my heart, repent of sinful attitudes, and prepare me for future ministry. The impact that this entire humiliating experience had on my counseling, writing, and speaking ministry was enormous—not that I would ever wish to go through anything like that again. From tangible improvements (such as the ability to show more compassion and the *extra* care I now take to not formulate an opinion without hearing both sides of a story) to intangible things (such as seeing the power of God change people through his Word), I'm seeing greater fruit in the ministry now than I ever did before. And the reputation that God has been pleased to bestow on me today seems to be far greater and broader than the one I had previously—and it is certainly *much* greater than I deserve.

When your reputation has been damaged, it's easy to spend inordinate amounts of time trying to repair it. Some people are so worried about protecting their reputations that at the slightest hint that someone may have said something bad about them, they would go into spin control (e.g., calling people in an attempt to assess the damage, going to other extreme measures to correct misinformation, letting the word out that the rumor was not true, or speaking evil about those who had besmirched their good names). I love what the psalmist did when proud people tried to tarnish his reputation: "The arrogant have forged a lie against me; with all my heart I will observe Your precepts" (Ps. 119:69). I'll make more of this point later, but for now remember this: if you want to clothe yourself with humility, look to your responsibilities and leave your reputation to God.

2. Redirect praise back to God and to those individuals whom God has used to help you accomplish your achievements.

> Thus says the LORD: "Let not the wise man glory in his wisdom, let not the mighty man glory in his might, nor let the rich man glory in his riches . . . (Jer. 9:23 NKJV)

If the essence of humility is the realization that God (and others) is responsible for one's achievements, it follows that a humble person will not take credit for things he did not do. Instead, he will see to it that those who are responsible for the good deeds will be given their proper credit.

After walking across the stage to receive our diplomas from Calvary Bible College, my entire graduating class made a receiving line so that families and friends could come by to congratulate us. Included in the line of congratulators were, of course, our professors and teachers. I was just standing there in line, smiling and saying "thank you" to everyone, when all of a sudden it hit me. I realized that thanking my instructors for congratulating me wasn't enough. I needed to thank them for their part in graduating me—for the time and effort that had gone into teaching me what I needed to know to graduate from that fine school. I immediately began expressing sincere appreciation for the impact they had on my life.

3. Associate with the humble. Romans 12:16 says in part, "Do not be haughty in mind, but associate with the lowly. Do not be wise in your own estimation." On what basis do you choose your friends? A people-pleaser chooses a friend largely based on how such a friend might improve his reputation. Are you willing to develop friendships with those individuals who, on one hand, can model genuine humility and, on the other hand, can do very little to enhance your social standing? If not, you are out of step with this verse.

And don't forget that another way you can "associate with the lowly" is to look in the Bible for models of humility. In his sermon "What Must We Do to Prevent and Cure Spiritual Pride," the Reverend Richard Mayo gives these directions:

> Set before your eyes the examples of humble and lowly persons. (Some are greatly influenced by examples—more than they are by precepts.) Jacob considers himself "unworthy of all the lovingkindness and of all the faithfulness which" God had shown him (Gen. 32:10). David speaks of himself as "a worm and not a man" (Ps. 22:6). Agur (the son of Jakch) says that he is "more stupid than any man" (Prov. 30:2). The Apostle Paul says of himself, "I am the foremost of all [sinners]" (1 Tim. 1:15) and "the very least of all saints" (Eph. 3:8) . . . The Apostle Peter said to the Savior, "Go away from me, Lord, for I am a sinful man" (Gk: *a man who is a great sinner*, Luke 5:8). Thus, the heaviest ears of corn always hang downward, as do the boughs of trees that are most weighed down with fruit."[10]

Although we've come to the end of this section, we haven't quite finished putting on humility. One more item of clothing is necessary to complete your outfit. This piece is so important that it deserves a chapter all its own.

---

10. *Puritan Sermons 1659–1689*, vol. 3 (Wheaton, IL: Richard Owen Roberts, Publishers, 1981), 391–92.

Eleven

WHOSE SERVE IS IT?

Part of the humility with which Christ clothed Himself was taking upon Himself the form of a servant:

> Have this attitude in yourselves which was also in Christ Jesus, who, although He existed in the form of God, did not regard equality with God a thing to be grasped, but emptied Himself, *taking the form of a bond-servant*, and being made in the likeness of men. (Phil. 2:5–7)

Servanthood is perhaps the most important article of clothing in your entire wardrobe.

Let's begin our look into servanthood by examining an example of its antithesis. The apostle John had to deal with a very proud man—a maniacal, micromanaging monster named Diotrephes. John described this man as someone who "loves to be first" (3 John 9). Here is the context.

At the time the epistle of 3 John was written, apostolic authority was still in effect. John, by virtue of his apostleship, had the superior oversight of the local church of which Diotrephes was a member (perhaps even the pastor). It was John who was the ultimate human authority in the church, not Diotrephes! In stark contrast to this man who loved to exalt himself, John refers to himself not as the apostle but as the elder (see 3 John 1).

John had written a letter to the church (probably not 2 John) in which he said something that Diotrephes did not want the congregation to hear. The letter apparently contained some reference to certain traveling preacher companions of John to whom Diotrephes was not partial. Diotrephes refused to show hospitality to John's missionary preacher friends. The letter of 3 John was written to Gaius, probably a member of the same or another church in the area, encouraging him to house these itinerant preachers. It is against this backdrop that we find these most unusual instructions given to Gaius:

> I wrote something to the church; but Diotrephes, who loves to be first among them, does not accept what we say. For this reason, if I come, I will call attention to his deeds which he does, unjustly accusing us with wicked words; and not satisfied with this, he himself does not receive the brethren, either, and he forbids those who desire to do so and puts them out of the church. (3 John 9–10)

Diotrephes had an intense desire to have preeminence in his church. A literal rendition of the Greek for the phrase *who loves to be first* is "who loves the presidency (or the chief place)." We might say in today's English, "He loves to be the boss," or "He loves to be in charge." The tense of this word is continuous. His continuous longing for *preeminence* and *rule* was the *preeminent* and *ruling* motive of his heart. A verbal form of this word in an ancient Greek manuscript was used to convey the idea "to domineer." Diotrephes' pride manifested itself not so much in the sin of people-pleasing but in the form of being a bully. He was probably not primarily an approval junkie but a control addict. That is, he coveted being in control to such an extent that he was in bondage to (under the control of) the sin of "lording it over the saints." As Jesus explained to the disciples, this is exactly the opposite of being a servant:

> But Jesus called them to Himself and said, "You know that the rulers of the Gentiles *lord it over them*, and their great men exercise authority

over them. It is not this way among you, but whoever wishes to become great among you shall be your servant . . . (Matt. 20:25–26)

Now, how do you suppose John had so much insight into Diotrephes' desire for preeminence? Of course, as an apostle, he may have been given special knowledge, but his insight into Diotrephes' problem may have come from the knowledge of his own heart. It is possible that John could personally relate to this desire for preeminence that Diotrephes turned into an idol. The Scripture records an incident in which the apostle John, as a young man, seemed to struggle with this preeminence problem. Let's look at the context of the passage quoted above:

> Then the mother of the sons of Zebedee came to Jesus with her sons [James and *John*], bowing down and making a request of Him. And He said to her, "What do you wish?" She said to Him, "Command that in Your kingdom these two sons of mine may sit one on Your right and one on Your left." (Matt. 20:20–21)

The parallel account given in the gospel of Mark reveals that Mrs. Zebedee was in cahoots with, if not under the direction of, her two sons when she made this infamous request; for she is not even mentioned in the narrative:

> James and John, the two sons of Zebedee, came up to Jesus, saying, "Teacher, we want You to do for us whatever we ask of You." And He said to them, "What do you want Me to do for you?" They said to Him, "Grant that we may sit, one on Your right and one on Your left, in Your glory." (Mark 10:35–37)

Now, what exactly was it that John and his brother were asking for? Simply to have the *preeminent position of honor* in the kingdom of heaven over all the saints of God who had *ever* lived before, were currently living, and would live after them. How's that for ambition?

187

Like Diotrephes, who presumed authority he did not have, these two sons of Zebedee were presumptuous. They presumed that they could influence Jesus to hand over to them the two top positions in the kingdom.

By the way, the indignation of the other ten disciples also underscores the obvious desire for preeminence apparent in this request:

> And hearing this, the ten became *indignant* with the two brothers. (Matt. 20:24)

Notice also that Jesus circumvents Mrs. Zebedee and gives his response directly to her sons, who he knew had instigated the arrogant request:

> But Jesus answered, "You do not know what you are asking. Are *you* able to drink the cup that I am about to drink?" They said to Him, "We are able." He said to them, "My cup you shall drink; but to sit on My right and on My left, this is not Mine to give, but it is for those for whom it has been prepared by My Father." And hearing this, the ten became indignant with the two brothers. (Matt. 20:22–24)

"Do you *really* understand what you're asking for?" he says. "Do you realize that to obtain such a place of honor in my kingdom will require the enduring of much suffering? Are you really up to that?"

The *cup* to which Jesus referred is the *agony* associated with the *crucifixion* of which He had just finished forewarning them in verse 18. The apostle John and his brother James, at this stage in their lives, did not yet understand the truth of Proverbs 15:33 and 18:12: "Before honor comes humility." They proudly and arrogantly assured the Lord that they could handle the suffering.

The Lord responded, "My cup you shall drink; but to sit on My right and on My left, this is not Mine to give, but it is for those for whom it has been prepared by My Father." Jesus explained that even *He* did not have the authority to make that decision. "Look," He said, "even if you are willing to suffer for my name, the decision is not mine to make. Not only are you asking the *wrong person*, but you are going about it in the *wrong way!*" This is the context in which the Lord, after calling together the rest of the disciples, said to them *all*:

> "You know that the rulers of the Gentiles *lord it over them*, and their *great men exercise authority* over them. It is *not this way among you*, but who-'ever *wishes* to become great among you shall be your *servant*, and whoever wishes to be first among you shall be your *slave*..." (Matt. 20:25–27)

"It is not this way among you." Jesus is saying, "This is not the way it works in My kingdom."

From his point of view, the Gentiles and the disciples had it backwards. Their selfish motives had inverted and perverted the only real way of obtaining greatness.

"But whoever *wishes* to become great among you shall be your servant, and whoever *wishes to be first among you* shall be your slave."

Does the phrase "wishes to be first among you" sound vaguely familiar? It should. "But Diotrephes, who *loves to be first among them*, does not accept what we say" (3 John 9).[1]

It is one thing to have a will to be great or even to be *first* in the kingdom of heaven when you also have a willingness to become the servant and the slave of all. It is quite another thing to love the *first place* among all the citizens in the kingdom of heaven because you desire to lord it over them all. I believe John knew firsthand, though to a lesser degree, the inordinate desire by which Diotrephes was being drawn away and enticed.

Jesus called *all* the disciples to Himself. Why did He do that? He did it to teach them all a lesson. The *indignation* of the other ten disciples in Matthew 20:24 underscores the obvious desire for preeminence on the part of John and James. But this indignation on the part of the other ten *also* reveals their own struggle with the desire

1. The phrase *loves to be first* is *philoproteuon* (*philos*: "to love" + *protos*: "the first place"). The phrase *wishes to be first* is *thelo einai protos* (*thelo*: "to will" + to be + *protos*: "first").

for preeminence. It doesn't say that they were concerned by, or puzzled by, but that they were *indignant with* the two brothers!

Now we come to the heart of the matter. Let's take a close look at verse 25:

> But Jesus called them to Himself and said, "You know that the rulers of the Gentiles lord it over them, and their great men exercise authority over them."

During the time of Christ, practically every Gentile government had as its system of administration some form of dictatorship. The disciples, therefore, were very well acquainted not only with autocracy, but with the abuse of power that often went along with it. The term *lord it over* is one word in the Greek Bible. It literally translates "to rule down on." The word means "to bring under one's power, to hold in subjection, to exercise lordship or dominion over."

Whereas the term *rulers of the Gentiles* refers to those who had positions of governmental authority, the term *great men* refers to those who had obtained positions of honor and distinction in society for reasons other than governing authority. They may have achieved the status of *great* men because of their wealth, or lineage, or intellect, or education, or charismatic personality. But regardless of how they had gotten there, they were held in high esteem by society and used their *greatness* to influence and control others in a way that Christ said was unchristian.

This verb is used to convey the idea of exercising one's authority *against* someone (in the sense of being antagonistic or oppressive). These great men, just like Diotrephes, used their influential positions to exercise an oppressive, domineering, dictatorial, tyrannical, self-serving kind of authority. But this is not the way Christians are to exercise the authority that has been given to them by God.

> It is not this way among you, but whoever wishes to become great among you shall be your *servant*, and whoever wishes to be first among you shall be your *slave* . . . (Matt. 20:26–27)

Jesus said that the Gentiles and the disciples had it backwards. Their selfish motives had inverted and perverted the only real way of obtaining greatness.

John MacArthur explains:

> Jesus . . . was speaking of an entirely different kind of greatness than the sort James and John were seeking and that the world promotes. This kind of greatness is pleasing to God, because it is humble and self-giving rather than proud and self-serving. The way to the world's greatness is through pleasing and being served by men; the way to God's greatness is through pleasing Him and serving others in His name. In God's eyes, the one who is great is the one who is a willing servant.[2]

Jesus uses two words metaphorically to illustrate what it means to be great in God's kingdom: *servant* and *slave*. What is the difference?

A servant was one who was paid to execute the commands of another. The term described a person who held the lowest position of *hired* labor at that time—such as one who served tables or cleaned houses.

A servant, however, was much better off than a slave. Here are a few definitions of the word *slave* from the Greek lexicon:

1. One who gives himself up to another's will.

2. One who is devoted to another to the disregard of his own interests.

3. One who is in a permanent relation of servitude to another, his will being altogether consumed in the will of another.[3]

The place of an unpaid slave in the time of Christ was considered even more undignified and demeaning than that of a servant. A *servant* could at least come and go as he pleased. He had some control over the

---

2. John MacArthur, *Matthew* (Matt. 20:28) (Chicago: Moody Press, 1989), electronic edition.
3. Spiros Zodhiates, *the Complete Word Study Dictionary* (Chattanooga, AMG International, 1993).

direction of his own life. He could buy and sell and possess and own whatever he could afford. But a *slave* was bought and sold and possessed and owned by someone other than himself. He could not come and go as he pleased, but only as his master pleased. He had *virtually no control* over his own life in comparison to a servant.

The voluntary humiliation of oneself to the lowest position among the saints is what is at the heart of verses 26 and 27. If you want to be considered great by God, to please Him more than you please man, then you will, like your Lord, take upon yourself the form of a servant.

This emulation of the mind of Christ is the very point Jesus emphasizes as He concludes this lesson to His self-serving disciples:

> . . . just as the Son of Man did not come to be served, but to serve, and to give His life a ransom for many. (Matt. 20:28)

Jesus was saying, "Follow my example. I did not come seeking a position. I did not come so that others could meet My needs but so that I could meet theirs." If anyone had the right to *demand* the service of others, He did. But rather than insisting on His right to be served, He gave His life in service to others.

Christ came not only "to serve" but also "to give His life a ransom for many." And as we have already seen, unselfish giving is the essence of love. It has to do with your *motive*.

By the way, do you think the disciples learned this lesson quickly?

They didn't. They were still arguing about who would be greatest among them days before Christ was crucified! Let's take a quick peek into the scene at the Last Supper:

> And *there arose also a dispute among them as to which one of them was regarded to be greatest*. And He said to them, "The kings of the Gentiles lord it over them; and those who have authority over them are called 'Benefactors.' But it is not this way with you, but the one who is the greatest among you must become like the youngest, and the

leader like the servant. For who is greater, the one who reclines at the table or the one who serves? Is it not the one who reclines at the table? But I am among you as the one who serves." (Luke 22:24–27)

It is very likely that the event of Christ's washing the disciples' feet occurred soon after He spoke these familiar words to the disciples. Look at this carefully:

[Jesus] got up from supper, and laid aside His garments; and taking a towel, He girded Himself. Then He poured water into the basin, and began to wash the disciples' feet and to wipe them with the towel with which He was girded . . .

So when He had washed their feet, and taken His garments and reclined at the table again, He said to them, "Do you know what I have done to you? You call Me Teacher and Lord; and you are right, for so I am. If I then, the Lord and the Teacher, washed your feet, you also ought to wash one another's feet. For I gave you an example that you also should do as I did to you. Truly, truly, I say to you, a slave is not greater than his master, nor is one who is sent greater than the one who sent him. If you know these things, you are blessed if you do them." (John 13:4–5, 12–17)

Jesus again turns to the slave metaphor, this time modeling it for them by clothing Himself in a special garment (sound familiar?) and performing one of the most humiliating functions of a slave— washing dirty, smelly feet. Then He gave them new instructions to follow this example.

But Jesus Christ gave His life not merely as an example, but as a ransom. That is, He paid with His life the redemption price for the sins of the world. His death on the cross satisfied God's requirement of death and eternal damnation for sinners who would otherwise have to pay the price for the punishment of their own sin. He gave His life as a ransom for (in Greek, *anti*: "over against, in exchange for, or as a substitute for") many. The ransom Christ paid made it certain that those who would believe in Him would not perish but have everlasting life.

His death and subsequent resurrection also enabled you and me to be set free from our slavery to sin so that we could become slaves to righteousness.

> Do you not know that when you present yourselves to someone as slaves for obedience, you are slaves of the one whom you obey, either of sin resulting in death, or of obedience resulting in righteousness? But thanks be to God that though you were slaves of sin, you became obedient from the heart to that form of teaching to which you were committed . . . (Rom. 6:16–17)

So if you want to overcome the love of approval, you must make it your ambition to become a servant and slave to God, to righteousness, and in some ways to others.

"But Lou, don't you remember? Part of my problem with being a people-pleaser is that I try *too* hard to serve others! Won't I be feeding my inordinate desire to please people if I try so hard to serve them?"

You will if you continue to serve people for the wrong reasons. Let me say it again (a little louder this time): *It has to do with your motive.* A servant's heart is an attitude that seeks to serve others—not for selfish reasons such as a desire to impress people (so that they'll like you) or a fear that if they are not coddled they will reject you, but for their good and for God's glory. It's a spirit of wanting to do what is best for others in light of eternity. It is giving without expecting anything back from anyone. It is serving, knowing that your reward for such service will be given to you not by man, but by God—not necessarily in this life, but in the next one. So if you learn to serve others not for self-exaltation, but because you love God and neighbor, you just may find a whole new joy in serving that you have heretofore never known.

SUGGESTIONS FOR DEVELOPING A SERVANT'S HEART

Here are a few suggestions to help you on your way to putting on the garments of a servant. This is only a short list to get you started. See if you can come up with some more ideas on your own. Ask your family members and close friends for some additional service projects.

1. **Make a list of the closest people in your life.** The disciples, who were told by Christ to wash *each other's* feet, were a tight-knit bunch of guys. Your list should include those with whom you have regular dealings: spouse, children, parents, brothers, bosses, employees, teachers, friends, working associates, or anyone else whom you have regular opportunities to serve.[4]

2. **Learn how to talk in terms of what is of interest to them.** When we selflessly and sacrificially invest time and effort discussing topics of interest to others, we are demonstrating biblical servanthood. We are "with humility of mind regard[ing] one another as more important than [ourselves], . . . not *merely* look[ing] out for [our] own personal interests, but also for the interests of others" (Phil. 2:3–4).

During my college years, I had occasion to sit next to a meteorologist at a fund-raising banquet. I picked his brain for close to two hours. I asked him virtually every question I ever had about the weather and weather forecasting. When the banquet was over, he shook my hand and said, "I can't remember the last time I enjoyed talking to someone as interesting as you." The truth is, we spent a very small portion of our time talking about me, and the great majority of the time talking about the weather. Yet I (a mere college student) was perceived by him as interesting because I focused on what interested him.

---

4. This is not to imply that you should serve *only* those who are close to you. The point of this exercise is to start with those closest to you so that you may have regular opportunities to train yourself to have a servant's heart. Then, when being a servant has become second nature, you should find it easier to serve those on the periphery of your life.

3. Learn how to ask them questions with the attitude of a learner and a servant. The servant asks questions because he loves people and wants to meet their needs if he can. He wants to pray for them, to minister to them, to help them grow spiritually, and, if they are not Christians, to proclaim the gospel to them. He also asks questions to communicate his care for them.

As a counselor, I was trained to "establish involvement" with my counselees. That's a fancy term for "breaking the ice." Some counselors will spend ten to twenty minutes "chatting" or "small-talking" with their counselees at the beginning of the first session just to establish a caring relationship. Not me! I figure that the best way to establish my love for my counselee is to simply roll up my sleeves and begin helping him solve his problem. I may make a couple of polite introductory comments or ask a few "ice-breaking" questions, but as a rule, three to four minutes into that first session, I'm intently looking my counselee in the eyes, asking vital questions, and listening very intently to what he is saying—trying to diagnose his problem biblically and then to offer help and hope from God's Word. He has little doubt that I truly care about him—even though I've minimized the small talk. In time, he will hear me tell of my own struggles with sin and how, by God's grace, I've been able to implement biblical solutions. The attitude I try to communicate is this: "I'm not an expert—I'm just one beggar showing another beggar where to find the bread. Tomorrow you may be on this side of the desk helping me to solve one of my own problems."

It is not enough for you to simply learn to ask the right questions. If you want to be a servant, you must learn to ask those questions with humility, not in a condescending "I'm the expert" sort of way. A wise and humble person will sincerely ask questions in the other person's area of expertise because his heart longs to acquire knowledge, and as long as that knowledge is biblical (or at least isn't unbiblical), its source doesn't matter much.

4. Regularly pray for them and for your attitude toward them. Find out what is going on in their lives (put those newfound question-asking skills to good use) so that you can pray specifically. Place their names on your prayer list. If you don't know how to pray specifically, try praying a prayer patterned after that of the apostle Paul for the Colossians:

> For this reason also, since the day we heard of it, we have not ceased to pray for you and to ask *that you may be filled with the knowledge of His will in all spiritual wisdom and understanding, so that you will walk in a manner worthy of the Lord, to please Him in all respects, bearing fruit in every good work and increasing in the knowledge of God; strengthened with all power, according to His glorious might, for the attaining of all steadfastness and patience; joyously giving thanks to the Father,* who has qualified us to share in the inheritance of the saints in Light. (Col. 1:9 12)

Don't forget to ask God to give you the wisdom, grace, and humility to be the kind of servant you've just read about. Ask him for opportunities to serve the people in your life.

5. Make it your goal to help them achieve their God-honoring goals. There is often more you can do to encourage others in this way besides praying. Faith without works is dead! Someone has said that the essence of being a servant is to become excited about helping others to succeed. The greatest area in which we are to succeed is our walk with Christ. Paul seemed to have this as a motive for those he served.

> We proclaim Him, admonishing every man and teaching every man with all wisdom, so *that we may present every man complete in Christ.* For this purpose also I labor, striving according to His power, which mightily works within me. (Col. 1:28–29)

Here are a few questions to ask yourself as you "consider how to stimulate one another to love and good deeds" (Heb. 10:24):

▤ Who are the people in and around my life whom the Lord might want me to help succeed?

- What are their goals?
- How can I help them meet their goals?
- How can I help them grow as Christians?
- How can I use the gifts, abilities, and other resources God has given me to serve and edify them?

6. Look for opportunities to minister to them. Keep your eyes peeled. Be attentive to what is going on in the lives of those around you. Find out what their needs are. See if God has given you any resources to meet those needs. Now, in the past, you may have done these things selfishly so as to manipulate those whom you wanted to please into liking you. From now on, you will endeavor to study and meet their needs so that you might be a blessing to them and bring pleasure to God.

Sometimes on my way to work, I think of the staff at our counseling center (who spend much of their time trying to please their boss, namely me, and make his job easier) and how I might encourage or do something special for each of them. On my way home from work, I might do that same thing for my wife and children. Meditate on ways in which you can become more of a servant to every person you know. Then begin ministering to them.

7. Ask their forgiveness. If you have ruled over others in a domineering way, ask forgiveness for lording your authority over them and for not having a servant's heart toward them. Here is a list of some of the common ways that authorities "lord it over" their subordinates. How many of these acts of pride have you committed?

- Being unwilling to grant requests
- Granting those requests begrudgingly and with much complaint
- Refusing to allow them to appeal (or question) your decisions
- Being discontented with the performance of their duties

- Responding to them in a discourteous or condescending manner
- Having a critical, condemnatory, judgmental attitude toward them
- Having unrealistic expectations of them (exacting too many demands from them)
- Being intolerant of their (nonsinful) idiosyncratic behaviors
- Prohibiting them from doing anything without your express knowledge or consent
- Micromanaging every aspect of their responsibilities
- Being unjustly suspicious of them (rather than trusting them)

So what are you wearing today? When you woke up this morning, did you make a conscientious effort to put on the attire of a servant? Or did you reach for that uniform with all those shiny medals—the one that will cause everyone who sees it to recognize how honorable and distinguished you are? That is the uniform of a people-pleaser. If you want to be a God-pleaser, do what Christ did: put on the garments of a servant and learn to serve others with a pure heart.

Twelve

ADDITIONAL REMEDIES

The Bible prescribes additional antidotes to the poison of pride. These are a bit broader in scope than those we have already considered but will help you in your quest to become less of a people-pleaser and more of a God-pleaser.

1. **Make it your goal to have others formulate their opinion of you based on your Christian character.** On what are you striving to have others formulate their opinion of you? What do you want to be the basis of your value in their eyes? Is it the character of Christ in you, or is it something more temporal, such as:

- Your good looks or well-toned body
- Your wealth
- Your company or business
- Your athletic abilities
- Your family name
- Your position at work
- Your intellectual prowess
- Your spiritual gifts and abilities
- Your ministry

Except for the last item (ministry done for God with the right motives), all of these are temporal things. You cannot take them with you. The moment you step into eternity, they will be worthless to you. Godliness, as we have previously seen, has value not only in this life, but also in the next.

> Discipline yourself for the purpose of godliness; for bodily discipline is only of little profit, but godliness is profitable for all things, since it holds promise for the present life and also for the life to come. (1 Tim. 4:7b–8)

If you build your life around these temporal things and they are taken away from you, you will be devastated. If you build your reputation on these things and you lose them, you could quickly find yourself to be rather unpopular.

True Christian character is the one thing with which most rational people find it difficult to be displeased. As Hugh Blair points out:

> There is no form of behavior that will please all men at all times. As a rule, what seems to please most people most of the time, and commands lasting praise is Christian character. Sincere devotion to God, the ability to demonstrate genuine love to others, the faithful fulfillment of life's responsibilities, a pure and undefiled conscience, an unwavering commitment to justice, mercy and truth . . . these are the qualities that render man truly respectable and great. Such character may, at times, incur unjust reproach. But the clouds which form as a result of man's prejudice and envy will gradually disperse; and its [Christian character's] brightness will in the end, shine through as the noon day sun. Throughout history, the truly illustrious men and women were those who did not court the praise of this world, but who performed the actions which deserved it.[1]

The apostle Paul was careful not to build his reputation on anything but what others could see him to be or hear him to say.

> I know a man in Christ who fourteen years ago—whether in the body I do not know, or out of the body I do not know, God knows—such

1. *Sermons by Hugh Blair, D.D.* (London: T. Cadell; C & J Rivington, 1827), 192.

a man was caught up to the third heaven. And I know how such a man—whether in the body or apart from the body I do not know, God knows—was caught up into Paradise and heard inexpressible words, which a man is not permitted to speak. On behalf of such a man I will boast; but on my own behalf I will not boast, except in regard to my weaknesses. For if I do wish to boast I will not be foolish, for I will be speaking the truth; but I refrain from this, so *that no one may credit me with more than he sees in me or hears from me.* (2 Cor. 12:2–6)

This included boasting about temporal accomplishments (see also Phil. 3:4–11). He wanted people to evaluate him on the basis of who he was on the inside. If he boasted at all, it was about his weaknesses so that people would glorify God for His power that is, in human weakness, perfected (1 Cor. 12:7–10).

So for you, as someone who is desirous of no longer glorifying self and becoming more proficient in glorifying God, learning to build a God-honoring reputation based on internal character is essential.

2. **Do not go fishing for compliments.** Fishing for compliments is manipulating someone into a compliment. It's attempting to evoke an admiring comment from another without having to embarrass yourself by directly asking for it.[2] It can take a number of creative forms. Here are a few of the more common ones:

How to Go Fishing for Compliments

A.	By intentionally putting yourself down in the presence of others in the hopes that they will disagree with your assessment.	"That was one of the worst performances I've ever had." "That was awful! I can't believe I did so poorly!"

2. Manipulators typically try to get what they want by attempting to evoke an emotional response (guilt, sympathy, etc.).

B	By asking people to assess your performance in one area in the hopes that they will praise you in another area.	"Tell me, do you think I held the microphone too close to my mouth?" "Don't you just love the lyrics to that song?"
C.	By continually bringing up as a topic for discussion the activity or achievement for which you want to be praised in the hopes that sooner or later you will be commended for your accomplishment.	"What did you enjoy most about the service this morning?" "Didn't you just love the pastor's sermon this morning?" "I sure did, but it paled in comparison with your solo you sang for the offertory." "I think the ministry in music before the message really enhances the quality of the sermon. Don't you?"
D.	By praising others who have similarly achieved success in the arena in which you excel.	"Doesn't Sister so-and-so have such a wonderful voice? I wish I could sing as well as she!"

An accolade-angler must be adept at his trade in order to successfully carry out the manipulative trick without giving himself away. This, of course, takes practice. And like most everything else we practice over and over again, a habit soon develops that (as we have learned) enables us to do things more comfortably, quickly, and even unconsciously. Some people-pleasers, therefore, go fishing for compliments without being very aware that that is what they are doing. They just know what they want and know (somewhat unconsciously) how to get what they want.

Sometimes the flattery-fisherman ends up getting *caught* himself because the fish he's trying to catch doesn't take the bait—he knows an artificial lure when he sees it. Solomon said, "It is not good to eat much honey, nor is it glory to search out one's own glory" (Prov. 25:27). When you fish for compliments, you are trying to seek out your own magnificence. If it backfires, it will be anything but magnificent for you.

So stop casting for compliments. Put up a large, colorful sign in your mind that says "No fishing," or perhaps one like this:

FISHING LIMITS
Fishing for men: no limit
Fishing for men's approval: strictly
prohibited under penalty of law!

Chances are, you'll inadvertently catch more and bigger fish that way than you will by trying to snag them with deceit.

3. Avoid developing friendships with those who are prone to flattery. The story is told of a young supermarket clerk working in the produce department. As he is stacking some fruit, an old woman approaches him with an unusual request.

"Sonny, I'd like to buy half a head of cabbage."

"I'm sorry, Ma'am, but we only sell them whole."

"I know, dear, but I was wondering if you could make an exception for me. You see, my husband died many years ago. My children live out of town, so I have no one else to help me eat the cabbage."

"Well, I know that must be difficult, but I just don't think we can sell you half a head of cabbage. How about if I go into the back and pick out the freshest head of cabbage I can find for you. That way, it will last for days and you'll be able to eat the entire head by yourself."

"Thank you, young man, but I'd rather just have half a head. Would you mind asking the produce manager if he would be willing to sell me half a head?"

At this the young clerk is incensed. So, with a polite smile and a "let me check," he storms off to the rear of the produce department. As soon as he steps through the swinging doors at the back of the store, he spies the produce manager.

"There's an *old hag* out there who wants us to sell her *half a head of cabbage!*"

Then, to his surprise, he notices that the old woman has followed him into the back room and has heard his sniping comment.

So, with a smile on his face, he extends his hand in a loving gesture toward the woman as if continuing his thought.

"And this *dear woman* would like the other half."

The manager decides to make an exception, sells the woman half a cabbage, and comments to the clerk, "Great recovery, kid! That was amazing. I've never seen anyone think on his feet as quickly as you just did."

"Thank you, sir. I grew up in Reading, Pennsylvania, and learned how to get out of jams quickly."

"You're from Reading, Pennsylvania?"

"That's right. Reading, Pennsylvania, the home of ugly women and great hockey players."

All of a sudden, the produce manager's face turns solemn (and red).

"Young man, I'll have you know that *my wife* is from Reading, Pennsylvania."

"Really?" says the clerk. "What team did she play for?"

We sometimes think of flattery as a compliment, but in reality it is deceitful. Henry Hurst, the sixteenth-century Puritan pastor whose sermon "How We May Best Cure the Love of Being Flattered," which I referenced earlier, had some rather radical advice for dealing with flatterers:

If you would be cured, resolutely and deliberately reject the friendship of the man who [after being warned], turns due praise into flattery. Let such persons know that they please least when they praise most. Determine beforehand, that you will make their first offense an opportunity to inform them of their sin, then warn them, that subsequent offenses may result in the loss of your friendship. I see no reason why I may not apply to these flatterers that which David said in Psalm 101:7, "He who practices *deceit* shall not dwell within my house; He who speaks *falsehood* shall not maintain his position before me." David knew that the best way to prevent the love of flatteries and flatterers, was to keep them out of his presence.[3]

This advice may sound a bit severe to those of us who have grown up hearing much more about God's love and acceptance than about His justice and wrath. But fundamentally, Pastor Hurst had it right: there are certain types of people with whom the Bible says we should not associate—especially if they are professing Christians.

Hurst is also correct when he applies Psalm 101:7 to the flatterer. The Bible equates the two: "A lying tongue hates those it crushes, and a flattering mouth works ruin" (Prov. 26:28). David wouldn't keep close company with liars. Neither should we.

Then there is Proverbs 29:5: "A man who flatters his neighbor is spreading a *net* for his steps." How much wisdom is there in hanging out with a person you know is going to set a booby trap for you? Do you really want to be friends with a minor-league terrorist?

As a rule, "it is useless to spread the baited net in the sight of any bird" (Prov. 1:17), but not when you're dealing with an approval junkie. His pride blinds him to the flatterer's danger. He doesn't see the trap because he craves the bait that is in the trap. Once again, "he is drawn away by his own desires and enticed" (James 1:14 NKJV).

And while we're on the subject of snares, let's not forget the warning about the adulterous woman spoken of in Proverbs chapter 7 "who flatters with her words" (v. 5) and says:

3. Henry Hurst, *Puritan Sermons 1659–1689*, vol. 3, *How We May Best Cure the Love of Being Flattered* (Wheaton, IL: Richard Owen Roberts, 1981), 195.

"I have come out to meet you, to seek your presence earnestly, and I
have found you. I have spread my couch with coverings, with colored
linens of Egypt. I have sprinkled my bed with myrrh, aloes and cin-
namon. Come, let us drink our fill of love until morning; let us delight
ourselves with caresses. For my husband is not at home, he has gone
on a long journey; he has taken a bag of money with him, at the full
moon he will come home." With her many persuasions she *entices*
him; with her flattering lips she *seduces* him. Suddenly he follows her
as an ox goes to the slaughter, or as one in fetters to the discipline of
a fool, until an arrow pierces through his liver; as a bird hastens to the
snare, so he does not know that it will cost him his life. (Prov. 7:15–23)

Years ago, I was counseling a woman in her pastor's office. The
pastor was present to learn how to use the Bible more effectively in his
counseling. The counselee was obviously a very sensual woman who
was very much of a people-pleaser—a man-pleaser. At one point in the
session, she began to make comments that were somewhat flattering
and even erotic in nature. The pastor looked at me as if to say, "Now
what are you going to do?" What I did was to "answer a fool according
to [her] folly" (Prov. 26:4–5). I exposed her remarks, turning them
around on her by using them to convict her of how much of an approval
junkie she really was. Her entire attitude changed as she immediately
began to weep. We spent most of the rest of the counseling session addressing this approval issue in her heart (which really was at the heart
of what had brought her in for counseling). The point of telling this
story is that had I been susceptible to flattery, I probably would have
minimized this woman's sensual smooth-talking and missed a wonderful opportunity to minister the Word of God to her.

So how do you respond when people flatter you (when they say
things about you that exaggerate your virtues or minimize your flaws)?
Do you believe them, or do you question the accuracy of their perceptions and the sincerity of their motives? Remember, the Bible forbids
you to judge their motives, but it does not forbid you from asking them
to judge their own motives. In light of the many biblical warnings about

being alert to flattery, you may lawfully suggest that your flattering neighbor examine his motives when you perceive in him a tendency (habitual or recurring pattern) to stretch the truth in your favor. If he doesn't repent of his ways, the most loving thing you can do is to somehow tell him that his flattery has (at least temporarily) cost him your friendship.

4. Learn to be content with the condition and proportion that God has given to you. If the essence of people-pleasing pride is covetous lust for others to esteem us above and beyond the condition and proportion that God has appointed for us, then the essence of God-pleasing humility is *contentment* with the condition and proportion that God has appointed for us.

The apostle Paul learned an important element of being content: the ability to regulate his level of desire to the condition and proportion (the circumstance) into which God chose to place him from day to day:

> I am not saying this because I am in need, for I have learned to be content whatever the circumstances. I know what it is to be in need, and I know what it is to have plenty. I have learned the secret of being content in any and every situation, whether well fed or hungry, whether living in plenty or in want. (Phil. 4:11–12 NIV)

Paul may have been living in plenty on one day, only to find himself the next day in want of something he had enjoyed the day before.

Thomas Watson unpacks a very helpful concept of "regulating our fancy" that has application to being content with God's appointed condition and proportion for our lives:

> It is the fancy which raises the price of things above their real worth. What is the reason one tulip is worth five pounds, another perhaps not worth one shilling? Fancy raises the price. The difference is rather imaginary than real. So, why should it be better to have thousands

than hundreds, is because men fancy it so. If we could fancy a lower condition better, as having less care in it, and less accountability, it would be far more desirable. The water that springs out of the rock drinks as sweet as if it came out of a golden chalice. Things are as we fancy them. Ever since the fall, the fancy is distempered. God saw that the imagination of the thoughts of his heart were evil. Fancy looks through the wrong spectacles. Pray that God will sanctify your fancy. A lower condition would make us content if the mind and fancy were set correctly.[4]

Another important element of being content is to fully understand that God is the one who has given us (and has set the limits on) the "esteem value" of our lives (our condition and proportion). And as I've explained in another place: contentment involves putting the best possible interpretation on God's dealings with you.

First Corinthians 13:7 says that love "believes all things." That means that we are to believe the best about others. In other words, if there are ten possible interpretations or explanations for why someone took a particular course of action, nine of them being evil and only one of them being good, the loving person will, in the absence of contradictory evidence, choose to reject the bad and believe the good. Now, if we are commanded to view other sinners with this kind of optimism, how much more should we interpret God's dealings with us in the best possible light? How much more should we forsake the harsh interpretations of His providence in our lives and accept the good ones?

How do you see the limitations that God has placed on the degree that others esteem you? He could have given you more of whatever it takes to raise your value in the eyes of man. Do you think God has limited your "esteem level" to do you harm or to do you good? Think about that as you read this quotation from another one of my favorite Puritan authors, Jeremiah Burroughs:

4. Thomas Watson, *The Art of Divine Contentment* (Ligonier, PA: Soli Deo Gloria, 2001), 104–5.

If any good interpretation can be made of God's ways towards you, make it. You think it serious if you have a friend who always makes bad interpretations of your ways towards him. You would take that rather hard . . . It is very tedious to the Spirit of God when we make such bad interpretations of His ways towards us. When God deals with us otherwise than we would have Him do, if one sense [which is] worse than another can be put on it, we will be sure to do it. Thus, when an affliction befalls you, many good senses may be made of God's works towards you. You should think this way: "It may be God intends only to test me by this," or "It may be God saw that my heart was too set on something, and He intends to show me what is in my heart," or "Perhaps God saw that if my wealth continued I would fall into sin (that the better my position was, the worse my soul would be)" or "It may be God intended only to bless me with some special grace" or "It might be that God intends to prepare me for some great work which He has for me." This is how you should reason.

But we, on the contrary, make bad interpretations of God's dealings with us, and say, "God doesn't mean [to bless me like] this. Surely the Lord intends to display His wrath and displeasure against me by this trial. This is just the beginning of further evil He has determined against me!" Just as they said in the wilderness [you say to the Lord]: "You have brought us here to slay us." This is the worst interpretation you can possibly make on God's ways. Oh, why will you make these the worst interpretations, when there may be better? . . .

I urge you to consider that God does not deal with you as you deal with Him. If God were to put the worst interpretation on all your ways towards Him as you put on His towards you, it would be very bad for you.[5]

5. Don't overvalue friendships. The fear of losing friends is one of the most powerful driving forces in the heart of the people-pleaser. As I'm writing this section, I'm in the midst of reading a useful book

5. Jeremiah Burroughs, *The Rare Jewel of Christian Contentment* (Edinburg: Banner of Truth Trust, 1979), 223–24.

on the value of making and keeping good Christian friends. So I want to be very careful not to *overstate* my case. Friendships are vital to the Christian life and walk. Most of us need more of them. Most of us need deeper ones.

The point I like to make is that we must learn to be more loyal to God and to His truth than to people. I have known too many Christians who craved friendships and even fellowship to the point of idolatry. Some people allow their friends to drag them down into sin. Others, who are fearful of losing friends, will not confront them about their sin. Sometimes confronting a friend will turn him into an enemy. But consider the alternative, that "friendship with the world is enmity with God." (James 4:4 NKJV)

Another danger of overvaluing friendships has to do with doctrinal purity. Our churches are full of cowardly Christians who will not objectively study the Scriptures because they are afraid they might change their views and consequently face rejection from their family, friends, and church leaders. In my own life, I was afraid to reexamine previously held fallacious doctrinal positions because I was afraid that if I changed my view, I would lose friends. And when I did clarify my views, I did lose a few. But my conscience is now clear, and God is glorified because my doctrine is now purer than it once was. Moreover, God gave me new friends, and our fellowship is sweeter because it is based on mutual love of the truth.

6. Learn how to glory in your weaknesses and glorify God for your strengths. Rather than trying to camouflage his weaknesses, the apostle Paul boasted about them. Why? He tells us in 2 Corinthians 12:8–10:

> Concerning this [thorn in my flesh] I implored the Lord three times that it might leave me. And He has said to me, "My grace is sufficient for you, for power is perfected in weakness." Most gladly, therefore, I will rather boast about my weaknesses, so that the power of Christ may dwell in me. Therefore I am well content with

weaknesses, with insults, with distresses, with persecutions, with difficulties, for Christ's sake; for when I am weak, then I am strong.

Paul boasted about the very things by which most of us are embarrassed (weaknesses, insults, distresses, persecutions, and difficulties) because he wanted Christ's power to be manifested in his life. The tense of the original Greek is continuous: "My power is being perfected in your weakness." Remember, Paul's thorn in the flesh was given to him not because he was proud but to prevent him from becoming so in light of all the special revelations he had received from God. Rather than wanting to appear strong, he longed to appear weak so that God's strength would be seen at work in his life. He didn't want to promote himself but Christ, so he magnified his weakness in the eyes of others, that they might see the glory of God.

When was the last time you did that? It can really take the sting out of embarrassing conditions in your life. Perhaps you've never thought through the specific benefits to God's kingdom and glory that could result from your weaknesses. The work sheet on the following page is provided to help you do just that. In the left-hand column, list the present weaknesses in your life—the things that cause you the greatest embarrassment. Next to each one, in the right-hand column, try to identify at least three ways in which Christ's power and glory may potentially be manifested through that weakness. Here are a few suggestions about the potential power of Christ to get you started with column 2:

1. Others will receive hope and encouragement as they realize the extent to which God has strengthened me in my weakened state.

2. God's power will be manifested in my life as He prepares me to minister in the future to others who have the same weakness.

3. God will use this weakness to strengthen my dependence on and my walk with Him.

4. God will be glorified as the Holy Spirit's power conforms me to the image of Christ through this weakness.

213

My Weaknesses	Christ's Power
The things in my life about which I am easily embarrassed	The specific ways in which God could receive glory through my weaknesses
▤	▤
▤	▤
▤	▤
▤	▤
▤	▤
▤	▤
▤	▤
▤	▤
▤	▤

The other side of this coin is to learn how to glorify God for your strengths. Perhaps the place to begin is to see your strengths as potential dangers. "Let him who thinks he stands take heed that he does not fall" (1 Cor. 10:12). While the realization of a God-given strength is not necessarily pride, the propensity to use it in dependence on the flesh or for fleshly purposes or with fleshly motives necessarily is.

Thankfulness is the key to keeping your strengths in proper biblical perspective. Thanking God regularly for the gifts and abilities He has given you will help you remember where they came from and safeguard your heart from proudly misusing them. And when you consider that He has placed all these treasures (and more) in such a weak and wretched vessel as yourself, it should further humble you and motivate you to glorify Him. "But we have this treasure in earthen vessels, so that the surpassing greatness of the power will be of God and not from ourselves . . ." (2 Cor. 4:7)

7. Learn to bring every people-pleasing thought captive to the obe-dience of Christ. The Proverbs say, "Watch over your heart with all dili-gence, for from it *flow* the springs of life" (Prov. 4:23). Everything we do flows from the heart. Our ability to correct the sinful thoughts and motives of our hearts is largely contingent upon our ability to recognize them in the first place.

Another tool can help you with this process. The Heart Journal is a work sheet on which you can record and evaluate the thoughts and motives behind each of your questionable people-pleasing behaviors. It is also designed to help you replace unbiblical thought patterns with biblical ones. In Appendix B, you will find detailed instructions on how to use this powerful tool to get to the heart of the people-pleasing prob-lem you want to conquer. This is a very helpful resource. Please don't overlook it.

8. Look to your responsibilities and leave your reputation to God. One of the best antidotes to the love of approval is to change the focus of your thoughts from your reputation to your responsibilities. Look again at 1 Thessalonians 2:4–9, noticing that the focus of Paul and his companions was not on their reputation but rather on their ministry:

> But just as we have been approved by God to be entrusted with the gospel, so *we speak, not as pleasing men, but God who examines our hearts.* For we never came with flattering speech, as you know, nor with a pretext for greed—God is witness—*nor did we seek glory from men,* either from you or from others, even though as apostles of Christ we might have asserted our authority. But we proved to be gentle among you, as a nursing mother tenderly cares for her own children. Having so fond an affection for you, *we were well-pleased to impart to you not only the gospel of God but also our own lives,* because you had be-come very dear to us.
>
> For you recall, brethren, our *labor* and hardship, how *working night and day so as not to be a burden to any of you, we proclaimed to you the gospel of God.*

We can see a very similar principle operating again in Paul's life in 2 Corinthians 4:1, where his focus on ministry kept him from discouragement: "Therefore, since we have this *ministry*, as we received mercy, *we do not lose heart . . .*" Rather than losing heart as a result of being "afflicted in every way," and "perplexed," and "persecuted," and "struck down" (vv. 8–9), he fulfilled the responsibilities God had given him to preach the gospel.

How about you? How many of your biblical responsibilities are you neglecting as a result of being preoccupied with man's approval? By shifting your attention from pleasing men to obeying God, you just might find yourself worrying less about your status among them and rejoicing more in the pleasure you are bringing to Him. Perhaps you would do well to make a list of those responsibilities you've been currently neglecting. You know—the ones you've been feeling guilty about lately. Then, when you find yourself focusing too much on your reputation, you can pull out your list and get busy pleasing God by faithfully fulfilling those items you've been heretofore neglecting.

If you are working harder at establishing and maintaining your reputation than at maintaining Christ's honor by being a faithful servant of His, you are working against yourself. More importantly, you're working against God. He is the only one who can give you that good name you're striving so hard to obtain. He can see to it that a good report about you travels far and wide. But He can and probably will frustrate your selfish attempts to promote yourself rather than His glory. "God is opposed to the proud, but gives grace to the humble" (James 4:6). Which option He chooses depends largely on your attitude. Are you seeking first His eternal kingdom and righteousness, or are you pursuing, like the pagans, temporal things that can be taken away and destroyed? The final chapter of this book will help you better answer this question.

Thirteen

WHERE'S YOUR TREASURE?

As I begin to write this chapter, I am sitting in a beautiful condominium on a golf course in Gulf Shores, Alabama,[1] overlooking the first fairway. It is a gorgeous day. The sky is clear. The sun is shining. The weather is perfect. Golfers are out in abundance. My wife and daughters are swimming at the outdoor pool of this resort. The small lake that separates the lawn of my condo from the first tee is surprisingly calm.

But all is not well in the Gulf of Mexico. It is Friday, August 13, 2004. Two Southern governors have declared states of emergency. Hurricane Charley is about to hit the coast of Florida. Two million people have been asked to evacuate.[2] Many of them woke up this morning and were told that Charley was going to hit in the Tampa Bay area. They were asked by Governor Jeb Bush to evacuate their homes. Many of them have fled to Orlando. The problem is, Charley (which was just upgraded to a category 4 hurricane) has changed course in the last few hours and is now headed toward the home of Walt Disney World (which, by the way, is now closed). The upper-level wind speeds of the hurricane were

1. *Alabama* means "Here we may rest!"
2. Imagine two million people preparing to leave home. They are making plans today to be somewhere tomorrow—somewhere safe, somewhere away from the rain, away from the wind, away from the floods, and away from the tornadoes that will be spawned in Charley's wake. Over two dozen people are going to die from Charley. They will pass from this life to the next. How many of these two million people do you suppose have prepared for life in their next town: eternity?

clocked last hour at about 145 mph. News anchor Shepard Smith just described Santa Bell Island, where the inner wall of Charley's eye just hit, as "a paradise."

The storm has just made landfall, and Neil Cavuto (author of a book entitled *More Than Money*) is already talking about the impact it could have on our nation's economy. Millions of people are running for their lives as a result of Charley, four people have already died in Cuba and the Caribbean, dozens more will lose their lives in the next few days, thousands will become homeless, and FOX News[3] is reporting on money! We live in the midst of an earthly-minded culture.

In this concluding chapter, I want to talk to you about the importance of being heavenly-minded. Specifically, I'd like you to think about the rewards that await you in eternity.

"But why? Why talk about heaven in a book about being a people-pleaser?"

Because being a people-pleaser is one of the strongest indicators that an individual has a temporal value system—that he is storing up treasure on earth rather than in heaven. As we've seen, when you do things "to be seen by men" (for the purpose of impressing people), you lose your eternal rewards: "Beware of practicing your righteousness before men to be noticed by them; otherwise you have *no reward* with your Father who is in heaven" (Matt. 6:1). The topic of heaven is also necessary to cover in this book because the ability to overcome[4] your people-pleasing penchant will depend on your cultivating an eternal value system.

If you want to dethrone the idol of approval, you must learn to value eternal heavenly rewards more than temporal earthly ones. I am amazed at the number of passages in Scripture that instruct us (directly and indirectly) to spend time thinking about heaven. It's really quite staggering. I'm sure it would take an entire chapter just to *cite* them all. In fact,

3. For the record (and in the interest of being "fair and balanced"), I *am* a Fox News fan.
4. Not so incidentally, did you know that "overcomers" will be getting a special reward in heaven? It's true. Check out Revelation 2:17.

it is going to be hard for me to give even a cursory treatment of this subject without seeming to go outside the boundaries of this book's thesis.

"OK, I suppose it *would* be rather interesting to learn more about what it's going to be like up there."

I'm *sure* it would be. To ponder the particular delights of heaven described in the Bible would make a powerful impression on our lives. But the passages I have in mind don't necessarily describe what heaven is like—although some of them do. Rather, they teach us that in our everyday decisions we are to keep eternity in view. Why? We are to fix our minds on heaven because we will be rewarded up there for what we do (or don't do) down here. Following are a few examples of those anticipatory passages to which I'm referring. Be prepared—I am about to unleash the "tiger" on you again, but this time in a most ferocious fashion.

> Do not store up for yourselves treasures on earth, where moth and rust destroy, and where thieves break in and steal. But store up for yourselves treasures in heaven, where neither moth nor rust destroys, and where thieves do not break in or steal; for where your treasure is, there your heart will be also. (Matt. 6:19–21)

> Do not work for the food which perishes, but for the food which endures to eternal life, which the Son of Man will give to you, for on Him the Father, God, has set His seal. (John 6:27)

> For our citizenship is in heaven, from which also we eagerly wait for a Savior, the Lord Jesus Christ; who will transform the body of our humble state into conformity with the body of His glory, by the exertion of the power that He has even to subject all things to Himself. (Phil. 3:20–21)

> Therefore, if you have been raised up with Christ, keep seeking the things above, where Christ is, seated at the right hand of God. Set your mind on the things above, not on the things that are on earth. For you have died

and your life is hidden with Christ in God. When Christ, who is our life, is revealed, then you also will be revealed with Him in glory. (Col. 3:1–4)

But have nothing to do with worldly fables fit only for old women. On the other hand, discipline yourself for the purpose of godliness; for bodily discipline is only of little profit, but godliness is profitable for all things, since it holds promise for the present life and *also* for the *life* to come. It is a trustworthy statement deserving full acceptance. For it is for this we labor and strive, because we have fixed our hope on the living God, who is the Savior of all men, especially of believers. (1 Tim. 4:7–10)

Therefore, prepare your minds for action, keep sober in spirit, fix your hope completely on the grace to be brought to you at the revelation of Jesus Christ. (1 Pet. 1:13)

Now, little children, abide in Him, so that when He appears, we may have confidence and not shrink away from Him in shame at His coming. (1 John 2:28)

Beloved, now we are children of God, and it has not appeared as yet what we will be. We know that when He appears, we will be like Him, because we will see Him just as He is. And everyone who has this hope fixed on Him purifies himself, just as He is pure. (1 John 3:2–3)

In light of these passages (and the others that will follow), do you think you now spend as much time as you ought thinking about heaven? Randy Alcorn, in his book *In Light of Eternity*, believes that the lack of heavenly contemplation is a serious problem:

The greatest weakness of the western church today is arguably our failure to think about the long tomorrow—to take seriously the reality that heaven is our home. Out of this springs our love affair with this world and our failure to live now in light of eternity.

When my family goes on a trip, we like to know in advance, something about where we're going. If we're planning a vacation, we study the brochures to know the destination's attractions.[5]

Puritan preacher Edward Griffin comments on the value of heavenly meditation:

> There is no need that the inhabitants of earth should remain so little acquainted with heaven. There is a ladder, such as Jacob saw, by which they may ascend and descend every hour. We ought daily in our thoughts to visit that delightful land and to make excursions through its glorious regions. The more we accustom ourselves to these flights the easier they will become. Why is it that we feel so little the impression of eternal glory, but because our thoughts are no more conversant with heaven? It is of the utmost importance that we should become more familiar with that blessed country. It would tend to wean us from this poor world, to support us under the trials of life and the delay of our hopes, to illumine us with the light of that land of vision, to transform us into the likeness of its blessed inhabitants, and to reconcile us to the self-denials and labors which we have here to endure for Christ.[6]

To what degree does eternity influence the way *you* live? Does it affect your thoughts, words, attitudes, and actions? More specifically, to what extent do thoughts of your eternal destiny motivate you to please God more than man?

Let's unpack a couple of the passages we looked at above.

"Wait a minute! Something troubles me about this notion of doing things for a heavenly reward. It just seems selfish or something."

It may *seem* selfish, but the truth is, rewards are biblical. Not only does God want us to anticipate rewards—He takes pleasure in our seeking them. "He who comes to God must believe that He is and that He is

---

5. Randy Alcorn, *In Light of Eternity* (Colorado Springs: WaterBrook Press, 1999), 6.
6. To read the entire sermon on heaven by Edward Griffin, go to the Fire and Ice Web site: http://www.puritansermons.com.

a rewarder of those who seek Him" (Heb. 11:6). Many passages in the Bible give us commands with promises and rewards attached to them. Some of the rewards are temporal (dealing with the blessings that our obedience will bring on earth); many are eternal (referring to the rewards that obedience in this life will render in heaven). Randy Alcorn explains:

> We're used to the idea that Satan tempts us by offering us power, possessions, and pleasures. But we forget it's God who made our desires for these things, not as part of our sin nature, but as part of our human nature. That's why Satan tempted the sinless Christ with pleasure, power, and possessions (Matthew 4:1–11), just as he tempted Adam and Eve before they were sinners . . .
>
> It's not wrong for us to be motivated by the prospect of reward. Indeed, something is wrong if we're *not* motivated by reward. To resist wanting rewards is pseudospiritual. It goes against the grain of the way God created us and the way he tries to motivate us.[7]

I think we're now ready to proceed with our two anticipatory passages. In 1 Peter 1:13, we are told in very emphatic terms how to think about this life in light of the next one:

> Therefore, prepare your minds for action, keep sober in spirit, fix your hope completely on the grace to be brought to you at the revelation of Jesus Christ.

This verse serves as a hinge connecting the first part of 1 Peter (which deals with the assurance of future glory through new birth in Christ) with the rest of the book (the expectation of righteous behavior in spite of unfair circumstances).[8] Peter admonishes his readers, who were suffering for their faith, to gird up the loins of their minds (to be mentally prepared),[9] to be sober (to view and interpret life in such a way as to be self-controlled

---

7. Alcorn, *In Light of Eternity*, 133–34.

8. James R. Slaughter, *The Importance of Literary Argument for Understanding 1 Peter*, vol. 152, *Bibliotheca Sacra* (Dallas: Dallas Theological Seminary, 2002), 84.

9. The idea here is to tuck in your garment so as not to be encumbered when you walk or race. We might say, "Roll up the sleeves of your mind and get ready to think."

and dispassionate—that is, undistorted by their emotions). Then he admonishes them with a Greek aorist imperative (once and for all) to *fix* their hope *completely* on the coming of Christ and the rewards that they will receive upon His arrival. He says to them, "Set your hope perfectly, wholly, unchangeably, and without doubt or despondency upon your future glorification."[10] This is how they were to endure suffering. This is how you, as a repentant people-pleaser, can endure threats to your reputation, rejection from others, and uncomfortable but unavoidable conflicts. The second coming of Christ was to be the motivation to live a righteous life for those resident "aliens" and visiting "strangers" to whom Peter was writing (1 Pet. 2:11). So, too, for you, the second coming of Christ can be a powerful motivation to fear God more than people, to love the approval of God more than the approval of men, and to live a life in light of eternal rewards rather than temporal ones.

"But I want to know what kind of rewards there will be in heaven."

Of course, entire books have been written in attempts to begin to describe what heaven will be like, and as I've said, this little volume is not capable of recounting them. But let me mention a few things. First is to live in the presence of Christ (the magnificence of which none of us can fully comprehend). Also, in heaven there will be no sin (our glorification involves our total sanctification), no sickness, no suffering, and no Satan. Then there will be our brand-new celestial bodies that are fashioned after Christ's resurrected body. And then there are those things called crowns. Randy Alcorn succinctly describes the various crowns that are available in heaven:

> Crowns are a common symbol of rulership. Five crowns are specifically mentioned as heavenly rewards.
>
> 1. *The Crown of Life*—for faithfulness to Christ in persecution or martyrdom (James 1:12; Revelation 2:10).
>
> 2. *The Incorruptible Crown*—for determination, discipline, and victory in the Christian life (1 Corinthians 9:24–25).

10. Kenneth Samuel Wuest, *Wuest's Word Studies from the Greek New Testament: For the English Reader* (1 Peter 1:13) (Grand Rapids: Eerdmans, 1997), electronic edition.

3. *The Crown of Glory*—for faithfulness representing Christ in a position of spiritual leadership (1 Peter 5:1–4).

4. *The Crown of Righteousness*—for purifying and readying ourselves to meet Christ at His return (2 Timothy 4:6–8).

5. *The Crown of Rejoicing*—for pouring ourselves into others in evangelism and discipleship (1 Thessalonians 2:19; Philippians 4:1).[11]

The second anticipatory passage that I think deserves a closer look is Colossians 3:1–4:

> Therefore if you have been raised up with Christ, keep seeking the things above, where Christ is, seated at the right hand of God. Set your mind on the things above, not on the things that are on earth. For you have died and your life is hidden with Christ in God. When Christ, who is our life, is revealed, then you also will be revealed with Him in glory.

The phrase *keep seeking*,[12] in verse 1, is a single Greek verb that means "to strive for earnestly." The present tense indicates a continuous action. As Christians who have been coresurrected with Christ, we are to habitually preoccupy ourselves with heavenly realities—to "seek first His kingdom and His righteousness" (Matt. 6:33). As a people-pleaser, you have (to a certain extent) perpetually occupied yourself with earthly realities. In some corner of your heart, you were seeking first your own kingdom and your own form of righteousness—a self-righteousness (or a "rightness," perhaps) that would impress men. But now that you have come to know Christ and have repented of being a people-pleaser, your interests are to be focused on Christ; your thoughts, your aims, your ambitions, in fact your entire outlook, are to be centered on that heavenly realm where Christ rules and where your

11. Alcorn, *In Light of Eternity*, 124.
12. "The things above be constantly seeking," as Wuest translates it. "The word 'things' is in the emphatic position, contrasting the above things with . . . earthly things." *Wuest's Word Studies from the Greek New Testament* (Col. 3:1), electronic edition.

life truly belongs.[13] Living to please Christ, therefore, will be far more important to you than striving to please people.

To *set your mind* (*on the things above*, v. 2) is to "direct your mind" toward (in the direction of) heaven—like the needle of a compass that always directs itself to the north. So, as J. B. Lightfoot explains, "You must not only *seek* heaven, you must also *think* heaven."[14] To *set your mind on the things above* is to "look not at the things which are seen, but at the things which are not seen" (2 Cor. 4:18). And of course, you should think biblically (not mystically) about heaven, allowing the Scriptures to guide you on your way through the streets of gold.

The King James Version of the Bible puts it this way: "Set your affection on things above, not on things on the earth." To set your affection on something is to love it, to be attentive to it, to desire it, to long for it, and to delight in it. Up to this point, you have been setting too much of your affection on earthly things—things that have to do with the status and honor you receive from your peers. Now, by God's grace, you will train yourself to spend more time thinking about, longing for, and delighting in Christ's status (as the risen Lord of lords and King of kings, seated in heaven at the right hand of God where He rules and reigns) and the honor due Him.

And "when Christ, who is our life, is revealed, then you also will be revealed with Him in glory" (Col. 3:4). This means that when Christ appears at His second coming, you will also appear with Him in your new glorified condition. To the degree that you are setting your affections on things above, you will not be inordinately concerned with the way you appear down here.

When is the best time to think about heaven? The contexts surrounding many of the anticipatory passages give us insight into the circumstances in which we may most profitably think about heaven. As you read through the list, ask yourself, "How often does heaven come

---

13. *New Bible Commentary: 21st Century Edition*, 4th ed., ed. Gordon J. Wenham, J. A. Motyer, D. A. Carson, and R. T. France (Col. 3:5) (Downers Grove, IL: InterVarsity Press, 1994), electronic edition.

14. J. B. Lightfoot, *St. Paul's Epistles to the Colossians and to Philemon* (1879; repr., Grand Rapids: Zondervan, 1959), 209.

to my mind when I am facing each of these situations?" Time and space will not permit me to fully develop each of these points, but my prayer is that this section will motivate you to further study as you examine the contexts of these passages on your own. The *italicized* phrases highlight each passage's eternal elements.

1. **We are to think of heaven when facing trials.** Trials prepare us for glory. Our faith is like gold (though much more precious to God). Its ore has impurities that must be burned off to produce something glorious. We do not know now exactly what God will make of us (what kind of ornament He will fashion us into), but in heaven, that glory will be revealed. Keeping this heavenly image in mind when facing trials will not only make them easier to endure, but also enable us to greatly rejoice with inexpressible joy.

> Blessed be the God and Father of our Lord Jesus Christ, who according to His great mercy has caused us to be born again to a living hope through the resurrection of Jesus Christ from the dead, *to obtain an inheritance which is imperishable and undefiled and will not fade away, reserved in heaven for you,* who are protected by the power of God through faith for a salvation ready to be revealed in the last time. In this you greatly rejoice, even though now for a little while, if necessary, you have been distressed *by various trials,* so that the proof of your faith, being more precious than gold which is perishable, even though tested by fire, *may be found to result in praise and glory and honor at the revelation of Jesus Christ;* and though you have not seen Him, you love Him, and though you do not see Him now, but believe in Him, you greatly rejoice with joy inexpressible and full of glory, obtaining as the outcome of your faith the salvation of your souls. (1 Pet. 1:3–9)

> Beloved, do not be surprised at the *fiery ordeal* among you, *which comes upon you for your testing,* as though some strange thing were happening to you; but to the degree that you share the sufferings of Christ, keep on rejoicing, *so that also at the revelation of His glory you may rejoice with exultation.* (1 Pet. 4:12–13)

2. We are to think of heaven when facing suffering and affliction. When Paul faced suffering, he looked to the future. He was totally convinced, in spite of his apostolic affliction, that God was powerful enough to enable him to faithfully fulfill his ministry until that day when he would be called upon to give an account for the stewardship of the gospel that had been entrusted to him.

> For this reason I also suffer these things, but I am not ashamed; for I know whom I have believed and I am convinced that He is able to guard what I have entrusted to Him *until that day*. (2 Tim. 1:12)

3. We are to think of heaven when facing persecution. The persecution we typically face today in western society is mild in comparison to that faced by our brethren in other places in the world. Perhaps this is why so few of us meditate on heaven as we should.

> Blessed are you when men hate you, and ostracize you, and insult you, and scorn your name as evil, for the sake of the Son of Man. Be glad in that day and leap for joy, for behold, *your reward is great in heaven*. For in the same way their fathers used to treat the prophets. (Luke 6:22–23; cf. 2 Thess. 1:4–11)

> The Lord will rescue me from every evil deed, *and will bring me safely to His heavenly kingdom*; to Him be the glory forever and ever. Amen. (2 Tim. 4:18)

4. We are to think of heaven when facing death. In 2 Timothy 4:6, Paul referred to his impending death as a "departure." When he thought about dying (having his earthly home torn down), he looked forward to his new and glorious resurrected body. It's not that Paul had a death wish. Indeed, he wanted to be alive at Christ's second coming (as the King James Version renders 2 Corinthians 5:2, "earnestly desiring to be clothed upon with our house which is from heaven") so that he would not have to see death. But if not, he would welcome death, knowing that it would be "very much better" (Phil. 1:23) than staying on in his earthly abode.

> For we know that if the earthly tent which is our house is torn down, we have a building from God, a house not made with hands, eternal in the heavens. For indeed in this house we groan, longing to be clothed with our dwelling from heaven, inasmuch as we, having put it on, will not be found naked. For indeed while we are in this tent, we groan, being burdened, because we do not want to be unclothed but to be clothed, so that what is mortal will be swallowed up by life. Now He who prepared us for this very purpose is God, who gave to us the Spirit as a pledge.
>
> Therefore, being always of good courage, and knowing that while we are at home in the body we are absent from the Lord—for we walk by faith, not by sight—we are of good courage, I say, and prefer rather to be absent from the body and to be at home with the Lord. Therefore we also have as our ambition, whether at home or absent, to be pleasing to Him. For we must all appear before the judgment seat of Christ, so that each one may be recompensed for his deeds in the body, according to what he has done, whether good or bad. (2 Cor. 5:1–10)

5. We are to think of heaven when facing the death of a loved one. It is a comfort to those whose relatives and friends have died in Christ to know that they will be seen again. But as Solomon reminds us, there is value in mourning the death even of those who are lost:

> It is better to go to a house of mourning than to go to a house of feasting, because that is the end of every man, and the living takes it to heart. (Eccl. 7:2)

> For if we believe that Jesus died and rose again, even so God will bring with Him those who have fallen asleep in Jesus. For this we say to you by the word of the Lord, that we who are alive and remain until the coming of the Lord, will not precede those who have fallen asleep. For the Lord Himself will descend from heaven with a shout, with the

voice of the archangel and with the trumpet of God, and the dead in Christ will rise first. Then we who are alive and remain will be caught up together with them in the clouds to meet the Lord in the air, and so we shall always be with the Lord. *Therefore comfort one another with these words.* (1 Thess. 4:14–18)

6. We are to think of heaven when facing temptation. Temptations to love pleasure more than God are powerful in our day. Fleshly gratifications are all around us. Moses, looking toward the future, was able to let go both of his affluence and of his reputation because he had an eternal value system:

> By faith Moses, when he had grown up, refused to be called [NIV: refused to be known as] the son of Pharaoh's daughter, choosing rather to endure ill-treatment with the people of God than to enjoy the passing pleasures of sin, considering the reproach of Christ greater riches than the treasures of Egypt; *for he was looking to the reward.* (Heb. 11:24–26)

7. We are to think of heaven when facing disappointments about life on earth. If there is one point to the book of Ecclesiastes, it is this: Life on earth (under the sun) is at best vanity (pain, toil, sweat, little or no justice, etc.). Solomon explains that the rewards in this life are few (a good meal, a glass of wine, a good marriage, the satisfaction that comes from our labor). The real reward for the believer is not in this life but in the next. So when you are discouraged with the things of this life, enjoy the temporal rewards down here, but remember that the best rewards are up there.

> Therefore we do not lose heart, but though our outer man is decaying, yet our inner man is being renewed day by day. For momentary, light affliction is producing for us *an eternal weight of glory* far beyond all comparison, while we look not at the things which are seen, but at the things which are not seen; for the things which are seen are temporal, *but the things which are not seen are eternal.* (2 Cor. 4:16–18)

8. We are to think of heaven when facing opportunities to show love to others. The second greatest commandment is to be obeyed with heaven in mind. One of my college professors used to define *love* as "doing what is best for another in light of eternity."

> And this I pray, that your love may abound still more and more in real knowledge and all discernment, so that you may approve the things that are excellent, *in order to be sincere and blameless until the day of Christ* . . . (Phil. 1:9–10)

> Now . . . may the Lord cause you to increase and abound in love for one another, and for all people, just as we also do for you; *so that He may establish your hearts without blame in holiness before our God and Father at the coming of our Lord Jesus* with all His saints. (1 Thess. 3:11–13)

> God is love, and the one who abides in love abides in God, and God abides in him. By this, love is perfected with us, *so that we may have confidence in the day of judgment*; because as He is, so also are we in this world. There is no fear in love; but perfect love casts out fear, because fear involves punishment, and the one who fears is not perfected in love. (1 John 4:16b–18)

9. We are to think of heaven when facing opportunities for ministry. There are quite a few of these ministry-oriented passages. Perhaps this is because of the incredible stress, disappointment, and special accountability that often accompanies work for God's kingdom.

> Do you not know that those who run in a race all run, but only one receives the prize? Run in such a way that you may win. Everyone who competes in the games exercises self-control in all things. They then do it to receive a perishable wreath, *but we an imperishable. Therefore I run in such a way, as not without aim; I box in such a way, as not beating the air; but I discipline my body and make it my slave, so that, after I have preached to others, I myself will not be disqualified.* (1 Cor. 9:24–27)

For to me, to live is Christ and *to die is gain*. But if I am to live on in the flesh, this will mean fruitful labor for me; and I do not know which to choose. But I am hard-pressed from both directions, *having the desire to depart and be with Christ, for that is very much better*; yet to remain on in the flesh is more necessary for your sake. Convinced of this, I know that I will remain and continue with you all for your progress and joy in the faith . . . (Phil. 1:21–25)

We proclaim Him, admonishing every man and teaching every man with all wisdom, so that *we may present every man complete in Christ. For this purpose also I labor*, striving according to His power, which mightily works within me. (Col. 1:28–29)

For God has not destined us for wrath, but for obtaining salvation through our Lord Jesus Christ, who died for us, so that whether we are awake or asleep, we will live together with Him. *Therefore encourage one another and build up one another*, just as you also are doing. (1 Thess. 5:9–11)

Fight the good fight of faith; take hold of the eternal life to which you were called, and you made the good confession in the presence of many witnesses. I charge you in the presence of God, who gives life to all things, and of Christ Jesus, who testified the good confession before Pontius Pilate, that you *keep the commandment without stain or reproach until the appearing of our Lord Jesus Christ*, which He will bring about at the proper time—He who is the blessed and only Sovereign, the King of kings and Lord of lords . . . (1 Tim. 6:12–15)

Also if anyone competes as an athlete, *he does not win the prize* unless he competes according to the rules. (2 Tim. 2:5)

For this reason *I endure all things for the sake of those who are chosen*, so that they also may obtain the salvation which is in Christ Jesus and *with it eternal glory*. It is a trustworthy statement: For if we died with Him, we will also live with Him; *if we endure, we will also reign with Him* . . . (2 Tim. 2:10–12a)

Therefore, I exhort the elders among you, as your fellow elder and witness of the sufferings of Christ, and a partaker also of the glory that is to be revealed, shepherd the flock of God among you, exercising oversight not under compulsion, but voluntarily, according to the will of God; and not for sordid gain, but with eagerness; nor yet as lording it over those allotted to your charge, but proving to be examples to the flock. *And when the Chief Shepherd appears, you will receive the unfading crown of glory.* (1 Pet. 5:1–4)

10. **We are to think of heaven when facing directives from our spiritual leaders.** We should think about the eternal rewards of those who are spiritually responsible for us. Their heavenly rewards are somehow tied to our spiritual success.

Do all things without grumbling or disputing; so that you will prove yourselves to be blameless and innocent, children of God above reproach in the midst of a crooked and perverse generation, among whom you appear as lights in the world, holding fast the word of life, *so that in the day of Christ I will have reason to glory* because I did not run in vain nor toil in vain. (Phil. 2:14–16)

For who is our hope or joy or crown of exultation? Is it not even you, *in the presence of our Lord Jesus at His coming*? For you are our glory and joy. (1 Thess. 2:19–20; cf. Phil. 4:17)

Obey your leaders and submit to them, for they keep watch over your souls *as those who will give an account.* Let them do this with joy and not with grief, *for this would be unprofitable for you.* (Heb. 13:17)

11. **We are to think of heaven when being influenced by doctrinal error.** Doctrinal error is serious. In the final analysis, it is sin. Moreover, the influence of others is a very powerful force (cf. Prov. 13:20; 1 Cor. 5:6; 15:33). People-pleasers are especially prone to believe error because they are often more loyal to people than to the

truth. Thinking about heaven and the potential loss of rewards is a powerful motivation to keep oneself from embracing heresy.

> Watch yourselves, that you do not lose what we have accomplished, but *that you may receive a full reward.* (2 John 8)

> But you, beloved, building yourselves up on your most holy faith, praying in the Holy Spirit, keep yourselves in the love of God, waiting anxiously for the mercy of our Lord Jesus Christ to eternal life. And have mercy on some, who are doubting; save others, snatching them out of the fire; and on some have mercy with fear, hating even the garment polluted by the flesh.
> *Now to Him who is able to keep you from stumbling, and to make you stand in the presence of His glory blameless with great joy,* to the only God our Savior, through Jesus Christ our Lord, be glory, majesty, dominion and authority, before all time and now and forever. Amen. (Jude 20–25; cf. 2 Thess. 2:2–3)

12. We are to think of heaven when facing discouragement in our Christian walk. One of the best cures for discouragement is a heavenly focus. The apostle Paul warned the Corinthians not to throw in the towel on their faith by reminding them of Christ's desire to see them in glory, holy and blameless and beyond reproach.

> And although you were formerly alienated and hostile in mind, engaged in evil deeds, yet He has now reconciled you in His fleshly body through death, *in order to present you before Him holy and blameless and beyond reproach*—if indeed you continue in the faith firmly established and steadfast, *and not moved away from the hope of the gospel* that you have heard, which was proclaimed in all creation under heaven, and of which I, Paul, was made a minister. (Col. 1:21–23; cf. 2 Cor. 4:1, 16–18)

13. We are to think of heaven when facing increased affluence. In Luke 12:16–21, Jesus told a parable about the man who "stores up treasure for himself, and is not rich toward God" (v. 21). He says to himself, "Soul, you have many goods laid up for many years to come; take your ease, eat, drink and be merry" (v. 19). But what did God say to him? "You fool! This very night your soul is required of you; and now who will own what you have prepared?" (v. 20).

> Instruct those who are rich in this present world *not to be conceited or to fix their hope on the uncertainty of riches*, but on God, who richly supplies us with all things to enjoy. *Instruct them* to do good, to be rich in good works, to be generous and ready to share, *storing up for themselves the treasure of a good foundation for the future*, so that they may take hold of that which is life indeed. (1 Tim. 6:17–19)

14. We are to think of heaven when facing spiritual apathy. Diligence is arguably the best antidote for apathy. Peter urges his readers to be diligent in light of the Lord's return. Forms of the word *look* occur three times in the following passage. It means "to eagerly or anxiously await" or "to hopefully anticipate." When you put the "blessed hope" of Christ's return out of mind, you will find yourself growing cold toward God, and apathetic in your Christian walk.

> But the day of the Lord will come like a thief, in which the heavens will pass away with a roar and the elements will be destroyed with intense heat, and the earth and its works will be burned up.
>
> Since all these things are to be destroyed in this way, *what sort of people ought you to be in holy conduct and godliness, looking for and hastening the coming of the day of God*, because of which the heavens will be destroyed by burning, and the elements will melt with intense heat! But according to His promise we are *looking* for new heavens and a new earth, in which righteousness dwells.
>
> Therefore, beloved, since you *look* for these things, *be diligent to be found by Him in peace, spotless and blameless* . . . (2 Pet. 3:10–14)

15. We are to think of heaven when facing arrogant thoughts about our past accomplishments. It is easy for us to sit back "on our laurels," as it were, and coast through the rest of our Christian walk, thinking that we have it made in the heavenly shade because of what God's Spirit has done through us in the past. Yet this was not the attitude of the great missionary Paul:

> But whatever things were gain to me, those things I have counted as loss for the sake of Christ. More than that, I count all things to be loss in view of the surpassing value of knowing Christ Jesus my Lord, for whom I have suffered the loss of all things, and count them but rubbish so that I may gain Christ, and may be found in Him, not having a righteousness of my own derived from the Law, but that which is through faith in Christ, the righteousness which comes from God on the basis of faith, that I may know Him and the power of His resurrection and the fellowship of His sufferings, being conformed to His death; in order that I may attain to the resurrection from the dead.
>
> Not that I have already obtained it or have already become perfect, but I press on so that I may lay hold of that for which also I was laid hold of by Christ Jesus. Brethren, I do not regard myself as having laid hold of it yet; *but one thing I do: forgetting what lies behind and reaching forward to what lies ahead, I press on toward the goal for the prize of the upward call of God in Christ Jesus. Let us therefore, as many as are perfect, have this attitude* . . . (Phil. 3:7–15a)

16. We are to think of heaven when facing self-exalting desires and circumstances. Our own desire to exalt ourselves leads us into the sin of people-pleasing. As James explains, "each one is tempted when he is carried away and enticed by his own lust" (James 1:14). Thinking about heaven and the possibility of losing eternal rewards can provide the extra motivation that some of us may need to clothe ourselves with humility by keeping silent during those times when we are tempted to exalt ourselves.

> Beware of practicing your righteousness before men to be noticed by them; otherwise *you have no reward with your Father who is in heaven* . . .
>
> When you pray, you are not to be like the hypocrites; for they love to stand and pray in the synagogues and on the street corners so that they may be seen by men. Truly I say to you, *they have their reward in full* . . .

235

> Whenever you fast, do not put on a gloomy face as the hypocrites do, for they neglect their appearance so that they will be noticed by men when they are fasting. Truly I say to you, *they have their reward in full.* (Matt. 6:1, 5, 16)

So where is your treasure? Jesus said:

> Do not store up for yourselves treasures on earth, where moth and rust destroy, and where thieves break in and steal. But store up for yourselves treasures in heaven, where neither moth nor rust destroys, and where thieves do not break in or steal; for where your treasure is, there your heart will be also. (Matt. 6:19–21)

If you value eternal things (if you are more concerned about storing up heavenly treasures than earthly ones), it will be a relatively simple thing for you to overcome your struggle with being a people-pleaser. Not that it will be easy. It will still require much effort, considerable amounts of time, and restructuring of your thoughts as you depend on the Holy Spirit for His enabling grace.

But to the degree that you have a temporal value system (to the extent that you are more focused on enjoying earthly pleasures than heavenly ones), you will find the teachings and reproofs of this book very hard to swallow, and the practical guidelines for correction and training in righteousness very tedious indeed. If you find yourself in this latter category, let me urge you to begin your journey by confessing your sin of worldliness to God. Then ask Him to give you the grace to love Christ "with all of your heart, soul, mind, and strength" (you will not be able to love God's approval more than man's approval if you don't love Him as you should), and to "set your affection on things above, not on things on the earth" (Col. 3:2 KJV). And be patient—God will probably not wean you of your love of the world overnight. It will take time, effort, and thought to refocus your spiritual eyes, but in the end it will be worth it.

Appendix A

PREREQUISITE TO PLEASING GOD[1]

There is a prerequisite to pleasing God: "Without faith it is impossible to please [God]" (Heb. 11:6). Many people believe that getting to heaven is accomplished by doing many good things and relatively few bad things. The truth is, however, that even one sin is enough to keep you out of heaven. It really doesn't matter how much good you do. Any sin—regardless of how great or small—is enough to keep you out of heaven and send you straight to hell. All sin displeases God.

> Through one man sin entered into the world, and death through sin, and so death spread to all men, because all sinned. (Rom. 5:12)

> For the wages of sin is death, but the free gift of God is eternal life in Christ Jesus our Lord. (Rom. 6:23)

> For whoever keeps the whole law and yet stumbles in one point, he has become guilty of all. For He who said, "Do not commit adultery," also said, "Do not commit murder." Now if you do not commit adultery, but do commit murder, you have become a transgressor of the law. (James 2:10–11)

---

1. A good portion of this appendix was taken from my previous book *Losing That Lovin' Feeling* (Wetumpka, AL: Pastoral Publications, 2003).

According to the Bible, for a person to be saved and go to heaven, there must first be the realization that his sin has caused a separation from God. God, who is both holy and just, must appropriately deal with sinners and their sin. God's holiness disposes Him to hate sin. His justice requires Him to punish sin. The wages or punishment of sin is death (cf. Gen. 3:19; Rom. 5:12; 6:23). For Him to simply overlook sin without requiring the proper punishment would go against His holy and just nature.

How just would you consider a judge to be if he, out of partiality to a convicted serial murderer, sentenced him to only a few days in jail rather than sentencing him to at least the minimum sentence required by the law?

Well, what kind of magistrate would God, "the Judge of all the earth" (Gen. 18:25), be if He didn't punish sinners who transgressed His law? For God to let sinners off the hook without demanding that they pay at least the minimum penalty for their crimes would render Him unjust (and unfit for the bench). Since the minimum sentence for sin, according to the Bible, is death, God must punish sinners. His justice requires Him to do so.

It is appointed for men to die once and after this comes judgment. (Heb. 9:27)

The Lord knows how to rescue the godly from temptation, and to keep the unrighteous under punishment for the day of judgment. (2 Pet. 2:9)

Then I saw a great white throne and Him who sat upon it, from whose presence earth and heaven fled away, and no place was found for them. And I saw the dead, the great and the small, standing before the throne, and books were opened; and another book was opened, which is the book of life; and the dead were judged from the things which were written in the books, according to their deeds. And the sea gave up the dead which were in it, and death and Hades gave up the dead which were in them; and they were judged, every one of them according to their deeds. Then death and Hades were thrown into the lake of fire. This is the second death, the lake of fire. (Rev. 20:11–14)

Now, other elements of God's nature dispose Him to be loving and merciful. In fact, the Bible says that God is "not willing that any should perish but that all should come to repentance" (2 Pet. 3:9 NKJV).

"But how can He forgive sinners in love and mercy when his justice requires Him to punish them for their sins?"

God had to find a substitute—someone who was willing to pay the penalty in the place of sinners.

> Men of Israel, listen to these words; Jesus the Nazarene, a man attested to you by God with miracles and wonders and signs which God performed through Him in your midst, just as you yourselves know—this Man, delivered over by the predetermined plan and foreknowledge of God, you nailed to a cross by the hands of godless men and put Him to death. But God raised Him up again, putting an end to the agony of death, since it was impossible for Him to be held in its power. (Acts 2:22–24)

If God could find someone willing to pay the price for man's sin, yet who did not have to die for his own sin, He could punish that substitute in the sinner's place. But who is without sin? Only God. So God, in His love and mercy, took upon Himself the form of a man in the person of Jesus Christ (Phil. 2:7). The Lord Jesus lived a sinless life and then sacrificed Himself on the cross as the substitute for sinners, who were incapable of redeeming themselves. After He was buried, He rose from the dead and in so doing demonstrated His power over death and sin and hell.

> For Christ also died for sins once for all, the just for the unjust, so that He might bring us to God, having been put to death in the flesh, but made alive in the spirit . . . (1 Pet. 3:18)

This resurrection power is available to those who are truly willing to let go of their sins and believe the gospel (the good news about what Christ did by dying on the cross). The gospel of Jesus Christ provides power not only over death and hell, but also over sin—the very sin that has enslaved them and caused them so much misery.

Have you ever turned away from your sin and asked God to forgive you once and for all on the basis of Christ's substitutionary death on the cross?

> For God so loved the world, that He gave His only begotten Son, that whoever believes in Him shall not perish, but have eternal life . . . He who

believes in the Son has eternal life; but he who does not obey the Son shall not see life, but the wrath of God abides on him. (John 3:16, 36)

If you confess with your mouth Jesus as Lord, and believe in your heart that God raised Him from the dead, you will be saved; for with the heart a person believes, resulting in righteousness, and with the mouth he confesses, resulting in salvation . . . For "Whoever will call on the Name of the Lord will be saved." (Rom. 10:9–10, 13)

When a person becomes a Christian, the Holy Spirit indwells (takes up residency inside of) him, giving him the power to obey God. Your ability to make use of the biblical resources contained in this book will be severely limited if you do not have the Spirit's enabling power in your life. He is the true Comforter. Only he can come alongside you and provide you with the supernatural power you need to love the approval of God more than the approval of men.

Therefore, having been justified by faith, we have peace with God through our Lord Jesus Christ, through whom also we have obtained our introduction by faith into this grace in which we stand; we exult in hope of the glory of God. And not only this, but we also exult in our tribulations, knowing that tribulation brings about perseverance; and perseverance, proven character; and proven character, hope; and hope does not disappoint, because the love of God has been poured out within our hearts through the Holy Spirit who was given to us.

For while we were still helpless, at the right time Christ died for the ungodly. For one will hardly die for a righteous man; though perhaps for the good man someone would dare even to die. But God demonstrates His own love toward us, in that while we were yet sinners, Christ died for us. (Rom. 5:1–8)

Appendix B

GETTING TO THE HEART OF PRIDE[1]

(DIRECTIONS FOR USING THE HEART JOURNAL)

The Heart Journal is a tool you can use to identify unbiblical thoughts and motives associated with the sinful behavior that attends the love of man's approval. It is a work sheet on which you can record the answers to five sets of self-examination questions after committing questionable people-pleasing behaviors. Each set of two questions will help you identify, examine, and correct the unbiblical thoughts and motives of your heart.

Photocopy as many journal pages as you think you'll need in a given two-week period. If all goes well, the frequency of your people-pleasing episodes will diminish, so you'll use fewer copies in subsequent weeks.

This journal can be used whenever you have responded to a situation in life as a people-pleaser rather than a God-pleaser. Here are a few instances when you might find it helpful to examine your heart for people-pleasing (proud) thoughts and desires:

1. Some of the material in this appendix has been adapted from my book *The Heart of Anger* (Amityville, NY: Calvary Press Publishing, 1998).

1. When you realize you should have said "no" to someone but didn't

2. When you go fishing for compliments

3. When you gossip about someone

4. When you worry what people think of you

5. When you face rejection

6. When you are willing to sin to avoid rejection

7. When you show personal favoritism to someone

8. When you avoid conflict

9. When you are contradicted by someone (especially in public)

10. When you meet a new person

11. When you are afraid to get too close to someone

12. When you have an intense longing to be noticed

13. When you give in to peer pressure

14. When you are critical of others (or hold them in contempt)

15. When you overreact to criticism

16. When you fail to witness to someone out of fear

17. When you flatter someone

18. When you lie

19. When you are discontented with the condition of your life

20. When you take credit for the achievements in your life

21. When you boast or brag

22. When you are defensive

23. When you blame someone else for your sin

24. When you are indecisive

25. When you talk too much

26. When you are contentious

27. When you are ungrateful

28. When you find yourself using your wisdom, abilities, and gifts for selfish purposes

Step 1: Identify the circumstantial trigger of your prideful response.

Question 1. What happened that enticed me to respond in pride? In other words, what circumstances led to my prideful response?

The answer to this question will make it easier to identify the circumstances in which you are most prone to be tempted. (By comparing this answer to the first answer of each of your other journal entries, you may discover a pattern of temptation to please people more than God.)

Step 2: Identify the specific expression of pride that you manifested in this circumstance.

Question 2. What did I do that might have been generated by an inordinate love of man's approval? In other words, what external manifestation of pride needs to be examined in light of God's Word?

By identifying the exact unbiblical way in which you responded (what sin you committed), you cooperate with the Spirit's ministry in your life. Most of the twenty-eight items listed above (lying, gossiping, fishing for compliments, avoiding necessary conflicts) qualify for possible entries.

Step 3: Identify specific thoughts and motives associated with your pride.

Question 3. What did I say to myself (in my heart) just before I responded this way? What did I want, desire, or long for when I responded as I did?

Unlike steps 1 and 2, steps 3, 4, and 5 require *two* separate answers. This is because each question is addressing a different issue of the heart. The first question of each set focuses on your thoughts. The second question focuses on your motives (desires).

The ability to discern the thoughts and motives of your heart (especially when experiencing intense emotion) is an essential skill for the believer. Recognizing thoughts and imaginations of the heart is a prerequisite of bringing them "captive to the obedience of Christ" (2 Cor. 10:5; see also Deut. 15:9; Ps. 15:2; Isa. 55:7; Jer. 4:14; Matt. 15:19). This process of recognition is made more difficult because of three factors:

1. "The heart is deceitful above all things" (Jer. 17:9 NKJV) and cannot be "known" apart from the Word of God, which is able to discern its "thoughts and intentions." (Cf. Heb. 4:12.)

2. The heart's voice is often camouflaged by its desires. That is, it is difficult to detect wrong thoughts because they are often based on desires that may seem legitimate when, in fact, they are either *wrong* desires or legitimate desires that are desired *inordinately*. (James 1:12–16; 4:1–2)

3. The heart has the capacity to speak to itself at the rate of over 1,200 words per minute, making such detection a bit complicated.

In answer to the first question of step 3 ("What did I say to myself [in my heart] just before I responded this way?"), record verbatim the thoughts that went through your mind at the moment your pride manifested itself. (Be honest and accurate.) Such thoughts typically involve frequent first-person references (*I, me, mine,* etc.). At first, you may be able to recognize only one or two sentences (some people also think with accompanying pictures). In time and with practice, you may be able to list half a dozen or more. Here are a few examples:

- "If I don't do this for her, she will be upset with me!"
- "I wonder how good my performance was. How can I get them to tell me without making it too obvious?"
- "If I put myself down, maybe they will disagree with my negative assessment."
- "I wonder what she thinks of me."
- "I'd better not ask too many questions or he will think I'm dumb."
- "I just couldn't go out in public looking like this."
- "I'll probably make a fool of myself."
- "I'd better not reveal too much about myself."
- "Being seen with a loser like her is going to ruin my reputation."
- "How dare he correct (or contradict) me in public!"
- "I just couldn't handle it if he rejected me."

■ "I'd rather have a root canal than face his rejection."

■ "How can I impress her?"

■ "How can I get her to notice me?"

■ "I can't believe she criticized me in front of my friends. My reputation is ruined, thanks to her!"

■ "I have to get away from this person as quickly as possible."

■ "I have to be careful not to say anything that might start a conflict."

■ "I can't bear the thought of being hurt again."

■ "My friends would really be impressed if they knew I had a friend like her."

The answer to the second question of step 3 ("What did I want, desire, or long for when I responded as I did?") may be a bit more difficult to determine. Motives (passions, desires and affections, etc.) are not always as easy to discern as are thoughts. It is often not until we stop and ask ourselves specific questions concerning these things that we can put our fingers on what they are. If you have difficulty identifying your motives by asking this question in the Heart Journal, try some of these questions:

1. What did I believe I couldn't be happy without when I responded as I did?

2. What did I believe I had to have when I responded as I did?

3. What was I worried most about losing when I responded as I did?

4. What did I delight in (seek my happiness in) the most when I responded as I did?

5. What was I loving more than God and my neighbor when I responded as I did?

What are some of the things that people-pleasers long for? Obviously, an excessive desire for the approval of men is at the heart of the matter. But this sinful craving often expresses itself in a variety of ways. Here are a few of them:

- I want to be loved
- I want to feel important
- I want to be respected
- I want to be noticed
- I want to be recognized
- I want to avoid a conflict
- I want him/her to be my friend
- I don't want people to know I'm such a sinner

- I want to be well thought of
- I want to have a good reputation
- I want others to look up to me
- I don't want to face his anger
- I don't want to be rejected
- I don't want to be labeled
- I want everyone to like me

Step 4: Biblically evaluate the exact nature of the thoughts and motives that produced your people-pleasing activities.

Question 4. What does the Bible say about the thoughts that led to my response? What does the Bible say about the desires that led to my response?

At this point you are going to analyze the thoughts and desires that led to your people-pleasing response. And you will want to do so biblically, "not in words taught us by human wisdom but in words taught by the Spirit, expressing spiritual truths in spiritual words" (1 Cor. 2:13 NIV). For a problem cannot be solved biblically until it is diagnosed using biblical terminology. Only then can you know where to look in the Scripture for directives and principles needed to solve the problem God's way. Only then can you identify the biblical alternatives that are to be put on in place of those that are to be put off.

For example, the thought that preceded an attempt to go fishing for compliments might be: "I wonder how good my performance was. How can I get them to tell me without making it too obvious?" How would you describe what is wrong (or right) with this ideation? Perhaps you would use biblical terms like this:

"My thought was *selfish* and *proud*. I was more concerned with what people thought of me than with how my performance might have benefited them. I was also being *deceptive* in that rather than asking them truthfully how they thought I did (which I would probably never do lest my pride become obvious to them), I wanted to manipulate the information out of them without disclosing what I was really looking for."

Or if you found this thought popping up in your heart, what biblical words would you use to describe it? "How dare he correct me in public!" Probably something like this would suffice: "I was *sinfully angry* because by correcting in public—even though he was right to do so and made the correction very graciously—he embarrassed me. No . . . actually, I *allowed myself* to be embarrassed because, in my *arrogance* and *selfishness*, I was more concerned about *my reputation* than I was that those who heard me walked away with accurate information. I *thought of myself more highly than I ought*" (Rom. 12:3).

Let's do one more. "I'd rather have a root canal than face his rejection." Here is how a journal entry for this thought might read: "The Bible says that 'the *fear* of man brings a snare.' This thought also reveals that I was *anxious* about what might go wrong in the future. God says that *worry* is a sin."

The second question in step 4 ("What does the Bible say about the desires that led to my response?") is there to help you biblically evaluate (classify) your motives.

If the desire *is in and of itself* sinful, the evaluation is relatively easy to make.

Motive	Biblical Evaluation
I wanted to get even.	Revenge
I wanted to look at pornography.	Lust
I wanted to kill him.	Murder
I wanted to exaggerate my achievements.	Pride/Deception
I wanted to avoid a biblical confrontation.	Fear

If the desire is not inherently sinful, however, the question then becomes, "Did I want something that God says is good *too much*?" or "Did I want some good thing so much that I was willing either to sin *in order to get it* or to sin *because I couldn't have it*?"

Remember, to desire the approval of others is not necessarily wrong (*it is not in all cases in and of itself a sin*). But as with money, pleasure, and anything else that is not inherently evil, to desire approval so much that it turns into the *love* of approval is wrong. The scribes and the Pharisees (like so many today and down through the ages) were approval addicts. That is, their desire for approval was so inordinate that they were in bondage to it. "For by what a man is overcome, by this he is enslaved" (2 Pet. 2:19b). They wanted approval so much that they spent much of their time and effort doing those things that would bring glory from men. As we have seen, even those things that are religious in nature (such as prayer, fasting, and giving) can be done with a motive to gain man's approval.

Step 5: Develop alternative biblical thoughts and motives to replace the unbiblical ones.

Question 5. What should I have said to myself when I was first enticed? What should I have wanted more than my own selfish or idolatrous desire?

It isn't enough to identify and remove (put off) wrong thoughts and motives from our hearts. In order for change to be biblical (effective, enduring, and pleasing to God), we must replace sinful thoughts and motives with righteous ones. We must make it our goal to:

- be pure in heart (Matt. 5:8);
- speak the truth in our hearts (Ps. 15:2);
- desire truth in our innermost being (Ps. 51:6);
- let our minds think on whatever is true, honorable, just, pure, of good repute, excellent, and worthy of praise (Phil. 4:8);
- renew our minds (Rom. 12:2; cf. Eph. 4:23); and
- have our loins girded with truth.

Step 5 is by far the most important element of the journal because it is where repentance (change of mind) is brought to fruition. It is where the Scripture can be best utilized for "correction [and disciplined] training in righteousness" (2 Tim. 3:16). It is the part of the process that best prepares you for biblically dealing with future people-pleasing temptations and situations. By identifying and rehearsing biblical alternatives to the sinful thoughts and motives of your heart, you can retrain yourself not only to think biblically in the future, but also to increasingly desire only those things that are good for you to have.

In response to the question, "What should I have said to myself when I was first enticed?," try to record as many biblically accurate alternative thoughts as you can in a reasonable amount of time (say five to ten minutes at first). These alternatives should reflect (1) theological accuracy (especially focusing on God's sovereignty as it relates to His ability to have prevented the tempting circumstances from occurring), (2) biblical hope (especially as it relates to God's promise to cause all things to work together for your good), and (3) the putting on of those antithetical concepts to pride, selfishness, the fear of man, and other sinful attitudes you identified in step 4 (humility, love, the fear of the Lord, etc.).

Let's repackage the three examples we looked at in step 4. When tempted to go fishing for compliments, what would be a more biblical thought than: "I wonder how good my performance was. How can I get them to tell me without making it too obvious?"

What about something like this: "My performance is not the issue. I should be more concerned with whether my performance was pleasing to God and edifying to my neighbor than I am with what they think of me. After all, I am performing on His stage. He is my ultimate audience. He is evaluating not only my external performance but also the internal performance of my heart. Besides, if the Lord wants me to know their opinion about this matter, He doesn't need my help to manipulate it out of them."

What would be a biblical alternative to "How dare he correct me in public"?

Perhaps this would be appropriate: "I should be thankful that God sent someone to clarify what I said so that those who heard me would not leave with the wrong impression. I should also be thankful for the fact that he corrected me so graciously (I probably wouldn't have been so gracious to him). I'm not going to play the fool by despising reproof and correction" (cf. Prov. 1:23; 3:11; 5:12; 10:17; 12:1).

"That might work for a public correction, but what if it was more of a contradiction?"

Then something like this might be more fitting: "OK, this *is* a little humiliating, but 'God gives grace to the humble.' I will take all the grace He wants to give me. Besides I have given my reputation to Him. He will do a better job of protecting it than I ever could. Now, how should I verbally respond to this contradiction in a way that will bring glory to God?"

How about putting a cap on that root canal cogitation? Instead of: "I'd rather have a root canal than face his rejection," why not: "Being rejected is not the worst thing in the world (neither is a root canal)—it is part of what being a Christian is all about." Or maybe: "If I am rejected, I will just have to be rejected. I'm not going to let sinful fear keep me from loving God and loving my neighbor by refusing to go where God wants me to go."

I recommend that you work to develop several alternative biblical thoughts for each unbiblical thought you have. The more options you develop, the easier it will be for you to reach back to the memory banks of your mind and find one when you need it.

The last question in the Heart Journal is: "What should I have wanted more than my own selfish or idolatrous desire?"

The ultimate answer to this question in every case ought to be: "To please and glorify God." This concept may be expressed in a variety of ways. Before identifying some of the forms of motivation that glorify God, let's consider some of those delights, loves, and longings that Scripture encourages the believer to develop.

A Christian's first love should be love for the Lord his God that emanates from his heart, mind, soul, and strength (Luke 10:27). This is the ruling motive for everything that the Christian does. He may have other good and noble motives in his heart, but love for God must be preeminent.

Another Christian motive should be to love one's neighbor with the same intensity as he loves himself. As everyone naturally "nourishes and cherishes" himself (Eph. 5:29), so the Christian is to love his neighbor to the same degree.

Using these two righteous loves, we may categorize the other lawful loves spoken of by name in the Bible. These are biblically legitimate to the degree that they are subordinate to loving God. Here is a partial list:

1. The love of the Word of God — Psalm 119:140
2. The love of wisdom — Proverbs 4:6; 8:17
3. The love of mercy — Micah 6:8
4. The love of truth — Zechariah 8:19; 2 Thessalonians 2:10
5. The love of peace — Zechariah 8:19
6. The love of that which is good — Amos 5:15
7. The love of the Lord's return — 2 Timothy 4:8
8. The love of life (not his own) — 1 Peter 3:10
9. The love of light — John 3:19
10. The love of one's spouse — Ephesians 5:25

By answering the final question in the Heart Journal, you will work to develop godly motivation and train yourself to set your affections on the things above rather than on the things that are on earth (Col. 3:2).[2] You will identify those desires that you ought to delight in, love, pursue, set your affection on, covet, etc. God will be using the "momentary, light affliction" to produce "an eternal weight of glory far beyond all comparison" as with the eyes of your heart you learn to "look not at the [temporal] things which are seen, but at the [eternal] things which are not seen" (2 Cor. 4:17–18).

In every situation that once tempted you to please people more than God, you can train yourself to increasingly delight (seek your happiness) more in pleasing God than in pleasing people.

> I delight to do Your will, O my God; Your Law is within my heart. (Ps. 40:8)

Rather than asking yourself, "What will people think of me if I do (or don't do) this?," you can learn to ask, "What will the Lord think if I do (or don't do) this?"

What, then, are some alternative biblical motives (desires) to put on in an effort to replace the idolatrous ones you've discovered in your heart? How can the desires to love and glorify and please God be expressed so that they may prayerfully be cultivated to maturity? What are the correct answers to the question, "What should I have wanted more than my own selfish desires?" Here are a few to get you started. Next to each response I've suggested a portion of Scripture. These passages (and others like them) can be memorized to help facilitate the development of each new godly motive.

Righteous Desires I could have wanted:	**Related Scripture**
▤ To love and glorify God by _____.	Matthew 5:16
▤ To delight in doing God's will, which was _____.	Psalm 40:8

---

2. When Peter rebuked the Lord after hearing His prophecy concerning Jesus' imminent death, he was himself rebuked: "You are not *setting your mind on God's interests*, but man's" (Matt. 16:23).

- To be more like Jesus
  Christ in this way:

  _____.

  2 Corinthians 3:18

- To love my neighbor as
  myself.

  Matthew 22:34–40

- To have wisdom and
  understanding.

  Proverbs 4:5–9

- To honor and obey my
  parents.

  Ephesians 6:1–3

- To delight in God's Word.

  Psalm 1:2

- To delight more in what
  I can give to others than
  in what I can get.

  Acts 20:35

- To minister to others.

  Matthew 20:25–28

- To offer a blessing.

  1 Peter 3:8–16

- To demonstrate to my
  parents that I am
  trustworthy.

  Proverbs 20:6

Let's plug our original three examples in to the last journal question: "What should I have wanted more than my own selfish or idolatrous desire?"

In the first example ("I wonder how good my performance was. How can I get them to tell me without making it too obvious?"), I should have wanted "to be more concerned about my performance on God's stage than on man's and to be more concerned with the pleasure my 'performance' brought to my neighbor. I should have been content with not knowing what they thought of me (if the only way to find out was to manipulate them)."

In the second example ("How dare he correct me in public!"), God would have been pleased for me "to love my neighbor by 'rejoic[ing] with the truth' [1 Cor. 13:6] and to long both for the grace that comes with humility [cf. 1 Pet. 5:5] and for the wisdom that comes from reproof" (cf. Prov. 9:7–9; 15:31).

And finally, let's look at our potential patient: "I'd rather have a root canal than face his rejection." (Imagine how rejected dentists must feel.)[3] What kind of godly desires might this person work on developing? She should have wanted to please God in any number of ways, such as:

- Learning how to see rejection as an opportunity to express the love of Christ to the person who rejects her (thus overcoming fear with love according to 1 John 4:18); or
- Developing courage to face potentially hurtful situations; or
- Not exaggerating the terribleness of the daily trials that God calls each believer to face.

Let me make one final suggestion for using the Heart Journal. Because it can take a considerable amount of time to completely fill out, why not consider doing the bulk of the work during your regular time of Bible study? To do this, answer questions 1 through 3 as soon after each people-pleasing episode as you can reasonably do. Then the next morning (or whenever your next "quiet time" is), open your Bible, concordance, and any other Bible study tool you think would be helpful, and get to work answering questions 4 and 5. Remember, the more Scripture you study and internalize in the process, the more the Holy Spirit will have to work with as He transforms you by the renewing of your mind.

---

3. I have a dentist friend who tells me that the suicide rate among dentists is very high compared to the general population. Think about how thankless a job being a dentist is. Patients are rarely happy to see you, they almost never express thanks to you, but rather complain about the pain (excuse me—I mean the "discomfort") you cause them, and they *totally forget* you until they are hurting again or they get one of those pesky little postcards in the mail reminding them that they are due for another exciting checkup.

HEART JOURNAL

---

1. What happened that enticed me to respond in pride? In other words, what circumstances led to my prideful response?

2. What did I do that might have been generated by an inordinate love of man's approval? In other words, what external manifestation of pride needs to be examined in light of God's Word?

3. What did I say to myself (in my heart) just before I responded this way? What did I want, desire, or long for when I responded as I did?

4. What does the Bible say about the thoughts that led to my response? What does the Bible say about the desires that led to my response?

5. What should I have said to myself when I was first enticed? What should I have wanted more than my own selfish or idolatrous desire?

Lou Priolo is the Director of the Eastwood Counseling Ministry in Montgomery, Alabama. He is a graduate of Calvary Bible College and Liberty University. Lou has been a full-time biblical counselor and instructor for more than twenty years, and is a Fellow of the National Association of Nouthetic Counselors. He lives in Wetumpka, Alabama, with his wife Kim and his daughters Sophia and Gabriella.